BARRON'S

ESL GUIDE TO

American Business English

ESL GUIDE TO
American Business English

Andrea B. Geffner

Former Dean,
Taylor Business Institute, New York

President,
ESCO, Inc., New York

BARRON'S

For Marcus

All inquiries should be addressed to:
Barron's Educational Series, Inc.
250 Wireless Boulevard
Hauppauge, New York 11788
http://www.barronseduc.com

Library of Congress Catalog Card No. 98-21252

ISBN: 978-0-7641-0594-4

Library of Congress Cataloging-in-Publication Data

Geffner, Andrea B.
    Barron's ESL guide to American business English / Andrea B.
Geffner.
        p.   cm.
    Includes index.
    ISBN 0-7641-0594-9
    1. English language—Business English.   2. English language—
Textbooks for foreign speakers.   3. Business writing.   I. Title.
PE1115.G38   1998
428.2'4'02465—dc21   98-21252
                                                                            CIP

PRINTED IN THE UNITED STATES OF AMERICA

20 19 18 17 16 15 14

Contents

Table of Model Letters

Part One

COMMUNICATIONS

1.
American Business Style

Words to Watch For

condescending (*adj*) with an attitude of superiority
dock (*v*) to take away part of or deduct from *residuos.*
efficient (*adj*) productive without <u>waste</u> *residuos.*
elicit (*v*) to draw out of; extract
exorbitant (*adj*) excessive
goodwill (*n*) the value of a business's public image and reputation
jeopardy (*n*) danger; risk
offensive (*adj*) insulting
reiterate (*v*) to repeat
sexist (*adj*) prejudiced or discriminating against women (or men)
subordinate (*n*) person of lower rank
tactful (*adj*) diplomatic; discreet

Tone

How do you achieve an appropriate business style when you write a business letter?

The first step is to relax! As you study this book, you will find that there is very little difference between correctly spoken English and business writing. Business letters may vary in tone from familiar to formal, but they should always sound natural. Written English should *sound* like spoken English.

A sure sign of an inexperienced writer is the obvious attempt to sound too "business-like" or "official."

> As per your request, please find enclosed herewith a check in the amount of $47.95.

This sentence is difficult to understand, making simple information seem complicated. It uses such expressions as "as per" and "herewith," which add nothing to the meaning. Instead of just making a point, it tries to sound overly important.

> As you requested, I am enclosing a check for $47.95.

In this version of the sentence, the meaning is clear. The sentence is more personal and friendly than the first version because it mentions "you" and "I." It is simple and <u>straightforward</u>. It is even more "business-minded" because it is more efficient. By using fewer words than the first version, it requires less time to compose and type as well as to read and comprehend.

Consider the difference between these two versions of the same letter:

VERSION I

Dear Mr. Pendleton:

With reference to your order for a Nashito camcorder, we are in receipt of your check and are returning same.

I beg to inform you that, as a manufacturer, our company sells camcorders to dealers only. In compliance with our wholesale agreement, we deem it best to refrain from direct business with private consumers.

For your information, there are many retailers in your vicinity who carry Nashito camcorders. Attached please find a list of said dealers.

Hoping you understand.

Yours truly,

VERSION II

Dear Mr. Pendleton:

We have received your order for a Nashito camcorder but, unfortunately, must return your check.

As a manufacturer, we sell only to dealers, with whom we have very clear wholesale agreements.

Nevertheless, we sincerely appreciate your interest in Nashito products. We are therefore enclosing a list of retailers in your community who carry a full line of our camcorders. Any one of them will be happy to serve you.

Sincerely yours,

Remember, within the limits of standard English, try to say things in a natural way.

Outlook

While striving for a natural tone, you should also aim for a positive outlook. Even when the subject of your letter is unpleasant, it is important to remain courteous and tactful. Building and sustaining the goodwill of your reader should be an underlying goal of nearly any letter you write. Even a delinquent account may someday become a paying customer.

A simple "please" or "thank you" is often enough to make a mundane letter more courteous. Instead of:

> We have received your order.

you might try:

> Thank you for your recent order.

Or, in place of the impersonal:

> Checking our records, we have verified the error in your November bill.

you could help retain a customer by writing:

> Please accept our sincere apologies for the error in your November bill.

Saying "We are sorry" or "I appreciate" can do much to build rewarding business relations.

On the other hand, you must be tactful when delivering unpleasant messages. NEVER accuse your reader with expressions such as "your error" or "your failure." An antagonistic letter would say:

> Because you have refused to pay your long overdue bill, your credit rating is in jeopardy.

A more diplomatic letter (and therefore one more apt to get results) might say:

> Because the $520 balance on your account is now over ninety days past due, your credit rating is in jeopardy.

Because the second sentence refrains from attacking the reader personally (and also includes important details), it will be read more receptively.

Consider the difference between these two versions of the same memo:

VERSION I

TO: Department Supervisors

FROM: Assistant Director

Inform your subordinates:

1. Because so many have taken advantage of past leniency, lateness will no longer be overlooked. Paychecks will be docked as of Monday, March 6.

2. As a result of abuses of employee privileges, which have resulted in exorbitant long-distance telephone bills, any employee caught making a personal call will be subject to disciplinary action.

As supervisors, you will be required to enforce these new regulations.

VERSION II

TO: _____

FROM: Wanda Hatch, Assistant Director

Unfortunately, a few people have taken advantage of lenient company policies regarding lateness and personal phone calls. As a result, we must all now conform to tougher regulations.

Please inform the members of your department that:

1. Beginning Monday, March 6, the paychecks of employees who are late will be docked.

2. Personal phone calls are no longer permitted.

It is a shame that the abuses of a few must cost the rest of us. But we are asking all department supervisors to help us enforce these new rules.

The "*You* Approach"

Courtesy and tact are sometimes achieved by what is called a *you* approach. In other words, your letter should be reader-oriented and sound as if you share your reader's point of view. For example:

> Please accept our apologies for the delay.

is perfectly polite. But:

> We hope you have not been seriously inconvenienced by the delay.

lets your reader know that you care.

The *you* approach does NOT mean you should avoid "I" and "we" when necessary. When you do use these pronouns, though, keep a few pointers in mind:

1. Use "I" when you are referring to yourself (or to the person who will actually sign the letter).
2. Use "we" when you are referring to the company itself.
3. DO NOT use the company name or "our company." This practice is rather like referring to oneself by one's name, rather than "I" or "me."

Also, you should be careful to use your reader's name sparingly in the body of your letter. Although this practice seems, at first glance, to personalize a letter, it can sound condescending.

Now, compare the two letters that follow, and see if you recognize the features that make the second letter more *you*-oriented.

VERSION I

Dear Ms. Biggs:

Having conducted our standard credit investigation, we have concluded that it would be unwise for us to grant you credit at this time.

We believe that the extent of your current obligations makes you a bad credit risk. As you can understand, it is in our best interest to grant charge accounts only to those customers with proven ability to pay.

Please accept our sincere regrets and feel free to continue to shop at Allen's on a cash basis.

Sincerely yours,

VERSION II

Dear Miss Biggs:

I am sorry to inform you that your application for an Allen's charge account has been turned down.

Our credit department believes that, because of your current obligations, additional credit might be difficult for you to handle at this time. Your credit reputation is too valuable to be placed in jeopardy. We will be delighted, of course, to reconsider your application in the future should your financial responsibilities be reduced. Until then, we hope you will continue to shop at Allen's where EVERY customer is our prime concern.

Sincerely yours,

Organization

One further word about style: A good business letter must be well organized. You must *plan in advance* everything you want to say; you must *say everything necessary* in your message; and then you must stop. In short, a letter must be logical, complete, and concise.

When planning a letter and before you start to write, jot down the main point you want to make. Then, list all the details necessary to make that point; these may be facts, reasons, or explanations. Finally, rearrange your list; in the letter, you will want to mention things in a logical order so that your message will come across as clearly as possible.

Making a letter complete takes place during the planning stage, too. Check your list to make sure you have included all the relevant details; the reader of your finished letter must have all the information he or she will need. In addition to facts, reasons, and explanations, necessary information could also entail an appeal to your reader's emotions or understanding. In other words, SAY EVERYTHING YOU CAN TO ELICIT FROM YOUR READER THE RESPONSE YOU'D LIKE.

On the other hand, you must be careful not to say too much. You must know when a letter is finished. If a message is brief, resist the temptation to "pad" it; if you've said what you have to say in just a few lines, don't try to fill the letter out. One mistake is to reiterate an idea. If you've already offered your thanks, you will upset the logical order and, therefore, the impact of your letter if you end with:

Thank you once again.

Tacking on a separate additional message will similarly weaken the effect of your main point. Imagine receiving a collection letter for a long overdue bill that concludes:

Let us take this opportunity to remind you that our January White Sale begins next week, with three preview days for our special charge customers.

Also, don't give your reader more information than is needed:

Because my husband's birthday is October 12, I would like to order the three-piece luggage ensemble in your fall catalog.

Certainly, an order clerk would much prefer to know the style number of the luggage than the date of your husband's birth.

Similarly, you should strive to eliminate repetitious words and phrases from your letters. For example:

I have received your invitation *inviting me* to participate in your annual Career Conference.

Since all invitations invite, the words *inviting me* are unnecessary. Another common mistake is to say:

> the green-colored carpet

or:

> the carpet that is green in color

Green *is* a color, so to use the word *color* is wordy.

Adverbs often cause the same problem:

> If we cooperate together, the project will be finished quickly.

Cooperate already means work together, so using the word *together* is unnecessary.

Also, when one word will accurately replace several, use the one word. Instead of:

> Mr. Kramer handled the job *in an efficient manner*.

write:

> Mr. Kramer handled the job *efficiently*.

Now consider the following two sample letters. Notice the repetitions in the first that are eliminated in the second.

VERSION I

Dear Ms. Rodriguez:

I am very pleased with the invitation that I received from you inviting me to make a speech for the National Association of Secretaries on June 11. Unfortunately, I regret that I cannot attend the meeting on June 11. I feel that I do not have sufficient time to prepare myself because I received your invitation on June 3 and it is not enough time to prepare myself completely for the speech.

Yours truly,

VERSION II

Dear Ms. Rodriguez:

I am pleased with the invitation to speak to the National Association of Secretaries. Unfortunately, I cannot attend the meeting on June 11.

I feel that I will not have sufficient time to prepare myself because I received your invitation on June 3.

I will be happy to address your organization on another occasion if you would give me a bit more notice. Best of luck with your meeting.

Sincerely yours,

Of course, as you exclude irrelevant details and repetitions, you should be careful NOT to cut corners by leaving out necessary words. For example, some writers, in a misguided attempt at efficiency, omit articles (*the*, *a*, and *an*) and prepositions:

> Please send order special delivery.

The only effect of omitting "the" and "by" here is to make the request rude and impersonal. The correct sentence is:

> Please send the order by special delivery.

Electronic Mail

When you use a computer terminal to communicate either inside or outside your organization, you should not abandon the basic principles of business writing. You should still strive for CLARITY, COMPLETENESS, CORRECTNESS, and COURTESY as you would in more traditional forms of correspondence. But when using electronic mail, there are a few additional guidelines:

1. Keep your message short: You want your message to fit on one screen, whenever possible, thus keeping all important information visible at once.
   DO use short phrases, abbreviations, and industry jargon known to your correspondent.
   DON'T be so brief that your meaning is lost or your approach seems unprofessional.
2. Be sure your message is easy to answer: Let your reader know at the start what your subject is *and* what you want done.
   DO ask questions that can be answered with one word.
   DON'T give long instructions that require your reader to leave the terminal or possibly clear the screen for information.
3. Beware of electronic eavesdroppers: Not only can your message be forwarded by the receiver or printed for others to read; it will also be stored in the computer's memory (even if you delete the message!).
   DO take advantage of the speed and efficiency of electronic mail.
   DON'T send any messages that could cast doubt on your character or capabilities.

Gender Neutral Language

As women have assumed a larger and larger role in the workplace, the words used to describe business roles have been reexamined. Since, for example, a "businessman" often turns out to be a woman, more and more people are opting for the sexually neutral term "businessperson."

The third person singular pronouns in English (*he/she*, *him/her*, *his/hers*) are divided by gender, so pronoun use presents a problem for the writer wishing to avoid "sexist" language. Traditionally, masculine pronouns have been used to refer to abstract, singular human nouns:

> *An employer* must be able to rely on *his* secretary.

But use of such masculine references is no longer considered the preferred form.

To avoid using gender-specific references, several solutions are possible. A common approach, if an awkward one, is to use both third person singular pronouns:

> *An employer* must be able to rely on *his* or *her* secretary.

This, however, can become extremely cumbersome, especially when a passage contains several pronouns. Some writers, therefore, revise their sentence to avoid singular human nouns in the first place; that way, a third person plural pronoun (with no gender reference) may be used:

> *Employers* must be able to rely on *their* secretaries.

Yet another way to handle the problem, perhaps the simplest, is to alternate the masculine and feminine pronouns throughout your writing.

Keep in mind, though, that many companies have policies regarding sexist language. Some, for instance, still discourage the use of the term *Ms.* on company correspondence; some retain old forms such as *chairman* or *congressman*. Similarly, a company may have a policy regarding pronoun use; before you revise your boss's or your own letters to eliminate all the sexist pronouns, find out how your company stands on the issue.

Summary

A successful business writing style will be

1. clear and simple so that facts and information are easy to understand.
2. polite and tactful so that the reader receives the message with a positive attitude.
3. reader-oriented so that the reader feels you understand each other's point of view.

Business letters will also be

1. logically organized, cantaining complete and accurate information.
2. concise, containing no unnecessary information.
3. gender neutral, containing no offensive or insulting language.

■■■■■■ PRACTICE CORRESPONDENCE

On another sheet of paper, rewrite these letters to make them more courteous, concise, and *you*-oriented.

A.

Dear Ms. Lawson:

I regret to inform you that we are completely booked up for the week of August 22. We have no rooms available because the National Word

Processors Association will be holding their convention at our hotel during the week of August 22. As you will surely understand, we have to reserve as many rooms as possible for members of the association.

If you can't change the date of your trip, maybe you could find the double room with bath that you want at another hotel here in Little Rock.

Cordially,

B.

Dear Mr. Ross:

With reference to your letter of Thursday last, I can't answer it because my boss, Ms. Leonard, is out of town. If I gave you any information about the new contract with Hastings Development Corporation, she might not like it.

If Ms. Leonard wants you to have that information, I'll have her write to you when she returns in two weeks.

Yours truly,

C.

Dear Ms. Graham:

The information you want having to do with filing for an absentee ballot for the upcoming Presidential election, is not available from our office.

Why don't you write your local Board of Elections?

Sorry.

Sincerely yours,

2.

Letter Format

Words to Watch For

ample (*adj*) enough to satisfy
consistent (*adj*) in agreement, harmonious
correspond (*v*) to agree with or match
ream (*n*) a quantity of paper, usually 500 sheets

Before we begin to discuss letter *content*, we must examine letter appearance because the physical condition of a letter makes the first impression on your reader. Before reading even one word you have written, the reader has formed an opinion based on the way your letter looks—the arrangement, the print quality, and so on.

When you have composed the body of your letter and are ready to type, keep in mind three things:

1. **Typing**—Letters should be single-spaced with double-spacing between paragraphs. Print should be clear and dark. Errors should not be erased or corrected after printing.
2. **Paragraphing**—Paragraph breaks should come at logical points in your message and should also result in an EVEN appearance. A one-line paragraph followed by an eight-line paragraph will not look balanced. Paragraphs of *approximately* the same length will please the eye.
3. **White space**—In addition to the space created by paragraphing, leave space by centering your letter on the page. An ample margin of white space should surround the message, top and bottom as well as both sides. If a letter is brief, avoid beginning to type too high on the page; if a letter is long, do not hesitate to use an additional sheet of paper. (See Figure 2–1 for recommended spacing between letter parts.)

Parts of a Business Letter

While the horizontal placement of letter parts may vary (see the next section, "Arrangement Styles"), the vertical order of these parts is standard. Refer to the model letter (Figure 2–1) as you study the following list of letter parts.

1. LETTERHEAD: This is printed and supplied by your employer. It is used only for the first page of a letter.
2. DATELINE: The date on which the letter is being prepared is typed a few lines below the letterhead.

3. INSIDE ADDRESS: The address of your reader is typed as it will appear on the envelope.
4. ATTENTION LINE: This is not always required. It should be used when the letter is addressed to a company or organization as a whole, but you want it to be handled there by a specific individual. It should be underlined or typed in capitals.
5. SALUTATION: You should use an individual's name whenever it is known, preceded by the word "Dear." When the reader's name is *not* known, the person's title is the next best term in a salutation. "Dear Sir," "Dear Madam or Sir," "Gentlemen," "Gentlemen and Ladies" are acceptable in cases of extreme formality.
6. SUBJECT LINE: Like the attention line, this is often omitted, but it is courteous to include it. It identifies the content of your message, so your reader may decide whether the letter requires immediate attention. It should be underlined or typed in capitals.
7. BODY: This is the actual message of your letter.
8. COMPLIMENTARY CLOSING: This is a polite, formal way to end a letter; standard forms are "Yours truly" or "Truly yours," "Sincerely yours," "Respectfully yours." Excessively familiar closings should be avoided, except in special situations. "Best wishes," for example, could be used when the reader is well known to you. Affectionate expressions, such as "Fondly" or "Love," should, obviously, be reserved for private correspondence.
9. COMPANY SIGNATURE: Another item often omitted from less formal correspondence, it should be used when the signer of the letter is writing as a spokesperson for the company, not as an individual. Since this information appears in the letterhead, some companies omit it altogether.
10. SIGNER'S IDENTIFICATION: Printed four lines below the previous item to allow space for the signature, this includes the signer's name and any relevant titles.
11. REFERENCE INITIALS: Consisting of the signer's initials in capitals followed by a slash or colon followed by the lowercase initials of the person preparing the letter, this item serves as a reminder of who prepared the letter.
12. ENCLOSURE REMINDER: Consisting of the word "enclosure," or the word "enclosure" followed by a list of the enclosed items, this is a practical courtesy to prevent your reader from discarding important matter with the envelope.
13. "CC" NOTATION: Also a courtesy, this tells the reader who has been sent a "carbon" copy (that is, a duplicate copy) of the letter.

Arrangement Styles

The horizontal placement of letter parts is flexible—within the limits of five basic styles. Often, however, a company will have a preferred arrangement style that employees are required to use.

① **Flanagan's** Department Store
12207 Sunset Strip
Los Angeles, California 91417

② June 7, 19—

③ Ketchum Collection Agency
1267 Hollywood Boulevard
Los Angeles, California 91401

④ ATTENTION: MS. TERRY ROBERTS

⑤ Gentlemen and Ladies:

⑥ Subject: Mr. Gary Daniels, Account # 69 112 003

We would like to turn over to your services the account of
Mr. Gary Daniels, 4441 Natick Avenue, Sherman Oaks, California
91418. The balance on Mr. Daniels' account, $829.95, is now
120 days past due; although we have sent him four statements
and five letters, we have been unable to collect his debt.

⑦ Mr. Daniels is employed by West Coast Furniture Showrooms, Inc.
He banks at the Natick Avenue branch of Third National City
Bank and has been our customer for four years. We have
enclosed his file for your reference.

We are confident that we can rely on Ketchum as we have in the
past. Please let us know if there is any further information with
which we can furnish you.

⑧ Sincerely yours,

⑨ FLANAGAN'S DEPARTMENT
STORE

Martha Fayman

⑩ Martha Fayman
Credit Manager

⑪ MF/wg
⑫ Enclosure
⑬ cc Mr. Norman Hyman

Figure 2–1
The Parts of a Business Letter

FULL-BLOCKED (Figure 2–2): All letter parts begin at the left margin. It is therefore the fastest traditional arrangement style to type.

BLOCKED (Figure 2–3): Like full-blocked, all letter parts begin at the left margin, *except* the dateline, complimentary closing, company signature, and writer's identification, which start at the horizontal center of the page. (Options—the dateline may end at the right margin; attention and subject lines may be centered or indented five or ten spaces.)

SEMI-BLOCKED *or* MODIFIED BLOCKED (Figure 2–4): This is the same as a blocked letter with one change: the beginning of each paragraph is indented five or ten spaces.

SQUARE-BLOCKED (Figure 2–5): This is the same as a full-blocked letter with two changes: the date is typed on the same line as the start of the inside address and ends at the right margin; reference initials and enclosure reminder are typed on the same lines as the signature and signer's identification. As a result, corners are squared off. This arrangement saves space, allowing longer letters to fit onto a single page. (Be sure to use a line at least 50 spaces long so that the inside address won't run into the dateline.)

SIMPLIFIED *or* AMS (Figure 2–6): Designed by the Administrative Management Society, this style is the same as full-blocked, except: (1) no salutation or complimentary closing is used; (2) an entirely capitalized subject line (without the word "subject") *must* be used; (3) the signer's identification is typed in all capitals; and (4) lists are indented five spaces unless numbered or lettered (in which case they are blocked with no periods after the numbers or letters). This style is extremely efficient, requiring much less time to type than other styles; however, it is also impersonal. For this reason, the reader's name should be mentioned at least once in the body.

Punctuation Styles

Regardless of punctuation style, the *only* letter parts (outside of the body) to be followed by punctuation marks are the salutation and complimentary closing. Within the body, the general rules of punctuation apply.

OPEN: No punctuation is used, except in the body. (See Figure 2–2.)

STANDARD: The salutation is followed by a colon; the complimentary closing is followed by a comma. (See Figure 2–3.)

> **Note:** The salutation and closing should be punctuated consistently: either *both* are followed by punctuation or *neither* is followed by punctuation. Note, too, that a comma is NOT used after the salutation; this practice is reserved for private correspondence.

NORP
NATIONAL ORGANIZATION OF RETIRED PERSONS
Freeport High School, Freeport, Vermont 66622

October 14, [*year*]

Ms. Iva Stravinsky
Attorney-at-Law
200 Center Street
Freeport, Vermont 66622

Dear Ms. Stravinsky

Subject: Guest Lecture

The members of the Freeport chapter of the National Organization of Retired Persons would indeed be interested in a lecture on "Proposed Changes in the Financing of Medicare." Therefore, with much appreciation, I accept your offer to address our club.

The NORP meets every Tuesday at 8 P.M. in the auditorium of Freeport High School. The programs for our meetings through November 20 have already been established. However, I will call you in a few days to schedule a date for your lecture for the first Tuesday after the 20th that meets your convenience.

The membership and I look forward to your lecture on a topic so important to us all.

Sincerely yours

NATIONAL ORGANIZATION OF RETIRED PERSONS

Henry Purcell
President

HP/bm

Figure 2–2
Full-Blocked Letter Style

NORP
NATIONAL ORGANIZATION OF RETIRED PERSONS
Freeport High School, Freeport, Vermont 66622

October 14, [*year*]

Ms. Iva Stravinsky
Attorney-at-Law
200 Center Street
Freeport, Vermont 66622

Dear Ms. Stravinsky:

Subject: Guest Lecture

The members of the Freeport chapter of the National Organization of Retired Persons would indeed be interested in a lecture on "Proposed Changes in the Financing of Medicare." Therefore, with much appreciation, I accept your offer to address our club.

The NORP meets every Tuesday at 8 P.M. in the auditorium of Freeport High School. The programs for our meetings through November 20 have already been established. However, I will call you in a few days to schedule a date for your lecture for the first Tuesday after the 20th that meets your convenience.

The membership and I look forward to your lecture on a topic so important to us all.

Sincerely yours,

Henry Purcell
President

HP/bm

Figure 2–3
Blocked Letter Style

NORP

NATIONAL ORGANIZATION OF RETIRED PERSONS

Freeport High School, Freeport, Vermont 66622

October 14, [*year*]

Ms. Iva Stravinsky
Attorney-at-Law
200 Center Street
Freeport, Vermont 66622

Dear Ms. Stravinsky:

Subject: Guest Lecture

The members of the Freeport chapter of the National Organization of Retired Persons would indeed be interested in a lecture on "Proposed Changes in the Financing of Medicare." Therefore, with much appreciation, I accept your offer to address our club.

The NORP meets every Tuesday at 8 P.M. in the auditorium of Freeport High School. The programs for our meetings through November 20 have already been established. However, I will call you in a few days to schedule a date for your lecture for the first Tuesday after the 20th that meets your convenience.

The membership and I look forward to your lecture on a topic so important to us all.

Sincerely yours,

Henry Purcell
President

HP/bm

Figure 2–4
Semi-Blocked Letter Style

NORP
NATIONAL ORGANIZATION OF RETIRED PERSONS
Freeport High School, Freeport, Vermont 66622

Ms. Iva Stravinsky   October 14, [*year*]
Attorney-at-Law
200 Center Street
Freeport, Vermont 66622

Dear Ms. Stravinsky:

SUBJECT: GUEST LECTURE

The members of the Freeport chapter of the National Organization of Retired Persons would indeed be interested in a lecture on "Proposed Changes in the Financing of Medicare." Therefore, with much appreciation, I accept your offer to address our club.

The NORP meets every Tuesday at 8 P.M. in the auditorium of Freeport High School. The programs for our meetings through November 20 have already been established. However, I will call you in a few days to schedule a date for your lecture for the first Tuesday after the 20th that meets your convenience.

The membership and I look forward to your lecture on a topic so important to us all.

Sincerely yours,

NATIONAL ORGANIZATION OF RETIRED PERSONS

Henry Purcell
President   HP/bm

Figure 2–5
Square-Blocked Letter Style

NORP
NATIONAL ORGANIZATION OF RETIRED PERSONS
Freeport High School, Freeport, Vermont 66622

October 14, [*year*]

Ms. Iva Stravinsky
Attorney-at-Law
200 Center Street
Freeport, Vermont 66622

GUEST LECTURE

The members of the Freeport chapter of the National Organization of Retired Persons would indeed be interested in a lecture on "Proposed Changes in the Financing of Medicare." Therefore, with much appreciation, I accept your offer to address our club.

The NORP meets every Tuesday at 8 P.M. in the auditorium of Freeport High School. The programs for our meetings through November 20 have already been established. However, I will call you in a few days to schedule a date for your lecture for the first Tuesday after the 20th that meets your convenience.

The membership and I look forward, Ms. Stravinsky, to your lecture on a topic so important to us all.

HENRY PURCELL, PRESIDENT

HP/bm

Figure 2–6
Simplified Letter Style

FRANKLIN AND GORDON OFFICE SUPPLIES, INC.
72-01 Lefferts Boulevard, Rego Park, New York, 11206

September 15, [*year*]

Robert Nathan, CPA
222 Bergen Street
New Orleans, Louisiana 77221

Dear Mr. Nathan:

We appreciate your interest in Franklin and Gordon office supplies
and are delighted to send you the information you requested:

>   Ruled ledger paper, by the ream only, costs $45; with the
>   purchase of six or more reams, the price is reduced to
> $42 per ream, a savings of at least $18.

>   Black, reinforced ledger binders are $25 each; with the
>   purchase of six or more binders, the price is only $23
>   each, a savings of at least $12.

Because we are the manufacturers of many other fine office
supplies, ranging from ballpoint pens to promotional novelties,
we have enclosed for your consideration a copy of our current
catalog. Should you decide to place an order, you may use the
convenient order form in the center of the catalog or call our
24-hour-toll free number (1-800-999-9000).

Please let us know if we may be of further assistance.

Sincerely yours,

FRANKLIN AND GORDON OFFICE SUPPLIES, INC.

George Gillian
Customer Service Manager

GG:jc
Enclosure

Figure 2–7
Special Paragraphing

Postscripts

It is best to avoid postscripts; when a letter is well planned, all necessary information will be included in the body. However, when a postscript is required, it is arranged as the other paragraphs in the letter have been, preceded by "P.S." or "PS":

> P.S. Let me remind you of our special discount on orders for a dozen or more of the same model appliance.

Special Paragraphing

When a message contains quotations of prices or notations of special data, this information is set in a special paragraph (see Figure 2–7), indented five spaces on the left and right, preceded and followed by a blank line.

The Envelope

An envelope should be addressed to correspond with the inside address. On an envelope, though, the state name should be abbreviated in accordance with the United States Postal Service ZIP-code style. On a standard business-size envelope, the address should begin four inches from the left edge, fourteen lines from the top (see Figure 2–8).

In accordance with Postal Service guidelines, the address should be blocked and single-spaced, and should include the ZIP code one space after the state. Because NO information should appear below the ZIP code, special instructions (such as *ATT: Mr. Smith* or *Please Forward*) should be placed four lines below the return address. Similarly, mailing services, such as *Priority Mail* or *Certified Mail*, should be placed below the stamp.

The return address, matching the letterhead, is usually printed on business envelopes.

Flanagan's Department Store

12207 Sunset Strip
Los Angeles, California 91417

Attention Ms. Terry Roberts   Registered Mail

　　　　　Ketchum Collection Agency
　　　　　1267 Hollywood Boulevard
　　　　　Los Angeles, CA 91401

Figure 2–8
The Envelope

Summary

There are several parts to a correctly written business letter. These parts must be arranged on the printed page following one of the five standard styles. Also, the envelope must be prepared to follow United States Postal Service guidelines.

REMEMBER, the appearance of your business letters sends a message about *you*!

■■■■■■ PRACTICE CORRESPONDENCE

Type this letter in each of the five arrangement styles: (A) Full-blocked, (B) Blocked, (C) Semi-blocked, (D) Square-blocked, and (E) Simplified.

Dateline: July 9, [*year*]
Inside Address: The Middle Atlantic Institute of Technology,
                        149 Danbury Road, Danbury, Connecticut 50202
Attention Line: Attention Dean Claude Monet
Salutation: Gentlemen and Ladies
Subject Line: Educational Exchange
Body:

The Commission for Educational Exchange between the United States and Belgium has advised me to contact you in order to obtain employment assistance.

I received my doctoral degree with a "grande distinction" from the University of Brussels and would like to teach French (my native language), English, Dutch, or German.

My special field is English literature; I wrote my dissertation on James Joyce, but I am also qualified to teach languages to business students. I have been active in the field of applied linguistics for the past two years at the University of Brussels.

I look forward to hearing from you.

Complimentary Closing: Respectfully yours
Signer's Identification: Jacqueline Brauer
Reference Initials: JB:db

3.
Request Letters

Words to Watch For

applicable (*adj*) relevant
closure (*n*) state of being concluded
discount (*n*) reduction from the regular price
fiscal (*adj*) financial
motivate (*v*) move to action
potential (*adj*) possible
recipient (*n*) one who receives
weather vane (*n*) a device for showing wind direction

As a businessperson, you will surely have to write request letters. The need for information or special favors, services, or products arises daily in almost every type of business. There are many reasons for writing a request letter:

1. To obtain information (such as prices or technical data)
2. To receive printed matter (such as booklets, catalogs, price lists, and reports)
3. To receive sample products
4. To order merchandise
5. To engage services (including repair or maintenance services)
6. To make reservations (at hotels, restaurants, theaters)
7. To seek special favors (such as permission, assistance, or advice).

Even though some requests, such as ordering merchandise, are routine matters, the general guidelines for business letter writing are especially important when writing any request. Tact and courtesy are essential when you want your reader to *act*. If you want your reader to act *promptly*, your letter must encourage prompt action; therefore, all requests should:

1. Be specific and brief.
2. Be reasonable.
3. Provide complete, accurate information.

Inquiries

More than anything else, an inquiry must be *easy to answer*. Usually, inquiries offer the reader no immediate reward or advantage. (*Maybe* you will become a future customer. *Maybe* answering your letter will build goodwill toward the business.) Therefore, you must express your inquiry so that your reader will answer even if he or she is very busy.

First of all, you should decide exactly what you want *before* you write. This should include the specific information that you need as well as the specific action you would like your reader to take. Consider this request:

Dear Sir or Madam:

Please send us information about your office copiers so that we will know whether one would be suited to our type of business.

Yours truly,

The recipient of this letter would not know how to respond. She could simply send a brochure or catalog, but she could not possibly explain the advantages of her company's machines without knowing your company's needs. You have *not* made it easy for her to act.

An inquiry should include specific questions worded to obtain specific facts as answers. The manufacturer in our example may make many models of copiers, so the inquiry must clearly identify the type your company would consider.

Notice how the revised letter (Figure 3–1) makes it easier for your reader to respond. It gives a clear picture of what you are looking for; therefore, she can determine which of the company's products might interest you. Also, by mentioning the REASON for your inquiry, you motivate her to respond. (The purchase you are planning is a potential sale for RBM.) Finally, by letting her know WHEN you intend to buy, you encourage her to reply promptly.

When a request does *not* involve a future sale, you should make your letter even more convenient for your reader:

1. List the specific facts you want.
2. Enclose a self-addressed, stamped envelope.
3. Suggest a way in which you can reciprocate.

Dear Mr. Greenbaum:

I am taking a course in Principles of Advertising at Smithville Community College in Smithville, Ohio, and am doing my term project on the ways in which American automobile manufacturers have been competing in the small-car market.

I would therefore greatly appreciate your sending me the following specifications on the new RX-7:

1. Fuel economy statistics.

2. Technological advances (such as steering system, brake system, and engine capacity).

3. Available options.

I would also find it very helpful if you told me in which magazine (or other mass media) you began your advertising campaign.

I am certain my classmates will find this information extremely interesting. I will be sure to send you a copy of my report as soon as it is complete.

Respectfully yours,

Mahoney and Millman, Inc.
1951 Benson Street
Bronx, New York 10465

May 2, [*year*]

RBM Manufacturing Company, Inc.
4022 Ninth Avenue
New York, New York 10055

Dear Sir or Madam:

We intend to purchase a new office copier before the end of the fiscal year. We would like to consider an RBM copier and wonder if you have a model that would suit our needs.

Our office is small, and a copier would generally be used by only three secretaries. We run approximately 3,000 copies a month and prefer a machine that uses regular paper. We would like a collator, but rarely need to run off more than 25 copies at any one time.

We would also like to know about your warranty and repair service.

Since our fiscal years ends June 30, [*year*], we hope to hear from you soon.

Sincerely yours,

William Wilson
Office Manager

WW/sw

Figure 3–1
Inquiry

Orders

Many companies use special forms for ordering merchandise or service. They may use their own, called a *purchase order*, or one provided by the seller, called an *order form*. These forms have blank spaces for the necessary information.

Nevertheless, there will be occasions when an order must be put into letter format. The letter must include COMPLETE, ACCURATE INFORMATION because incomplete orders result in delayed deliveries, and incorrect information results in the shipping of the wrong merchandise.

Every order should include:

1. the name of the item being ordered
2. the item's number (catalog number, style number, model number, and so on)
3. quantity desired (often in large units such as dozens, cases, reams)
4. description (such as size, weight, color, material, finish, extra features)
5. unit price
6. applicable discounts
7. applicable sales tax
8. total price
9. method of payment (such as charge account, including the account number, c.o.d., check)
10. desired delivery date
11. method of shipment (such as parcel post or air express)
12. delivery address (which may vary from the billing address)
13. authorized signature

In addition, if your order is in response to an advertisement, you should mention its source (such as the title and issue date of a magazine or newspaper).

The following letter is too vague:

Dear Sirs:

Please send me one of your weather vanes that I saw advertised for $34.95. We have recently repainted our garage, and a weather vane would be a wonderful finishing touch.

My check is enclosed.

Sincerely,

First of all, an order clerk would not know what to send this customer unless the company manufactured only one style of weather vane for $34.95. Also, instead of providing the NECESSARY FACTS, the writer included unnecessary details. Generally, it is NOT NECESSARY TO MENTION A REASON FOR AN ORDER. Orders are routine and handled in quantity. The seller does not care why you are buying.

While the preceding letter would require additional correspondence before the order could be shipped, the letter in Figure 3–2 assures prompt delivery.

---

250 Commonwealth Avenue
Boston, Massachusetts 02118
February 14, [*year*]

Cape Cod Ornaments, Inc.
94 State Road
West Yarmouth, Massachusetts 02757

Dear Madam or Sir:

I have seen your ad in the Boston <u>Globe</u> of Sunday, February 12, and would like to order the following weather vane:

   Model EPC-18" eagle with arrow, copper, $34.95.

I would like the weather vane sent to the above address by parcel post and charged, with any applicable sales tax and handling costs, to my VISA account (number 003 0971 A109; expiration date, 3/99).

   Yours truly,

Figure 3–2
Order

Summary

A request letter must be:

1. specific.
2. brief.
3. reasonable.

The information in the request letter must be:

1. complete.
2. accurate.

Most important, a request letter must be:

1. courteous.
2. easy to answer.

███████ **PRACTICE CORRESPONDENCE**

For each of the following activities, prepare a request letter using appropriate arrangement and punctuation styles.

A. You are the program chairperson of the Harrisburg Civic Association. Write a letter to Margaret Belmont, mayor of Harrisburg, asking if she would be willing to attend a future meeting of the association and address the members on a topic of general interest. Meetings are held the second Wednesday of every month at 7:30 P.M. in the basement meeting room of the community center. Previous speakers have included Raymond Delacorte, president of Grand Northern Motels, Inc., who spoke on the topic "Increasing Tourism in Harrisburg," and Gregory Lardas, CPA, who spoke on the topic "Local Property Tax: Boost or Burden?" You may explain that meetings are attended by approximately 75 community-minded people and that the lecture segment of the meeting usually lasts about one hour.

B. As assistant buyer for Fenway's Toy Store, 1704 North Broadway, Richmond, Virginia 23261, write a letter to the Marco Toy Company, Inc., 223 Sunrise Highway, Glen Cove, New York 11566, to order two dozen Baby Jenny dolls (at $10 each), one dozen Baby Jenny layette sets (at $15 each), and three dozen 18-inch Tootsie-Wootsie teddy bears (at $7 each). You would like to have these items in stock in time for the pre–Christmas selling season. You want to make this purchase on account and have it shipped air express. If Marco has available any special Christmas displays for their merchandise, you would like to receive these, too.

C. As assistant finance manager of your company, it is your responsibility to report to your supervisors about year-end tax-saving measures that can be taken within the organization. Write a letter to Wilda Stewart (Stewart and Stewart CPA's, 466 Main Street, Eugene, Oregon 84403), an accountant you met recently at a seminar on the new federal tax laws. Ask her for information for your report, including pointers on deferring income and accelerating deductions as well as year-end expenditures.

D. Answer the following advertisement in the current issue of *Office Workers' Weekly:*

COPY KWIK COPYSTAND

America's most widely used copystand: Functional, good-looking . . . saves precious desk space . . . relieves neck and eye strain . . . attaches easily to any computer monitor . . . comes with copy clip and magnetic line guide. One-year warranty. $24 plus $2.95 postage and handling (New Jersey residents please add appropriate sales tax). CKC, Inc., 2019 Logan Street, Paramus, New Jersey 70622.

E. You are a sales supervisor at the Am-Lux Company, Inc., 529 Eaton Avenue, Bethlehem, Pennsylvania 18115. You recently read an article by Louisa Sanchez entitled "From Lead to Deal: Ten Over-Looked Steps to Closure" in *High Commission* magazine. You believe the twenty-five salespeople in your department would benefit from reading the article. Write a letter to Ms. Sanchez, in care of *High Commission*, 705 Tenth Avenue, New York, New York, 10077, requesting her permission to make twenty-five copies of her article for circulation only within your company.

4.
Replies

Words to Watch For

dispatch (*n*) a message
divulge (*v*) to reveal or disclose
salvage (*v*) to save from destruction
savvy (*n*) insight, understanding
superfluous (*adj*) extra, more than necessary
unsolicited (*adj*) unrequested

ANSWERING the mail is an important job at most companies; therefore, knowing how to write a reply is a valuable and marketable skill.

There are many types of replies, including:

1. acknowledgments
2. follow-ups
3. confirmations
4. remittances
5. order acknowledgments
6. stopgap letters
7. inquiry replies
8. referrals
9. refusals

Some companies use form letters for certain types of replies, such as order acknowledgments. Nevertheless, a reply is often a good sales opportunity, so a personal, carefully worded letter can lead to both profits and goodwill.

A request is similar to a reply. It should be *specific* and *complete*. However, it is not necessary for a reply to be brief. Because a reply must be both *helpful* and *sales oriented*, it is often difficult to be brief.

On the other hand, a reply must be *prompt*. You may even point out your promptness to the reader directly in an effort to achieve a "*you* approach."

Dear Mr. Mechanic:

I received your letter this morning and wanted to be sure you would have our current price list before the end of the week. . . .

This type of sentence is a modest way to let your reader know you are *interested* and want to be *helpful*. In fact, whenever possible, a response should go a little further than the original request. An extra bit of information or unsolicited help can turn an inquirer into a steady customer.

Acknowledgments

An acknowledgment (Figure 4–1) should be written when you receive merchandise, material, money, or information. Such a letter is a courtesy, letting your reader know that his communication has reached its destination. When the matter received was not an order, an acknowledgment can also serve as a thank-you note.

Markham's Cards and Gifts
400 Paseo de Peralta, Santa Fe, New Mexico 87501

October 23, [year]

Mr. Herbert Benjamin
Sales Representative
Newmart Cards, Inc.
399 North Canon Drive
Beverly Hills, California 90210

Dear Mr. Benjamin:

Thank you for arranging for us to receive our Christmas card displays a bit early this year. We installed them as soon as they arrived on Monday, and we've already sold out two lines!

The two months between now and Christmas seem destined to be busy ones, and I suspect you'll be hearing from us again soon.

Best wishes,

Hedy Rosen
Assistant Buyer

Figure 4–1
Acknowledgment

Follow-Ups

After a decision or agreement has been made, either at a meeting or in conversation, it is a good idea to send a follow-up letter (Figure 4–2) to establish a written record of the transaction.

THE COMMITTEE TO KEEP MINNESOTA GREEN
24 NORTH MAIN STREET, BLACKDUCK, MINNESOTA 56630

June 3, [*year*]

Ms. Christine Solars
Solars, Solars, and Wright
62 Onigum Road
Walker, Minnesota 56484

Dear Ms. Solars:

We are pleased that you will be participating in the Ecology Colloquium sponsored by The Committee to Keep Minnesota Green. As we discussed in our telephone conversation this morning, the Colloquium will take place on June 29 in the convention room at the Blackduck Inn.

The Colloquium will begin with the keynote address at 10:30 A.M. At 11:00, you will join our other guests of honor in a debate on the topic, "The Cost of Conservation: Public or Private Responsibilities?" Following the debate, luncheon will be served in the main dining room, where you will, of course, be a guest of the Committee.

Along with the other members of the Committee, I am looking forward to our meeting on the 29th.

Sincerely yours,

Figure 4–2
Follow-Up

Confirmations

Confirmations are routine for such businesses as hotels and travel agencies, but other businesses may also need to send them. For example, doctors and repair services can avoid wasted time by contacting patients and customers a day or so in advance of scheduled appointments. Such confirmations are frequently made by telephone, but a form letter or postcard also effectively transmits *clear, correct,* and *complete* information, particularly when the type of business requires large numbers of confirmations. As is often the case, however, a letter written to a specific individual (see Figure 4–3), can turn that customer into a *regular* customer by adding a personal touch.

The Barclay

5500 South 96th Street, Omaha, Nebraska 68127

August 10, [*year*]

Mr. Albert Durrell
2233 Connecticut Avenue, N.W.
Washington, D.C. 20008

Dear Mr. Durrell:

This letter will confirm your reservation for a single room with bath for August 24–27. Your room will be available after 2 P.M. on the 24th.

Since you will be arriving in Omaha by plane, you may want to take advantage of The Barclay's Shuttle. Our limousine departs from the domestic terminal every hour on the half hour, and the service is free for guests of the hotel.

Cordially yours,

Figure 4–3
Confirmation

Remittances

Companies often request that their bill, or a portion of their bill, accompany a remittance. When this is not the case, a cover letter is necessary to explain what your enclosed check is for. This letter should contain any information regarding your order that is needed for the proper crediting of your account: include your account number, the invoice number, and the amount of the check. DO NOT include extra information that may confuse an accounts receivable clerk. Remarks not directly related to the remittance should be reserved for a separate letter.

Dear Gentlemen and Ladies:

The enclosed check for $312.68 is in payment of invoice no. 10463. Please credit my account (no. 663-711-M).

Yours truly,

Order Acknowledgments

Many companies today have abandoned the practice of acknowledging orders, particularly when the order will be filled promptly. Some companies respond to orders by immediately sending an invoice, and some use printed acknowledgment forms. But, no matter how it is handled, the confirmation of an order helps to establish goodwill by reassuring the customer that the order has been received.

The initial order from a new customer SHOULD be acknowledged. This acknowledgment welcomes the new customer and encourages further business (Figure 4–4). Similarly, an unusually large order by a regular customer deserves a note of appreciation.

Any order acknowledgment, whatever the circumstances, should contain specific information. It should let the customer know exactly how the order is being handled by:

1. mentioning the date of the order.
2. including the order or invoice number.
3. explaining the date and method of shipment.
4. acknowledging the method of payment.

All order acknowledgments should also express your appreciation for the order and assure the customer that it will be filled.

An acknowledgment is often an opportunity for a sales pitch. If a salesperson was involved in the order, his or her name should appear somewhere in the letter. The letter may also include a description of the merchandise to reaffirm the wisdom of the customer's purchase. Other related products may also be mentioned to generate customer interest in your company's products.

_pp_

PAYTON'S PLASTICS, INC.
1313 Spruce Street
Philadelphia, PA 17512

September 16, [*year*]

Ms. Cybel Megan
FRAMES-BY-YOU
26 Frith Street
London, WC2, England

Dear Ms. Megan:

We are please to have received your order of September 15 and
would like to welcome you as a new customer of Payton's Plastics.

Your order (No. 62997) for one dozen 4' × 5' sheets of 1/8" clear
Lucite and two dozen 4' × 5' sheets of 1/8" smoked Lucite is being
processed. It will be shipped in two separate consignments. The
first consignment will be shipped September 23, expected to arrive
in London October 5. You may contact the freight forwarder, Global
Transhippers Ltd. (171–327–7757), for further details.

We are sure you will appreciate the fine finish and tensile strength
of our entire line of plastics. Ms. Julie Methel, your sales representative, will be in London next week. She will call on you with a catalog and samples.

Cordially,

PAYTON'S PLASTICS, INC.

Howard Roberts
Customer Relations

Figure 4–4
Order Acknowledgment

Because orders cannot always be filled promptly and smoothly, situations arise in which a wise businessperson will send more than just an acknowledgment.

Customers, for example, do not always place complete orders. When an essential piece of information has been omitted, the order must be delayed and a tactful letter sent. Although the customer in such a case is at fault, the letter must neither place any blame nor express impatience. Indeed, the customer's own impatience must be avoided with a positive, friendly tone. A bit of reselling—reminding the customer of the order's desirability—is often useful in a letter of this kind.

Dear Mr. North:

Thank you for your order of October 22 for 6 rolls of black nylon webbing. We are eager to deliver Order 129 to your store as soon as possible.

But first, please let us know whether you'd like the webbing in 1-, $1\frac{1}{3}$-, or $2\frac{1}{2}$-inch widths. If you note your preference on the bottom of this letter and mail it back to us today, we can have your order ready by the beginning of next week.

Olsen's Upholstery products are among the finest made, and we're sure you'd like to receive your purchase without further delay.

Sincerely yours,

Sometimes a *delayed delivery* is caused by the seller, not the buyer—a delicate situation that requires a carefully written letter (Figure 4–5). When an order cannot be filled promptly, the customer deserves an explanation. You must explain that the delay is unavoidable and that everything is being done to speed delivery.

A delayed-delivery letter must be especially *"you-*oriented." It should express that you understand the customer's disappointment and regret the inconvenience. At the same time, the letter must avoid a negative tone. It should stress that the merchandise is worth waiting for and assume that the customer is willing to wait. The form letter in Figure 4–5 could be used in a mass mailing, but sounds, nevertheless, as if it has been individualized to the customer.

1066 Third Avenue

American Electric Company, Inc.

New York, New York 10081

August 10, [*year*]

Dear

Requests for our pamphlet, "10 Points to Consider When Buying Home Video Equipment," have been overwhelming. As a result, we are temporarily out of copies.

Nevertheless, the new printing is presently being prepared, and I have added your name to the mailing list to receive a copy as soon as it is available.

In the meantime, you may find an article by Professor Leonard Mack, of the Pennsylvania Institute of Technology, to be of some help. The article, entitled "The Latest Crop of Home Video Centers," will appear in the September issue of Consumer Digest.

Sincerely,

Figure 4–5
Delayed Delivery

When a *partial shipment* can be made, the customer must be informed that certain items have been *back ordered*. Again, the letter should assume the customer's willingness to wait. It should also make an attempt to "resell" the merchandise by stressing its finer features without emphasizing the delayed items (see Figure 4–6).

Silver Imports, Ltd.
609 San Anselmo Avenue
San Anselmo, California 94960

March 4, [*year*]

Ms. Bonnie Corum
Bonnie's Baubles
4091 West Ninth Street
Winston–Salem, North Carolina 27102

Dear Ms. Corum:

Thank you for your recent order, number 622. We are always especially delighted to serve an old friend.

Your six pairs of Chinese Knot earrings (item 15b) and one dozen Primrose pendants (item 8a) have been shipped by United Parcel and should arrive at your boutique within the week.

Unfortunately, our stock of cloisonné bangle bracelets (item 9d) has been depleted because of a delay in shipments from China. Our craftsmen have been at great pains to keep up with the demand for these intricate and finely wrought bracelets. We have put your one dozen bracelets on back order and hope to have them on their way to you before the end of the month.

Very truly yours,

Chun Lee Ng
Manager

Figure 4–6
Partial Delivery

When an order cannot be filled at all, a letter suggesting a *substitute order* (Figure 4–7) is occasionally appropriate. Naturally, the suggested merchandise must be comparable to the original order. The letter should give the impression of helping the customer, not trying to save the sale. The letter must include a sales pitch for the suggested item, and it should emphasize the customer's needs. Of course, the letter should also explain why the ordered merchandise is not available.

Books-By-Mail   P.O. Box 799   Dallas, Texas 75220

April 10, [*year*]

Mrs. Donna Phillips
RFD 2
Crosby, Texas 77532

Dear Mrs. Phillips:

Thank you for ordering Indra Madhur's outstanding book, <u>An Introduction to Indian Cooking</u>. As you know, in the fifteen years since its first publication, Mr. Madhur's book has become a classic and a standard for great cooks everywhere.

Sadly, <u>An Introduction</u> is no longer in print, and I am returning your check for $15.95. But to satisfy your interest in Indian cuisine, I would like to suggest an alternative, Purnamattie Jaffre's <u>Indian Gourmet</u>. Ms. Jaffre was a student of Mr. Madhur, and her recently published volume has been widely hailed by both food and cookbook critics.

If you would like a copy of <u>Indian Gourmet</u>, which costs only $13.95, please let me know, and I will immediately send it to you.

Cordially,

David Ewing
Order Department

Figure 4–7
Substitute Delivery

Stopgap Letters

When a thorough response to an incoming letter must be delayed, receipt of the letter must be acknowledged. These acknowledgment letters are called STOPGAP LETTERS. They let your customer know that the inquiry will not be ignored and that it will be responded to as soon as possible.

Similar to a delayed delivery letter, a stopgap letter informs your customer that you need time to process the request. Necessary information or materials, for example, may not be immediately available. Or your company may have set procedures for responding to certain inquiries. Credit applications and insurance claims, for instance, take time to be processed. They are often answered promptly with a stopgap acknowledgment.

A stopgap letter can also be helpful if your immediate supervisor is out of town. You can assure your reader that his letter will be given to your employer as soon as he returns. You should be careful NOT to commit your employer to any action, nor should you explain his absence.

Dear Reverend Hollingsworth:

Your request to meet with Rabbi Tucker to discuss his participating in an interfaith symposium on world peace arrived this morning. However, Rabbi Tucker is out of town and is not expected back before the 15th.

I will be sure to inform Rabbi Tucker of the planned symposium as soon as he returns.

Yours truly,

Inquiry Replies

All inquiries should be answered, even those that, for some reason, cannot be given a complete response. An inquiry indicates interest in your company, and an inquirer is a potential customer. The inquiry reply should not only increase that interest, but also inspire the inquirer to action.

An inquiry reply should begin by thanking the reader, acknowledging the interest in your company and end by offering further assistance—but ONLY if you actually want additional inquiries from this person (see Figure 4–8).

The purpose of an inquiry reply is usually to give *information*. You should include not only the specific facts requested, but any others that may be of help. (This is, of course, assuming that the original inquiry or request was reasonable.) If you cannot provide all the relevant data right away, you should promise to send it later.

A&M Sewing Supplies, Inc. 40–04 Summit Avenue, Fairlawn, NJ 07662

June 2, [*year*]

Mr. Samuel Long
Maxine Sportswear Manufacturing Co., Inc.
842 Seventh Avenue
New York, New York 10018

Dear Mr. Long:

Thank you for your interest in A & M equipment. We are happy to supply you with the information you requested.

The following prices are quoted per dozen. Individual units are slightly higher:

Item	1 Dozen @:
A-1 Garment Turner	$180.00
A-1 Automatic Winder	90.00
Ace Thread Trimmer	120.00
No-Slip Feed Puller	132.00

In case you have any further questions, Mr. Long, please do not hesitate to call. I can be reached between 8:30 A.M. and 6:00 P.M. at (201) 881-9412.

Sincerely yours,

Figure 4–8
Inquiry Reply I

If the information requested cannot be provided at all (as in Figure 4–9), if it is confidential, you should explain this in your letter. You must be careful, however, to word your explanation tactfully. Never suggest that your reader is trying to gather information to which she is not entitled. Assume the inquiry was innocent and maintain the customer's goodwill.

Maxine Sportswear Manufacturing Co., Inc.
842 Seventh Avenue, New York, NY 10018

June 10, [*year*]

Mrs. Sharon Klein
693 Pelham Parkway
Bronx, New York 10422

Dear Mrs. Klein:

We certainly appreciate your interest in Maxine Sportswear. Nevertheless, I am afraid I cannot supply you with the information you request.

Because we do not sell our garments directly to the consumer, we try to keep our wholesale prices between ourselves and our dealers. It is our way of meriting both the loyalty and good faith of those with whom we do business. Clearly, divulging our wholesale prices to a consumer would be a violation of a trust.

However, I have enclosed for your reference a list of our dealers in the Bronx and Manhattan. A number of these dealers sell Maxine Sportswear at discount.

Very truly yours,

Figure 4–9
Inquiry Reply II

Sometimes a request for information may be answered by sending a brochure or catalog. Such materials, though, must always be accompanied by a personalized cover letter. Explain why you have sent the brochure and stimulate your reader's interest in it. Also, call attention to the details of the brochure and attempt to encourage a purchase.

Dear Mr. Godonov:

Thank you for your request for information about the Teaneck Tennis Center. One of New Jersey's newest facilities, we are a full-service tennis club just 15 minutes from Manhattan.

The enclosed brochure describes our special features, including championship-size courts and professional instruction. You may find the section on our Businessperson's Special of particular interest.

If you drop by Teaneck Tennis any time between 7 A.M. and 10 P.M., we would be delighted to give you a personal tour of the Center—at no obligation of course.

Cordially yours,

Referrals

Business people often receive inquiries that can best be answered by another person. In that case, the correspondent must be directed elsewhere.

A letter of referral *acknowledges receipt* of the inquiry and *explains* why and to whom it is being referred. Alternately, you may find it more efficient to tell the correspondent exactly where and to whom he should write.

Dear Mrs. Simpson:

Your request for information regarding marriage counselors in your community can best be answered by the Board of Community Services.

I am therefore referring your letter to Mr. Orlando Ortiz at the Whitestone Community Board. He will, I am sure, be in touch with you soon.

Yours truly,

Refusals

There are many times when a businessperson must say "no." When granting a favor, awarding a contract, hiring an applicant, or making any decision, saying "yes" to one person often means saying "no" to another. The key, however, is to say "no" gracefully. Here, as in all correspondence, maintaining goodwill is extremely important.

When saying "no," you should never actually use the word "*no*." Your letter should be as positive as you can make it. The actual refusal should be stated once and briefly. The rest of the letter should be reader-oriented and very friendly.

No matter what the request, your reader deserves an explanation of your refusal. Your reason should be based on facts, not emotions, although an appeal to your reader's sense of fairness or business savvy is often appropriate (see Figure 4–10). NEVER make the reader himself the reason for your refusal.

Rarely will you want in a refusal to sever all business connections; therefore, you should be careful to keep your letter "open-ended." Express appreciation for the request even though it is being denied, and if possible suggest an alternative course of action. A "not-at-this-time" refusal keeps open the possibility of future business.

AGNES CAFIERO, M.D.

California Institute of Psychiatry
629 Seventh Avenue
San Francisco, California 94120

September 1, [*year*]

The Honorable Nelson McKenzie
The State Capitol Building
Sacramento, California 91400

Dear Mr. McKenzie:

Thank you for your recent request for my endorsement of your campaign for United States Senator. I am honored that you believe my name could be of value to you.

My professional policy, however, is to refrain from public endorsements. In my practice, I treat patients of all political parties, and I strongly believe that it is in their best interest that I maintain a nonpartisan position.

Privately, of course, I allow myself more leeway. I have always been impressed by your stand on the issues, particularly your support for national health insurance. I wish you all the best in your campaign and am enclosing a personal contribution of $100.

Sincerely yours,

Agnes Cafiero, M.D.

Figure 4–10
Refusal

Summary

Because replies should be helpful and sales-oriented, they must be:

1. specific.
2. complete.
3. prompt.

They must also be polite and express appreciation for the inquiry or order they are answering.

REMEMBER, replies are opportunities to maintain and develop business contacts and goodwill.

■■■■■■ PRACTICE CORRESPONDENCE

Prepare a letter of response for each of the following situations.

A. You are employed in the shipping department of Kinbote Products, Inc., 200 Southeast Fourth Street, Miami, Florida 33131. Write a letter acknowledging the following order from Ellen Minsky, buyer for Gold's Specialty Shops, 3636 West Grace Street, Tampa, Florida 33607.

> Dear Gentlemen and Ladies:
>
> Please send me two dozen exercise suits (Style L-29) in the following assortment of sizes and colors:
>
> Vanilla–3 petite, 3 small, 4 medium, 2 large
> Chocolate–2 petite, 4 small, 4 medium, 2 large
>
> Charge my account (882GSS) for the wholesale price of $35 per suit.
>
> I would like the order shipped air express and would appreciate your letting me know how soon I may expect delivery.
>
> Yours truly,

B. Cornell Peal, vice-president of the General Communications Corporation, 600 North Milwaukee Street, Milwaukee, Wisconsin 53202, is out of town attending a four-day meeting of the regional directors of the company. As his administrative assistant, send a stopgap letter in response to the following request from Professor Anne Boleyn, Department of Media and Communications, University of Wisconsin, Menomonie, Wisconsin 54751.

> Dear Mr. Peal:
>
> Last month, I telephoned your office to invite you to give a guest lecture to my graduate seminar in teletronics. You said you would be pleased to give such a lecture but asked that I contact you again, in writing, later in the semester.

If you are still interested in visiting the class, I would very much like to set a date for the lecture. The class meets on Tuesdays from 4:30 to 6:00 P.M. and runs for six more weeks.

I would appreciate your letting me know as soon as possible which Tuesday would be most convenient for you.

Sincerely yours,

C. You have just made a luncheon engagement for your employer Nancy Carson, an architect with Fulson Contractors, Inc., 4444 Western Avenue, Boulder, Colorado 80301. The appointment is with a prospective client, Justin Michaels, 622 Garth Street, Boulder, Colorado 80321. Write a letter to Mr. Michaels to confirm the lunch date, which will take place at Trattoria di Marco, at the corner of Tenth Street and Western Avenue, on April 7 at 1 P.M.

D. You are employed by the Lawsen Linen Company, P.O. Box 762, Bloomfield, New Jersey 07003. Write a letter to Mrs. Marianne Rollins, 444 Ross Avenue, Caldwell, New Jersey 07006, to explain a delay in shipping her order for one set of Floral Mist queen-size sheets and pillowcases. Because of a factory strike, all orders have been held up, but assure her that negotiations are progressing and a settlement is expected soon. Convince her to wait and not cancel her order.

E. Pacific Growth Properties L.P. (2785 Kimberley, Melbourne, Australia) owns or manages 97 supermarkets in Australia and New Zealand. The company is in the process of upgrading the bar-code scanning equipment in all of its stores. The president of Pacific Growth, Arthur Edwards, has been negotiating the purchase of this equipment from Horizon Technologies Inc. (325 Bedford Highway, Nashua, NH 03051) and has requested a 25 percent volume discount. As a representative of Horizon Technologies, write a letter to Mr. Edwards refusing the discount.

5.
Social Business Letters

Words to Watch For

appreciation (*n*) recognition of someone or something's value
awkwardness (*n*) clumsiness, gracelessness
bland (*adj*) mild, lacking flavor
condolence (*n*) sympathy
engraved (*adj*) printed with raised lettering
etiquette (*n*) prescribed forms of behavior
hospitality (*n*) generous treatment of guests
sincerity (*n*) genuineness, honesty
uplifting (*adj*) cheering, rousing

Social business letters do not promote immediate business. Nevertheless, writing a letter of congratulations or appreciation can be a good opportunity to build goodwill.

There are many occasions that call for social business letters. Such letters may express congratulations, sympathy, or thanks, or they may extend an invitation or make an announcement. These messages may be sent to friends and personal acquaintances, to co-workers and employees, and to business associates. They may even be sent to persons who are unknown to the writer but who are potential customers.

While the tone of a social business letter will depend upon the relationship between the correspondents, all such lettters must sound SINCERE. Also, with the possible exception of an announcement, they should avoid any hint of a sales pitch.

Social business letters are often written on smaller stationery than letterhead. Some may be handwritten or formally engraved, rather than typed. Moreover, to be more personal, the salutation in a social business letter may be followed by a comma instead of a colon.

The language of a social business letter must demonstrate a delicate balance between the personal and professional, the friendly and formal. Therefore, it is a good idea to refer to a current book of etiquette for proper wording. These are reference books, guides to customs, and accepted forms of social and professional behavior. They are invaluable tools, especially when composing formal invitations and letters of condolence.

Letters of Congratulations

Since everyone likes to have accomplishments acknowledged, a letter of congratulations is a great opportunity to build goodwill.

The occasions for congratulatory messages are numerous: promotions (Figure 5–1); appointments, and elections; achievements, awards, and honors; marriages and births (Figure 5–2); anniversaries and retirements.

Dear Alan,

Congratulations on your promotion to senior accounts executive. You have worked hard for Rembow Consultants, and I am delighted that your efforts have been rewarded.

As you move into your new office and assume the weight of responsibilities that go along with your new position, please let me know if I can be of any assistance.

Sincerely,

Figure 5–1
Letter of Congratulations I

Ruth T. Travis
1156 Clearview Avenue
Cold Spring Harbor, New York, 11798

Dear Monica,
Congratulations on the birth of your grandchild, David Gary. You and Jim must be thrilled by the experience of becoming grandparents.
Please extend my warmest wishes to your daughter Jane and her husband. May this new addition to your family bring you all joy.
Sincerely,
Ruth

Figure 5–2
Letter of Congratulations II

Letters of congratulations must be SINCERE and ENTHUSIASTIC, whether written to a close friend or a distant business associate. They may be short, but they should contain PERSONAL remarks or references.

There are three essential ingredients to a letter of congratulations; it should:

1. begin with the expression of congratulations.
2. mention the reason for the congratulations with a personal or informal comment.
3. end with an expression of goodwill (such as praise or confidence—NEVER say "Good luck," which implies chance rather than achievement).

Letters of Condolence

When an acquaintance experiences the death of a loved one, it is proper, although difficult, to send a message of condolence (see Figures 5–3 and 5–4). To avoid awkwardness, many people send commercially printed sympathy cards, but a specially written note is more PERSONAL and GENUINE.

A message of condolence lets your reader know that you are aware of his personal grief and wish to offer sympathy and support. The message, therefore, should be SIMPLE, HONEST, and DIRECT, and it should express SORROW with DIGNITY and RESPECT.

The message of condolence should begin by referring to the situation and the people involved. This should be a bland statement that avoids unpleasant reminders. The note may use the word *death* but should NOT describe the death.

Dear Mr. Summers,

I would like to extend the deep sympathy of all of us at Jason Associates.

We had the privilege of knowing and working with Edith for many years, and her friendly presence will be sadly missed.

Please consider us your friends and telephone us if we can be of any help.

Sincerely,

Figure 5–3
Letter of Condolence I

Michael Barrett
2368-83 Street, Brooklyn, New York 11214

Dear Hal,

Roseann and I were deeply saddened to learn of your great loss. We hope the love you and Edith shared will help comfort you in the days ahead.

If there is anything we can do for you now or in the future, please let us know.

With much sympathy,
Michael

Figure 5-4
Letter of Condolence II

The rest of the note should be brief—an encouraging reference to the future (which should be uplifting but realistic), or, if appropriate, a gesture of goodwill (such as an offer of help).

> **Note:** A letter of sympathy is also sent to someone who is ill or who has suffered an accident or other misfortune.

Letters of Appreciation

In business, as in life, it is important to say "thank you."

We have already seen (see page 37) that letters of appreciation should be sent to new customers upon the opening of an account or the making of a first purchase. But many other occasions call for a "thank you." A note of appreciation should always be sent after receiving:

1. gifts
2. favors
3. courtesies
4. hospitality
5. donations

A note of thanks should also be sent in response to a letter of congratulations.

Dear Mr. Yoshimura,

Thank you very much for referring Natalie Slate to us. We are, of course, pleased to take on a new client. But even more, we appreciate your confidence in our legal services and your willingness to communicate this confidence to others.

Be assured that we will continue to make every effort to live up to your expectations.

Cordially,

Figure 5–5
Letter of Appreciation I

Lisa Longo
9 Nutmeg Lane
Framingham, Massachusetts 01708

Dear Lucy,
Thank you for the beautiful paperweight. As it sits on my desk, I shall always be reminded of your valuable support when I was being considered for promotion.
Sincerely,
Lisa

Figure 5–6
Letter of Appreciation II

A thank-you note may be BRIEF, but it must be PROMPT, and it must, like all social business letters, sound SINCERE.

A proper letter of appreciation (see Figures 5–5 and 5–6) contains three key elements; it:

1. begins by saying "thank you."
2. makes a sincere personal comment.
3. ends with a positive and genuine statement (NEVER say "Thank you again.")

Invitations

While such events as openings, previews, and demonstrations may be advertised in newspapers or on handbills, guests can be more carefully selected if invitations are sent by letter.

A formal event, such as a reception, open house, or formal social gathering, *requires* a formal invitation. This invitation can be engraved or printed, or it can be handwritten on note-size stationery.

A general invitation (Figure 5–8) should be cordial and sincere; a formal invitation (Figure 5–7) should be less personal, written in the third person. Both kinds of invitation, however, must have three purposes:

1. Invite the reader to the gathering.
2. Offer a reason for the gathering.
3. Give the date, time, and place of the gathering.

A formal invitation should, in addition, include an R.S.V.P. notation. This abbreviation stands for *répondez s'il vous plaît;* it asks the reader to please respond, that is, "Please let us know if you plan to attend." Alternatively, the notation "Regrets Only" may be used, asking only those who can NOT attend to notify the host in advance.

The Brookdale Chamber of Commerce
requests the pleasure of your company
at a dinner honoring
the Honorable Stacy Coughey
Wednesday, the third of June
at seven o'clock
The Stardust Room of the Excelsior Hotel
R.S.V.P.

Figure 5–7
Invitation I

Jaco Films, Inc.
1120 Avenue of the Americas, New York, New York 10036

January 3, [*year*]

Dear

In a few weeks, JACO will proudly release its new feature-length film, <u>The Purchase</u>, starring Amanda Theriot in her first appearance in seventeen years.

A special preview showing of <u>The Purchase</u>, for friends of Ms. Theriot and of JACO Films, will be held on January 19, at 8 P.M., at the Regent Theater on Broadway and 52nd Street.

You are cordially invited to attend this preview. Admission will be by ticket only, which you will find enclosed. Following the film, refreshments will be served.

Sincerely yours,

Figure 5–8
Invitation II

Announcements

In some ways, announcements are more similar to public relations messages than to social business letters. They may take the form of news releases, advertisements, or promotional letters. But *formal announcements* resemble invitations in both tone and format. Indeed, the combination formal announcement/invitation (Figure 5–10) is not an uncommon form of correspondence.

Business events such as openings (see Figure 5–9), mergers, and promotions (see Figure 5–11) may be the subject of both formal and informal announcements.

Dr. Richard Levine
announces the opening of his office
for the practice of pediatric medicine
1420 North Grand Street
Suite 1B
Miami, Florida
(402) 889-7626

Figure 5–9
Formal Announcement

The ESCO Corporation
is pleased to announce the appointment of
Ms. Roberta Jenkins
as its new executive vice-president
and requests the pleasure of your company
at a reception in her honor
Friday, the twelfth of April
at four o'clock
The President's Suite   Room 510

Figure 5–10
Combination Announcement/Invitation

TO: All Personnel

FROM: George Hart, President

DATE: April 3, [*year*]

SUBJECT: The New Executive Vice-President

We are please to announce the appointment of Ms. Roberta Jenkins to the position of executive vice-president.

Ms. Jenkins has been with ESCO for eight years, first as assistant manager of marketing and then, for the past five years, as manager of marketing. She attended Baruch College and Pace University, where she earned a master's degree in business administration.

I'm sure you will all join me in extending hearty congratulations to Ms. Jenkins and best wishes for her future here at ESCO.

GH

Figure 5–11
Informal Announcement

Summary

Social business letters are messages to business acquaintances mostly concerning non-business topics; therefore, these letters are forms of both personal and professional communications.

The most important quality of a good social business letter is SINCERITY. The feelings expressed must convey honesty and genuineness. In addition, these letters are commonly SIMPLE and BRIEF, but they must be TIMELY! When an occasion calls for a social business letter, write it as soon as possible after the event.

■■■■■ PRACTICE CORRESPONDENCE

For each of the social situations described, prepare a correspondence that is appropriate to business relationships.

A. You are administrative assistant to the president of Burton and Doyle, Inc., 355 Bond Street, Oshkosh, Wisconsin 54901. Your boss, Mr. Arthur J. Burton, asks you to write a letter of congratulations, which he will sign, to Theodore Manning, 72 North Eden, La Crosse, Wisconsin

54601, a junior executive who has just been named "Father of the Year" by the La Crosse Boy Scouts Council.

B. You are employed by American Associates, Inc., 2870 North Howard Street, Philadelphia, Pennsylvania 19122. Your boss, Jacqueline Austin, 450 Poplar Street, Hanover, Pennsylvania 17331, has not been in the office for several days, and it has just been announced that her mother died. Since Ms. Austin will not be returning to work for a week or two, write a letter to express your condolence.

C. You have worked for the law firm of Lederer, Lederer and Hall, 407 East 23 Street, New York, New York 10013, for many years. On the occasion of your tenth anniversary with the company, an office party is held in your honor, and Mr. Gerald Hall presents you with a wristwatch as a token of the company's appreciation. Write a letter to Mr. Hall thanking him and the entire company for the party and the gift.

D. The Merchants Insurance Company of Tucson is holding its annual executive banquet on September 8, at 7 P.M. It will be held in the Gold Room of the Barclay Country Club, 700 Country Club Road, Tucson, Arizona 85726. Design a *formal* invitation that the company can send to all its executives. Include a request for response by August 24th.

E. A baby, Angela May, has been born to Mr. and Mrs. Andrew Lopato. She was born at Community General Hospital on February 9 at 7 A.M. and weighed seven pounds seven ounces. Prepare a *formal* announcement that the Lopatos could use to inform friends and business associates of Angela's birth.

6.
Sales and Public Relations Letters

Words to Watch For

facilitate (*v*) to make easier
flair (*n*) unique style
flashy (*adj*) showy, attractive
gimmick (*n*) clever device or trick
grab (*v*) to take quickly
nuance (*n*) delicate difference
patronage (*n*) trade of customers
promotion (*n*) advancement in position
scope (*n*) extent, range
solicit (*v*) to seek, request

All business letters are in a sense sales letters, as we have already observed. All business letters are also public relations letters in that one must always seek to establish and maintain goodwill. However, some letters are written for the *purpose* of selling, and others are written just to earn the reader's goodwill.

These letters—*sales* letters and *public relations* letters—require a highly specialized style of writing. Both demand a writer with *flair* and the ability to win the reader with words. For this reason, most large companies employ professional writers—advertising and public relations specialists— who handle all the sales and publicity writing.

Not only do advertising or public relations writers know how to appeal to people's buying motives; they know how to *find* potential buyers. They must know how to acquire mailing lists (such sources as a company's own files, telephone books, and directories are good starts) and how to select the right audience from those lists.

Nevertheless, there are times when almost any businessperson will have to compose either a sales letter or a public relations letter, especially in smaller companies. While the nuances of style may be beyond the scope of this chapter, certain basic guidelines can help you win a desired sale or earn an associate's goodwill.

Sales Letters

Sales letters may be divided into three categories: Direct Mail, Retail, and Promotion. While the manner of the sale is different for each, all share a common purpose—to sell a product or service.

AP All-Pro Sporting Supplies, Inc.
Box 8118, Phoenix, Arizona 85029

March 3, [*year*]

Dear

What do Miss Universe and Mr. America have in common? They
both lift weights to keep in shape—with very different results, of
course. And many women across the country are discovering—
just like Miss Universe—that weight lifting is an effective and fun
way to a better-looking body and better health in the bargain.

All-Pro has put together a special package to help women get
started. We will send you a pair of three-pound dumbbells and a
fully illustrated body-building regime. In just 45 minutes a day,
three days a week, these easy-to-follow exercises will firm up
every muscle of your body from your deltoids to your calves.

Despite the myths that have grown up around body-building, lifting weights will <u>not</u> make a woman look like a man. Does Demi
Moore look like Bruce Willis? And weight lifting is completely
safe. According to Dr. Leonard Paddington of the Phoenix Sports
Medicine Institute, "Weight lifting, which strengthens the cardio-
vascular system, is safe for people of all ages. If you start a
weight-lifting program now, you will be able to continue to whatever age you want."

Weight lifting shows results faster than any other form of exercise. Get started now and you'll be all set for your bathing suit
and the beach this summer.

Our Women'n'Weights package, with the two dumbbells and complete exercise regime, at the low, low price of $21.95, is available
only through the mail. You can't buy it in any store. And for a
limited time only, we will send you, along with your purchase, an
exercise mat FREE. This 100% cotton, quilted mat is machine
washable, a $6.96 value.

To order your Women'n'Weights package, and your free exercise
mat, SEND NO MONEY NOW. Just fill in the enclosed postage-
paid reply card, and your better body will be on its way to you.

Yours truly,

Figure 6–1
Direct Mail Sales Letter

Direct Mail Sales Letters

Direct mail, or mail order, attempts to sell directly to the customer *through the mail* (Figure 6–1). The direct mail sales letter, therefore, does the entire selling job. A salesperson never calls on the customer; the product is never even seen in person. Solely on the basis of the description and inducements in the letter, the customer is urged to buy—to mail a check and wait for his purchase to arrive.

A direct mail letter must, consequently, include a "hard sell." It must grab the reader's attention with its physical appearance; for example, it may use a flashy envelope or include a brochure or sample. To develop the reader's interest, it may use appealing headlines. To provide a thorough physical description of the product, it might include several pictures, from different angles.

Moreover, a direct mail letter must convince the reader of the product's quality and value. Such evidence as details and statistics, testimonies, and guarantees are essential when a customer cannot see or test a product for herself. And finally, to close the deal, a direct mail letter must facilitate action: clear directions for ordering plus a reply card and postage-paid envelope make buying easy. A "send-no-money-now" appeal or the offer of a premium provides additional inducement.

Retail Sales Letters

Retail sales letters (Figure 6–2) are commonly used by retail businesses to announce sales or stimulate patronage. They have an advantage over other forms of advertising (such as television, radio, or newspaper ads) because letters can be aimed selectively—at the specific audience most likely to buy. If an electronics store, for example, is holding a sale on electronic phone books and digital diaries, it might send letters only to businesspeople and professionals instead of, say, homemakers or educators. By doing this, they would reach customers with the clearest need for the product.

A letter announcing a sale must contain certain information:

1. the reason for the sale (a seasonal clearance, holiday, special purchase).
2. the dates on which the sale will take place.
3. an honest description of the sale merchandise (including a statement of what is and is not marked down).
4. comparative prices (original price versus sale price or approximate markdown percentages).
5. a statement encouraging the customer to act quickly.

Sales Promotion Letters

A sales promotion letter (Figure 6–3) solicits interest rather than an immediate sale. It is written to encourage inquiries rather than orders. For example, a product that requires demonstration or elaborate explanation can be introduced in a promotional letter. If interested, the customer will make an inquiry about the product. Similarly, products requiring expensive descriptive

Winston–Salem, NC 27106

January 24, [*year*]

Dear Customer:

Now that the scaffolds are down and the hammering has stopped, you are probably aware that Justin's has opened a new store in the Bethabara Shopping Center. We are extremely proud of this gleaming new addition to the Justin family.

To celebrate the occasion, we are having a Grand Opening Sale, and every Justin store will be in on it.

EVERYTHING in ALL our stores will be marked down 10–30%. Designer jeans that were $60–$90 are now $40–$60. An assortment of 100% silk blouses, originally $60–$95, are on sale for $40–$65. The savings are incredible.

The sale is for one day only, January 31. But the doors will open at 9 A.M., so you can shop early for the best selection. And, of course, your Justin's and VISA cards are always welcome.

Sincerely yours,

Figure 6–2
Retail Sales Letter

material (for example, a large brochure or sample) can be introduced in a promotional letter; uninterested names on a mailing list can then be eliminated, leaving only serious potential customers and thereby reducing costs.

Like other sales letters, a promotional letter stimulates the reader's interest and describes the product. But it need not be detailed: customers desiring further information are invited to send in a reply card, contact a sales representative, or visit a local dealer. Of course, such inquiries MUST be answered promptly by either a salesperson or a letter. The follow-up letter (which could include a leaflet or sample) should provide complete information, including specific answers to questions the customer may have asked. The follow-up attempts to convince the reader to buy and tells how to make the purchase.

All of the sales letters described in this chapter have certain features in common: they convey *enthusiasm* for the product and employ *evocative language*. They demonstrate the writer's knowledge of both product and customer. And they illustrate the advertising principles known as AIDA:

Smith & Marcus

Financial Consultants

732 Commonwealth Avenue

Boston, Massachusetts 62633

February 10, [*year*]

Dear

In times of economic uncertainty, personal financial planning can pose more challenges than running your own business. Determining the investment vehicles that will protect your own and your family's future requires financial insight and information.

That is why many successful business owners like yourself have engaged the services of the personal financial consultants at Smith & Marcus. We have both the expertise and objectivity to help you sort out your long- and short-term financial goals and then select the investment strategies that will meet those goals. Whether your immediate concerns are tax planning or estate planning, we believe we have the answers to your financial questions.

To introduce you to the sort of answers we have, you are cordially invited to a seminar, "What a Personal Financial Planner Can Do for You." The seminar will take place on Wednesday, March 1, [*year*], at 7 P.M. in the Essex Room of the Essex–Marlboro Hotel. Because seats are limited, we would appreciate your letting us know if you plan to attend by telephoning Dorothy Phillips at 771-3102, extension 222.

Yours truly,

Figure 6–3
Sales Promotion Letter

1. *A*ttention: The letter opens with a gimmick to grab the reader's attention and create the desire to know more.
2. *I*nterest: The letter provides information and plays up certain features of the product to build the reader's interest.
3. *D*esire: The sales pitch appeals to one or more personal needs (such as prestige, status, comfort, safety, or money) to stimulate the reader's desire.
4. *A*ction: The letter makes it easy for the reader to buy and encourages immediate action.

Pine & White   100 Massachusetts Avenue
Boston, Massachusetts 02116

June 12, [*year*]

Ms. Beverly May
100 Gould Street
Needham, Massachusetts 02194

Dear Ms. May:

Now that you've used your Pine & White credit card for the very first time, we are sure you have seen for yourself the convenience and ease a charge account provides. So we won't try to "resell" you on all the benefits you can take advantage of as a new charge customer.

We'd simply like to take this time to thank you for making your first charge purchase and assure you that everyone at Pine & White is always ready to serve you. We are looking forward to a long and mutually rewarding association.

Welcome to the "family."

Sincerely yours,

Christine Popoulos
Customer Relations

Figure 6–4
Public Relations Letter I

Public Relations Letters

Public relations involves the efforts of a company to influence public opinion and to create a favorable company image. Its purpose is NOT to make a sale or stimulate immediate business; its purpose is to convey to the public positive qualities such as the company's fair-mindedness, reliability, or efficiency.

Public relations is big business, and large corporations spend millions of dollars a year on their public relations campaigns. When a major oil company sponsors a program on public television, that is public relations. When a large chemical company establishes a college scholarship fund, that is public relations, too.

Public relations specialists know how to use all the mass media (television, radio, magazines, newspapers, films, and the Internet). They know how to compose press releases and set up press conferences, prepare broadcast announcements, and arrange public receptions.

But public relations exists on a smaller scale as well. It is a local butcher's remembering a shopper's name, and it is a local hardware store's purchase of T-shirts for the Little League. Basically, public relations is the attempt to establish and maintain GOODWILL.

Public relations letters, therefore, are those letters written for the purpose of strengthening goodwill. Some of these can be considered *social business letters* (see page 51), such as invitations, thank-you notes, and letters of congratulations. Others are similar to advertising, such as announcements of openings or changes in store facilities or policies. Still others are simply friendly gestures, such as a note welcoming a new charge customer or thanking a new customer for her first purchase (Figure 6–4).

A specific kind of public relations letter is designed to demonstrate a company's interest in its customers. This letter (Figure 6–5) is written *inviting* complaints. Its purpose is to discover causes of customer dissatisfaction before they become too serious. (Responses to such letters must always get a prompt follow-up to assure the customer that the reported problem will be investigated.)

Similarly, to avoid complaints (and of course encourage business), large companies frequently send *informative* letters that *educate* the public (Figure 6–6). For example, a supplier of gas and electricity may include an explanation of new higher rates with the monthly bill. Or a telephone company will enclose a fact sheet on ways to save money on long distance calls.

Whatever the main purpose for a public relations letter—to establish, maintain, or even revive business—remember that *all* public relations letters must be *friendly*. Their real purpose is to create a friend for the company.

Pine & White

100 Massachusetts Avenue
Boston, Massachusetts 02116

May 26, [*year*]

Mrs. Addison Tanghal
14 East Elm Street
Brookline, Massachusetts 02144

Dear Mrs. Tanghal:

It's been more than six months since you charged a purchase at Pine & White, and we can't help worrying that we've done something to offend you. We are sure you are aware of the convenience and ease your charge account provides, but we would like to assure you once again that everyone at Pine & White is always ready to serve you.

If you have encountered a problem with our service or merchandise, we want to know. It is our sincere desire to give you the personal attention and satisfaction you have come over the years to expect from Pine & White. And we welcome the advice of our customers and friends to keep us on our toes.

Please fill out the enclosed reply card if something has been troubling you. We will give your comments immediate attention, as we look forward to seeing you once again at our Brookline store and all our other branches.

Sincerely,

Christine Popoulos
Customer Relations

Figure 6–5
Public Relations Letter II

Murgano's Office Equipment, Inc. • Montgomery, Alabama • 36044

October 19, [*year*]

Dear Office Manager:

Few business folks these days would deny that the fax machine has become an indispensable tool. Instead of waiting days for a letter to cross the country by mail, you can push a button and fax it in seconds. Instead of paying the high price for an overnight courier to deliver your document, you can fax the same document anywhere in the world for the price of a phone call.

Short for <u>facsimile</u>, a fax machine consists of three parts. A <u>scanner</u> reads your original document and converts the images on the page into a digital code. A <u>modem</u> translates this code into a transmittable analog signal. Finally, a <u>telephone</u> calls the receiving fax machine and sends the message. When you receive a document, the process reverses. The telephone answers the call and receives the message. The modem translates the message back to a digital code, and then this code is converted to images on a page and printed. Thus, the received document is a <u>facsimile</u> of the original, transmitted document.

Fax machines are available with a wide range of useful features, from conveniences such as autodialer and on-hook dialing to qualities such as fine mode and half-tone (for sending finely detailed documents). Our on-staff experts can help you determine which features will best meet your business's needs.

Indeed, everyone at Murgano's is eager to make your fax purchase as uncomplicated as possible. Just give us a call or drop by our showroom. We'll put a fax in your future fast.

Sincerely yours,

Figure 6–6
Public Relations Letter III

Summary

To make a sale through the mail, a sales letter must be enthusiastic and descriptive. It:

1. gains the reader's attention with visual appeal or a clever opening statement.
2. arouses the reader's interest with information.
3. builds the reader's desire with personal appeals.
4. simplifies the reader's job by making it easy to respond.

A public relations letter focuses on a way in which your organization is customer- or community-minded. It enhances your company's public image by presenting the company as reliable and public-spirited. It is an opportunity to make people want to do business with you. It is a chance to be friendly and helpful and, therefore, to build goodwill.

■■■■■■ **PRACTICE CORRESPONDENCE**

On another sheet of paper, prepare either a sales or public relations letter as called for in each of the following situations.

A. Select a product (such as kitchen gadgets, magazines, or cosmetics) that you have considered purchasing or have actually purchased by mail. Write a letter that could be used to stimulate direct mail sales for the product.

B. Geoffrey's, a fine men's clothing store located at 10 Arlington Street, Boston, Massachusetts 02116, is having its annual fall clearance sale. All summer and selected fall merchandise will be on sale with discounts up to 60% on some items. The sale will begin on September 10. Write a letter to be sent to all charge customers, inviting them to attend three presale days, September 7–9, during which they will find a full selection of sale merchandise before it is advertised to the public.

C. You work for the ABC Corporation, Fort Madison, Iowa 52622, manufacturer of electronic typewriters. Write a letter to be sent to the heads of all business schools in the area, inviting them to inquire about your latest model. Describe some of the machine's special features and tell the reader how to receive additional information.

D. You are employed by the First National Bank of Dayton, 1742 Broad Street, Dayton, Ohio 45463. You recently opened both a savings and a checking account for Claire Paulsen, a new resident of Dayton. Write a letter to Ms. Paulsen (222 Elm Street, Dayton, Ohio 45466) to welcome her to the city and to the bank.

E. Imagine that you work in the customer relations department of a large furniture store. Write a letter that could be sent to customers who have bought furniture for one room of their home, encouraging them to buy furniture for another room. Remind them of the quality and service they received when they did business with you in the past. Encourage them to shop with you again.

7.
News Releases

Words to Watch For

camera ready (*adj*) ready to be printed or reproduced
dissemination (*n*) spreading or broadcasting
elaborate (*v*) to develop in detail
institute (*v*) to establish, initiate
layout (*n*) arrangement, design
newsworthy (*adj*) of interest to the public
successively (*adv*) consecutively

A *news release* is a form of publicity writing. It is usually an announcement of an event or development within a company. Meetings, appointments, promotions, and expansions are typical topics of news releases. The introduction of new products or services and the dissemination of financial information are also subjects for news releases.

News releases are sent to company publications and the mass media (specifically newspapers, radio, and television). There, the editor decides whether or not to approve the release for publication or broadcast. In order to be accepted by an editor, a release must do more than promote a company's image and goodwill. It must be NEWSWORTHY and TIMELY; that is, it must interest the audience.

News releases are not written in standard business letter format. Nor are they written in the "*you*-oriented" tone of voice referred to in this book. Both the layout and language of a news release are aimed at making it "copy ready." The less revision a release requires, the more likely an editor will accept it.

A news release is concise and straightforward. It contains no superfluous words; nor does it contain confusing words. Its meaning is easily understood. Moreover, it is written in an impersonal style. Your company, for example, is referred to by name, not as "our company" or "we." Individuals, including yourself, are similarly referred to by name—almost as if an outsider or reporter had written the story. References to dates and times, as well, are specific. (Words like *today*, *tomorrow*, and *yesterday* are meaningless if you are not sure when your release will be published.)

The first, or lead, paragraph of a news release is the most important. If space is needed for a more newsworthy item, an editor may cut parts of your release from the bottom up. Therefore, the lead paragraph must be capable of standing on its own. It summarizes the event and contains all the essential details. Following paragraphs elaborate on the first paragraph, giving additional information in order of importance. As in all business writing, ACCURACY and COMPLETENESS of details are essential, but in a news release, even a spelling error could cause an editor to doubt your reliability and therefore reject your story.

A news release may be prepared on either letterhead or plain paper. Ideally it should be limited to one page. If you must use more than one sheet, the word *MORE* should appear in the lower right corner of every page but the last, and all pages should be numbered successively in the upper right corner. The end of the release is indicated with one of the following symbols:

```
-xxx-
000
# # #
-30-
```

The heading for a news release includes a release date:

FOR RELEASE
February 2, [*year*]

FOR RELEASE AFTER
4 P.M., February 1, [*year*]

FOR IMMEDIATE RELEASE

Also, if letterhead is not used, the heading includes the company name and address. Also mention the telephone and fax numbers of people whom an editor could contact for additional information. Following the heading you may either provide a tentative title or leave an inch of white space for an editor to insert a title.

The body of the news release is double spaced. Paragraphs are indented five spaces. Margins are at least one inch on all sides to allow for copyeditors' comments. If photographs are provided with the release, they should be clearly labeled with a description of the event and the names of any people in the photo.

Finally, the release is addressed to The Editor, if sent to a newspaper, or to The News Director, if sent to a radio or television station. Of course, use the editor's or director's name if you know it. The envelope that contains the release shoud be identified by the words: NEWS RELEASE ENCLOSED.

NEWS RELEASE

Ericson Electronics, Inc.
1111 Maitland Plaza
Tremont, Massachusetts 52131
(606) 555-7777

April Frank
Editor-in-Chief
Audio-Video Dealer Monthly
(803) 666-2222

FOR IMMEDIATE RELEASE   7/7/—

Sales, Net Up At Ericson

Tremont, July 7, 19—. Ericson Electronics announced significantly higher second-quarter earnings despite slightly lower revenues. A spokesperson for Ericson credited a combination of improved sales mix and operating efficiencies in North America as well as a generally stronger overseas performance for the improvement.

For the three months, the TV and radio manufacturer had a net of $56 million, up 21.7% from last year's $46 million, while revenue of $2.81 million declined 1.3%.

Ericson said its unit shipments in North America were down, but less than the industry's overall 3% decline, and a combination of product mix, manufacturing efficiencies, and more favorable material costs resulted in improved margins. The company expects that, along with the industry, its total shipments will be down from last year's record because of the currently high level of TV inventories at retail.

"Overall, we're pleased with the quarter and with the progress it represents toward our full-year goals," said chairman Kwow Joong. "Our North and Latin American divisions again put up outstanding numbers, and our European and Asian results met our expectations. We look forward to significant operating improvement through this year."

-30-

Figure 7–1
News Release I

NEWS RELEASE

National Organization of Retired Persons
Fort Worth, Texas 76111
Zenaida Plonov, Publicity Director
(804) 771-1227

Alicia Hidalgo
The Editor
Fort Worth Gazette
(804) 771-2235

FOR RELEASE AFTER
3 P.M., April 7, [*year*]   4/4/—

ALVIN BANKS NAMED RETIRED PERSON OF THE YEAR

Fort Worth, April 7, [*year*]. Alvin Banks, outgoing president of the Fort Worth Chapter of the National Organization of Retired Persons, was named "Retired Person of the Year" at a luncheon in his honor on April 7.

During his two years in office, Mr. Banks, the retired owner and manager of Banks Building and Supply Company, helped the Fort Worth Chapter grow from 53 members to its present high of 175 members. He instituted a number of the organization's current programs, including a part-time job placement service and a guest lecture series.

Mr. Banks will be succeeded as president by Mrs. Beatrice Toller, a retired buyer for Grayson's Department Store.

The Fort Worth Chapter of the National Organization of Retired Persons meets Wednesday evenings at 7 P.M. at the Presbyterian Church on Humboldt Street. Meetings are open to the public and all retired persons are welcome to join.

# # #

Figure 7–2
News Release II

Summary

A news release resembles a newspaper article more than a business letter. It is a means of gaining publicity for your company. To earn this publicity, a news release must be:

1. newsworthy and timely. (Will the topic interest the public?)
2. objective. (Could an outsider or reporter have written it?)
3. accurate and complete. (Is all the essential information included and correct?)

▰▰▰▰ PRACTICE CORRESPONDENCE

For each of the following situations, prepare a publicity-minded news release.

A. As director of the accounting department of the Waterford Stores, send a news release to the company newsletter announcing the addition of a new member to your staff. Marlon Strong, a certified public accountant, earned his bachelor's degree at Brockton College, where he was president of the Young Accountants Club during his junior and senior years. Before coming to Waterford, he was a junior accountant with Moyer and Moyer, a private accounting firm. Quote yourself as praising Mr. Strong's background and expertise and welcoming him to the company.

B. Hajenius N.V. (32–34 Keizersgracht, Amsterdam, The Netherlands), the largest Dutch chemical compay, has agreed to acquire Butterworth P.L.C., a major British manufacturer of industrial paints and sealants. As public relations director of Hajenius, write a news release announcing the acquisition. In your release, include the following information.

- Hajenius has agreed to pay ₤1.78 billion to acquire Butterworth.
- The deal will make Hajenius the world's largest producer of paints and sealants.
- The Hajenius bid for Butterworth amounted to 430 pence a share.
- Due to the deal, Hajenius will take over the No. 1 position in the global paint market from Continental P.L.C.
- Butterworth's chairman, Reginald Epping, will become chief executive of the new sealant unit, which is to be spun off the rest of the business.

In your release, include remarks made by Jan Berlage, Hajenius's chairman: "This acquisition will clearly establish us as the European leader in paints and sealants while also providing a good base in Asia."

C. The Reliable Drug Store, 120 Franklin Street, Roscoe, New York, has been serving the community for more than twenty years. On Monday, May 3, there will be the grand opening of a Health Food Annex to be located in what used to be Fred's Barber Shop, just to the right of Reliable's main store, at 118 Franklin Street. According to Marjorie Mansfield, present owner and daughter of the founder of Reliable Drug,

Hiram Mansfield, the expansion was prompted by widespread interest in health foods as well as by increasing demand for top-quality vitamins and minerals. Ms. Mansfield said, "We intend to offer to small-town residents the variety of a big-city health food store and plan to carry everything from powdered yeast and protein to frozen yogurt and dried fruit." Write a news release to be sent to the local radio station making the expansion sound as newsworthy as possible.

8.
Complaints, Claims, and Adjustments

Words to Watch For

clientele (*n*) customers
compensation (*n*) payment, repayment
restitution (*n*) reparation, repayment
subsequently (*adv*) afterwards

Business transactions are not always successful; the exchange of money, merchandise, or service is not always smooth. When problems occur, the customer must promptly notify the company by letter. Such a letter is called a *complaint*. A complaint that calls upon the company to make restitution is called a *claim*. The company, responding to the claim, will write a letter of *adjustment*.

Complaints

When a customer is dissatisfied with goods or services, a complaint letter will inform the company or organization of the problem. The letter presents the facts and expresses the customer's dissatisfaction (see Figure 8–1).

Because a complaint, unlike a claim, does not necessarily call for action or compensation from the company, it should be answered gracefully. Indeed, the writer of a complaint is offering help to the offending organization, an opportunity to improve its operations. Therefore, the response to a complaint (Figure 8–2) is concerned and courteous, but *not* defensive. It may offer an explanation and suggest remedies that are being followed. It definitely should extend an apology.

Claims

Many aspects of business deals can cause errors, but the most common causes for claims are:

1. an incorrect bill, invoice, or statement (Figure 8–3)
2. a bill for merchandise ordered but never received
3. delivery of unordered merchandise
4. delivery of incorrect merchandise

21 West Main Street
Cochecton, NY 11222
October 9, [*year*]

Dr. Linda Peters, Director
County General Hospital
Route 97
Callicoon, New York 11203

Dear Dr. Peters:

On the afternoon of October 8, my neighbor's son, Kevin Sawyer, was raking leaves in his family's yard when he tripped and fell. From the degree of pain he was obviously experiencing, I suspected he might have broken his ankle. Thus, as the only adult around at the time, I drove him to your hospital.

When we arrived at the emergency room, no one was available to help Kevin from the car, and I had to help him hobble in as best I could. The effort increased his pain, yet when we were inside, the receptionist, without looking up, told us to take a number and wait our turn. We waited for more than two hours before Kevin was seen by a doctor.

As a member of the community your hospital serves, I am outraged by the treatment my young neighbor received. The lack of concern was upsetting; the lack of attention could have been life threatening. All of us in Wayne County deserve better treatment, and I hope you will look into the situation to see that the suffering caused Kevin Sawyer is never again inflicted by an employee of your institution.

Yours truly,

Michelle Sussman

Figure 8–1
Complaint

County General Hospital
Route 97
Callicoon, NY 11203

October 12, [*year*]

Ms. Michelle Sussman
21 West Main Street
Cochecton, New York 11222

Dear Ms. Sussman:

Thank you for bringing to my attention the inexcusable wait you and Kevin Sawyer endured in the emergency room on October 8. I am extremely sorry for any additional pain Kevin may have experienced and any emotional stress you may have felt under the circumstances.

Allow me, however, to offer an explanation. Shortly before you arrived, an automobile accident just outside Callicoon resulted in four seriously injured people being rushed to County General. Since we are, as you know, a small rural hospital, our emergency staff was stretched to its limits to assist these people simultaneously.

Nevertheless, you and Kevin should not have been ignored for two hours. I have spoken to the receptionist with whom you dealt and I can assure you that in the future, arrivals to our emergency room will be treated with concern and prompt attention.

Again, I apologize for the events of October 8 and greatly appreciate your letting me know about them.

Yours truly,

Linda Peters, M.D.

Figure 8–2
Complaint Response

5. delivery of damaged or defective merchandise (Figure 8–4)
6. an unusually delayed delivery

Two other more specialized types of claims are:

1. a request for an adjustment under a guarantee or warranty
2. a request for restitution under an insurance policy

A claim is written to *inform* the company of the problem and *suggest* a fair compensation. No matter how infuriating the nature of the problem nor how great the inconvenience, the purpose of a claim is NOT to express anger. The purpose is to get results.

Therefore, it is important to avoid a hostile or demanding tone. A claim must be calm and polite. Of course, it should also be firm.

A claim should begin with the facts, first explaining the problem (such as the condition of the merchandise or the specific error made). Then all the necessary details should be recounted in a logical order. These details

811 Regent Street
Phoenix, Arizona 99087
December 3, [*year*]

Gleason's Department Store
2297 Front Street
Phoenix, Arizona 99065

Dear Sir or Madam:

I have just received the November statement on my charge account (No. 059-3676). The statement lists a purchase for $83.95, including tax, which I am sure I did not make.

This purchase was supposedly made in Department 08 on November 12. But because I was out of town the week of the tenth and no one else is authorized to use my account, I am sure the charge is in error.

I have checked all the other items on the statement against my sales receipts, and they all seem to be correct. I am therefore deducting the $83.95 from the balance on the statement and sending you a check for $155.75.

I would appreciate your looking into this matter so that my account may be cleared.

Sincerely yours,

Figure 8–3
Claim I

may include the order and delivery dates, the order or invoice number, the account number, the method of shipment, and so on. A copy of proof of purchase, such as a sales slip or an invoice, should be included whenever possible. (Always, of course, keep the original.)

<u>Remember</u>: You are more likely to receive a favorable response from an adjuster who understands your problem thoroughly.

The second part of the claim emphasizes the loss or inconvenience that has been suffered. Again, the account should be factual and unemotional. You should NOT exaggerate.

Jack's Hardware Store
72 Elm Street
Kennebunk, Maine 06606

April 12, [*year*]

Eterna-Tools, Inc.
Route 9
Saddlebrook, New Jersey 07666

Dear Gentlemen and Ladies:

On March 1, we ordered and subsequently received one case of handsaws, model 88b. We paid for the order with our check no. 7293, a photocopy of which is enclosed.

When we decided to order these saws instead of model 78b, it was at the urging of your sales representative, Harold Saunders. He assured us that the new saws were more durable and efficient than the older model.

However, we have now had the saws on our selling floor for three weeks, and already six have been returned with broken teeth by extremely dissatisfied customers.

We are therefore returning the entire order of 88b saws and would like to be refunded for their full purchase price plus shipping expenses.

Yours truly,

Figure 8–4
Claim II

Finally, you should propose a *reasonable* adjustment. This should be worded positively and communicate your confidence that the company will be fair.

As you read the sample claims, notice especially how they state all the facts calmly. *The writer never expresses anger, never makes a threat, and never attempts to place blame.* At all times, the letter is directed toward the solution.

Adjustments

Claims should be answered *promptly* with a letter that will restore the customer's goodwill and confidence in the company. Like a claim, a letter of *adjustment* emphasizes the solution rather than the error and convinces the customer that you understand and want to be fair.

An adjustment letter begins with a positive statement, expressing sympathy and understanding. Near the start, it lets the reader know what is

Gleason's
DEPARTMENT STORE
2297 Front Street
Phoenix, Arizona 99065

December 8, [*year*]

Ms. Rosetta Falco
811 Regent Street
Phoenix, Arizona 99087

Dear Ms. Falco:

As you mentioned in your letter of December 3, you were indeed billed for a purchase you had not made.

According to our records, you should not have been charged the $83.95, and the sum has been stricken from your account.

Thank you for bringing this matter to our attention. We hope you have not been inconvenienced and will visit Gleason's soon so that we may again have the pleasure of serving you.

Sincerely yours,

Figure 8–5
Letter of Adjustment I

being done, and this news, good or bad, is followed by an explanation. The letter ends with another positive statement, reaffirming the company's good intentions and the value of its products, but NEVER refers to the original problem.

Whether or not your company is at fault, even the most hostile claim should be answered politely. An adjustment letter should NOT be negative or suspicious. NEVER accuse the customer. NEVER grant any adjustment reluctantly. Remember, your company's image and goodwill depend on how you respond, even to unjustified claims.

When the facts of a claim have been confirmed, one of three fair solutions is possible:

1. The requested adjustment is granted.
2. A compromise adjustment is proposed.
3. Any adjustment is denied.

Eterna-Tools, Inc. Route 9, Saddlebrook, NJ 07666

April 19, [*year*]

Mr. Jack Patterson
Jack's Hardware Store
72 Elm Street
Kennebunk, Maine 06606

Dear Mr. Patterson:

We are sorry that the model 88b handsaws you purchased have not lived up to your expectations. Frankly, we are surprised they have proved so fragile and appreciate your returning them to us. Our lab people are already at work trying to discover the source of the problem.

We are glad to assume the shipping costs you incurred, Mr. Patterson. But may we suggest that, instead of a refund, you apply the price of these saws to the cost of an order of model 78b saws. Your own experience will bear out their reliability, and we are sure your customers will be pleased with an Eterna-Tool Product.

If you will drop us a line okaying the shipment, your 78b handsaws will be on their way within the week.

Sincerely yours,

Figure 8–6
Letter of Adjustment II

Atlas Photocopiers, Inc.

81 Warren Street
New York, New York 10003

August 28, [*year*]

Mr. Thomas Shandy
Finance Director
Handleman & Burns, Ltd.
41 Maiden Lane
New York, New York 10002

Dear Mr. Shandy:

We are sorry that you are not completely satisfied with your Atlas photocopier. You are entirely justified in expecting more than eighteen months of reliable performance from an Atlas office machine, and we are always eager to service any product that does not for some reason live up to standards.

We appreciate your giving us the opportunity to inspect the malfunctioning copier. According to our service representative, two problems contributed to the unit's breakdown. It is apparently being used for a significantly higher volume of copying than it was built for (as is clearly indicated in both the sales material and user's manual with which you were provided). Furthermore, there are indications that a number of people in your department are not properly closing the cover before copying documents. The resultant "sky shots" can lead to the burnout of a number of mechanical parts.

Although we are not prepared to offer you a replacement copier as you suggested (indeed the one-year warranty has been expired for six months), we would be happy to take the damaged copier as a trade-in on another, larger-capacity Atlas copier. We believe this arrangement would better meet your department's needs and be more economically advisable than additional repairs on the old unit. Please let us know if you would like to speak to a sales representative about the terms of a trade-in.

Yours truly,

Figure 8–7
Letter of Adjustment III

Responsibility for the problem, reliability of the customer, and the nature of the business relationship are all considered in determining a fair adjustment. But the ultimate settlement must always be within the bounds of *company policy*.

Granting an Adjustment

This letter is cheerful. It freely admits errors and willingly offers the adjustment. It expresses appreciation for the information provided in the claim. The letter *may* include an explanation of what went wrong. It includes an indication that similar errors will be unlikely in the future. Finally, it *resells* the company, perhaps by suggesting future business (see Figure 8–5).

Offering a Compromise Adjustment

This letter is written when neither the company nor the customer is entirely at fault. It expresses an attitude of pleasant cooperation. It is based on facts and offers a reason for refusing the requested adjustment. As in Figure 8–6, it should immediately make a counteroffer that meets the customer halfway. Of course, it should leave the decision to accept the adjustment to the customer and suggest a course of action.

Refusing an Adjustment

Like all refusals, this adjustment letter is most difficult to write. You must say "no" but also try to reestablish your customer's goodwill. You must say "no" graciously but firmly while you convince the customer of the company's fairness and responsibility.

A letter refusing an adjustment begins by expressing the customer's point of view (see Figure 8–7). It demonstrates your sympathy and desire to be fair. It emphasizes the careful consideration that the claim received.

When saying "no," it is often tactful, moreover, to present the explanation *before* the decision and to include an appeal to the customer's sense of fairness. Also, an effective conclusion often suggests an option that the customer could take.

Summary

A complaint is written to inform an organization about a problem. A claim is a complaint that also requests a remedy to the problem.

A claim letter has three parts:

1. a complete, detailed account of the problem
2. a clear explanation of the consequences of the problem
3. a request for a reasonable solution to the problem

Both complaints and claims are based on facts. They should not be written simply to express anger or hostility.

Adjustments, as well as claim responses, must be prompt. They must also communicate concern and be courteous. The four parts of an adjustment letter are:

1. an expression of sympathy about the problem
2. a statement of what is being done about the problem
3. an explanation of the problem
4. a positive remark to restore goodwill

Adjustments are never defensive or suspicious. They emphasize a solution to a problem.

■ PRACTICE CORRESPONDENCE

The situations described in these problems call for either a claim or an adjustment letter. Prepare the appropriate letter as instructed.

A. In order to entertain and impress an important out-of-town business associate, you made dinner reservations at Club Cammarata, a prestigious restaurant known to cater to a business clientele. Your reservations were for 7:00 P.M. on June 8, and you and your guest arrived promptly. Your table, however, was not ready, and you were kept waiting for one hour and fifteen minutes. Intermittent inquiries were received by the maître d' with rude indifference. Consequently, your guest became extremely annoyed with the restaurant as well as with you. Write an appropriate complaint letter to the restaurant's owner (Enrico Cammarata, Club Cammarata, 2 Merrimack Road, Merrimack, New Hampshire 03113).

B. Refer to Exercise A and write the response that Enrico Cammarata should send to placate his dissatisfied customer and preserve his reputation in the Merrimack business community.

C. On September 5, Arnold Hayes received a monthly statement from Nayak & Nolan (10 French Market Place, New Orleans, Louisiana 70153), where he has had a charge account for eight years. The statement included a "previous balance" from the August statement. However, Mr. Hayes had promptly paid that balance (of $81.23) on August 7 and has a canceled check to prove it. Write the claim from Mr.

Hayes, 80 Arch Drive, New Orleans, Louisiana 70155, asking that his account be cleared up. Mention his enclosure of a check to cover the remaining balance on his account ($107.80).

D. Refer to Exercise C and write the letter of adjustment from Nayak and Nolan, acknowledging the error.

E. On October 7, the Kitchen Korner, 47-03 Parkway Drive, St. Paul, Minnesota 55104, placed an order for two dozen poultry shears from the Northridge Cutlery Company, 2066 Yellow Circle, Minnetonka, Minnesota 55343. By November 30, the shears have still not arrived, and there has been no letter from Northridge Cutlery explaining the delay. Write the claim from Kitchen Korner inquiring about the order. Emphasize these concerns: Did the order arrive? Why was neither an acknowledgment nor a stopgap letter sent? Will the shears arrive in time for pre–Christmas shopping?

F. Refer to Exercise E and write the letter from Northridge Cutlery answering Kitchen Korner's claim. Explain the delay as caused by a strike of local truckers. Apologize for failing to notify the customer.

9.
Credit and Collection Letters

Words to Watch For

adequate (*adj*) sufficient, enough
confidential (*adj*) secret, private
discreet (*adj*) showing good judgment, prudent
libel (*n*) giving an unjustly unfavorable impression of a person or thing
outstanding (*adj*) unpaid
rebate (*n*) discount, return of part of a payment

Credit Letters

Credit involves purchasing and receiving goods without immediate payment. Buying on credit enables a purchaser to acquire desired merchandise even when cash is not currently available. Selling can increase a company's volume of sales. Therefore, credit transactions are common and essential in business.

Of course, before granting credit, a company must be reasonably sure of the customer's financial stability, her ability and willingness to pay. These are checked by the exchange of credit information. There are five types of credit correspondence:

1. applications for credit
2. inquiries about creditworthiness
3. responses about creditworthiness
4. letters granting credit
5. letters refusing credit

Applications

Consumer applications for charge accounts, with businesses such as department stores or gasoline companies, are usually made by filling out an application form. A typical form asks for home and business addresses, names of banks and account numbers, a list of other charge accounts, and, perhaps, a list of references.

Business account applications are more often made by letter (Figure 9–1). A new business, for example, may wish to establish a credit line or open account when it places a first order with a supplier or manufacturer. A letter of this kind should include credit references (such as banks and other businesses that have extended credit).

Credit Inquiries

Department stores usually turn credit applications over to a *credit bureau*. Such bureaus keep files on people and businesses whose credit references and histories they have investigated. When they determine an applicant's *credit standing* (that is, reputation for financial stability), they give the applicant a *credit rating*. This rating is the bureau's evaluation of the

---

KRETCHMER'S APPLIANCE STORE
1135 STATE STREET, CHICAGO, ILLINOIS 60688

February 3, [*year*]

Standard Electric Corporation
2120 Oak Terrace
Lake Bluff, Illinois 60044

Dear Madam or Sir:

Enclosed is our purchase order 121 for 6 four-slice toasters, model 18E.

We would like to place this order on open account according to your regular terms. Our store has been open for two months, and you may check our credit rating with Ms. Peggy Sawyer, branch manager of the First Bank of Chicago, 1160 State Street, Chicago, Illinois 60688.

You may also check our credit standing with the following companies:

The Kenso Clock Company, 150 Ottawa, N.W., Grand Rapids, Michigan 49503

National Kitchen Products, Inc., 55 East Main Street, Round Lake Park, Illinois 60733

Eastern Electric Corporation, 750 East 58 Street, Chicago, Illinois 60637

Please let us know your decision regarding our credit as well as an approximate delivery date for our first order.

Sincerely yours,

Bruce Kretchmer

Figure 9–1
Credit Application

credit standing. On the basis of this rating, the store decides whether or not to grant the applicant credit.

When checking the credit standing of a business, a company may contact the references. The letter of credit inquiry (see Figure 9–2) is sent. It contains all the credit information known about the applicant, and it assures the reference that all information will remain confidential. The inclusion of a reply envelope is a wise courtesy.

Standard Electric Corporation
2120 Oak Terrace
Lake Bluff, Illinois 60044

February 7, [*year*]

Ms. Peggy Sawyer
Branch Manager
The First Bank of Chicago
1160 State Street
Chicago, Illinois 60688

Dear Ms. Sawyer:

Kretchmer's Appliance Store, 1135 State Street, Chicago, has placed an order with us for $120 worth of merchandise and listed you as a credit reference.

We would appreciate your sending us information regarding Kretchmer's credit rating. We would especially like to know how long the owner, Bruce Kretchmer, has had an account with you and whether or not any of his debts are past due. We will, of course, keep any information we receive in the strictest confidence.

A reply envelope is enclosed for your convenience.

Sincerely yours,

STANDARD ELECTRIC CORPORATION

Milton Smedley
Credit Department

Figure 9–2
Credit Inquiry

Credit Responses

Companies that receive large numbers of credit inquiries often use an in-house form for responding. This is a way by which they can control the information given out and, especially, limit the information to verifiable facts: the amounts owed and presently due, maximum credit allowed, the dates of the account's opening and last sale, and the degree of promptness in payment.

The First Bank of Chicago
1160 State Street
Chicago, Illinois 60688

February 14, [*year*]

Mr. Milton Smedley
Credit Department
Standard Electric Corporation
2120 Oak Terrace
Lake Bluff, Illinois 60044

Dear Mr. Smedley:

We are happy to send you, in confidence, the credit information you requested concerning Mr. Bruce Kretchmer, owner of Kretchmer's Appliance Store.

Mr. Kretchmer, who was appliance department supervisor at Lillian's Department Store until last fall, has had personal checking and savings accounts with us for the past ten years. His accounts were always in order, with adequate balances to cover all checks drawn.

His appliance store, at 1135 State Street, was opened last December. For this undertaking, he borrowed $8,000 from this bank and has begun making regular payments against the loan. We are unaware of any further outstanding debts he may have.

On the basis of our experience with him, we believe Mr. Kretchmer to be creditworthy.

Yours truly,

THE FIRST BANK OF CHICAGO

Peggy Sawyer
Branch Manager

Figure 9–3
Credit Reference

Because the reputation of an individual or a business is at stake, opinions should be expressed discreetly, if at all. Especially when a credit reference is unfavorable, it is advisable to state only objective facts in order to avoid a possible libel suit. Most companies, moreover, repeat somewhere in the letter (see Figure 9–3) that they expect the provided information to remain confidential.

Credit-Granting Letters

When all credit references are favorable, a letter is sent granting credit to the customer (Figure 9–4). Whether for a consumer charge account or a dealer open account, the acceptance letter:

1. notifies the customer of the credit approval.
2. welcomes the customer and expresses appreciation.
3. explains the credit terms and privileges.
4. establishes goodwill and encourages further sales.

Credit-Refusing Letters

Sometimes, of course, credit must be denied (Figure 9–5). A letter refusing credit must give the customer a reason; however, in an effort to be tactful and to protect references, the reason may be expressed vaguely.

The credit-refusal letter must also try to encourage business on a cash basis. Therefore, the tone must be positive and in some way "*you*-oriented." In addition, it is a good idea to suggest that the customer reapply for credit in the future, thereby letting him know that you desire and appreciate his business.

Standard Electric Corporation

2120 Oak Terrace
Lake Bluff, Illinois 60044

February 18, [*year*]

Mr. Bruce Kretchmer
Kretchmer's Appliance Store
1135 State Street
Chicago, Illinois 60688

Dear Mr. Kretchmer:

It is my pleasure to welcome you as an SEC credit customer since your request for credit has been approved.

Your first order, for 6 Model 18E toasters, will be ready for shipment on Monday, February 22.

On the first of each month, we will prepare a statement of the previous month's purchases. Your payment is due in full on the tenth. With each statement, you will also receive a supply of order forms and return envelopes.

Arlene Ryan, your personal SEC sales representative, will visit you some time next week. In addition to bringing you catalogs and samples, she will explain our special dealer options, such as advertising campaigns and rebate programs.

We are delighted that SEC can be a part of your store's beginnings and look forward to serving you for many years to come.

Sincerely yours,

Milton Smedley
Credit Department

Figure 9–4
Credit-Granting Letter

H&M HANS & MEYER'S • Suppliers to the Plumbing Trade • 1010 Broadway, New York, NY 10033

August 10, [*year*]

Mr. Donald Cortland
Cortland Hardware Store
20-67 Kissena Blvd.
Queens, NY 11203

Dear Mr. Cortland:

Thank you for your recent application for Hans & Meyer's 60-day terms of credit; however, we believe it would not be in your best interest to grant you credit at this time.

An impartial credit investigation indicates that your company's present financial obligations are substantial. We fear that adding to those obligations could jeopardize your sound credit standing in the community.

Of course, Mr. Cortland, you are always welcome to buy from Hans & Meyer's, on a COD basis. We will try our best to serve you in all ways possible. And if, in the future, your obligations should be reduced, feel free to apply again for terms of credit. We shall be delighted to reconsider.

Cordially yours,

Figure 9–5
Credit-Refusing Letter

Collection Letters

No matter how carefully a company screens its credit customers, there will be times when a bill goes unpaid and steps to collect must be taken. The problem when writing a collection letter is how to demand payment and still keep a customer. The writer of a collection letter wants to get the money owed *and* maintain goodwill.

Collection letters, therefore, should be *persuasive* rather than forceful, *firm* rather than demanding. A fair and tactful letter gets better results than a sarcastic or abusive one. In fact, even collection letters should be "*you-oriented*": courteous, considerate, and concerned about the customer's best interest.

Collection letters are usually sent in a series. The first letter is mildest and most understanding, with the letters becoming gradually more insistent. The final letter in a series, when all previous letters have failed, threatens to turn the matter over to a lawyer or collection agency. Of course, the tone of any letter in the series will vary, from positive and mild to negative and strong, depending upon the past payment record of the customer. The time between the letters may also vary, from ten days to a month at the start, from one to two weeks later on.

Every letter in a collection series contains certain information:

1. the amount owed
2. how long the bill is overdue
3. a specific action the customer may take

Some companies also like to include a SALES APPEAL, even late in the series, as an extra incentive for payment.

In general, most bills are paid within ten days of receipt, with nearly all the rest being paid within the month. Therefore, when a bill is a month overdue, action is called for. Still, the collection process must begin gently.

Step 1

The *monthly statement* reminds the customer of outstanding bills. If it is ignored, it should be followed (about a week or ten days later) by a second statement. The second statement should contain a notice (in the form of a rubber stamp or sticker) stating "Past Due" or "Please Remit." An alternative is to include a card or slip with the statement, alerting the customer to the overdue bill. This notice should be phrased in formal, possibly even stilted language; it is an *objective* reminder that does not prematurely embarrass the customer with too early a personal appeal.

> Our records indicate that the balance of $_____ on your account is now past due. Payment is requested.

Step 2

If the objective statement and reminder fail to get results, the collection process must gradually become more emotional and personal. (Form letters may be used, but they should *look* personal, adapted to the specific situation.) The second collection message, however, should still be friendly. It should seek to excuse the unpaid bill as an oversight; the tone should convey the assumption that the customer intends to pay. At this stage, too, a stress on future sales, rather than on payment, may induce action.

COLLECTION LETTER I

Dear _____ :

Snow may still be on the ground, but the first signs of spring are already budding. And we know you will be planning your Spring Sales soon. You may already have your order in mind.

When you send us a check for $ _____ , now _____ past due, you will guarantee that your next order will be promptly filled.

Oversights, of course, do happen, but we know you won't want to miss the opportunity, not only of stocking up for the coming season, but of taking advantage of our seasonal ad campaign as well.

Sincerely yours,

Step 3

The next letter in the series is still friendly, but it also now is firm. While expressing confidence in the customer's intention to pay, it inquires about the *reason* for the delay. The third collection message also makes an appeal to the customer's sense of:

1. fairness
2. cooperation
3. obligation

or desire to:

1. save her credit reputation.
2. maintain her credit line.

This letter should stress the customer's self-interest by pointing out the importance of prompt payment and the dangers of losing credit standing. The letter should communicate the urgency and seriousness of the unpaid account.

COLLECTION LETTER II

Dear _____ :

We are truly at a loss. We cannot understand why you still have not cleared your balance of $ _____ , which is now _____ overdue.

Although you have been a reliable customer for _____ years, we are afraid you are placing your credit standing in jeopardy. Only you, by sending us a check today, can insure your reputation and secure the continued convenience of buying on credit.

We would hate to lose a valued friend, Mr./Ms. _____

Please allow us to keep serving you.

Sincerely,

Step 4

Ultimately, payment must be demanded. The threat of legal action or the intervention of a collection agency is sometimes all that will motivate a customer to pay. In some companies, moreover, an executive other than the credit manager signs this last letter as a means of impressing the customer with the finality of the situation. Still, the fourth collection letter allows the customer one last chance to pay before steps are taken.

> **Note:** Before threatening legal action, it is advisable to have a FINAL COLLECTION LETTER reviewed by an attorney.

FINAL COLLECTION LETTER

Dear _____ :

Our Collection Department has informed me of their intention to file suit as you have failed to answer any of our requests for payment of $ _____ , which is now _____ overdue.

Before taking this action, however, I would like to make a personal appeal to your sound business judgment. I feel certain that if you telephone me, we can devise some means to settle this matter out of court.

Therefore, I ask that you get in touch with me by the _____ of the month so that I may avoid taking steps which neither of us would like.

Truly yours,

> **Note:** If a customer responds to a collection letter, STOP THE COLLECTION SERIES, even if the response is not full payment.

A customer may, for example, offer an excuse or promise payment; he may make a partial payment or request special payment arrangements. In such cases, the series would be inappropriate.

For instance, if your customer has owed $600 on account for two months and sends you a check for $150, you may send a letter similar to the following:

PARTIAL PAYMENT ACKNOWLEDGMENT

Dear Mr. Marsh:

Thank you for your check for $150. The balance remaining on your account is now $450.

Since you have requested an extension, we offer you the following payment plan: $150 by the 15th of the month for the next three months.

If you have another plan in mind, please telephone my office so that we may discuss it. Otherwise, we will expect your next check for $150 on September 15.

Sincerely yours,

Summary

The most important element of credit letters is *discretion*. Because they contain confidential financial information about a person or business, credit letters can seriously affect the financial reputation of that person or business.

Therefore, credit letters are both:

1. factual, based on data, not an opinion, and
2. tactful, emphasizing the confidentiality of the information.

The most important element of collection letters is *persuasion*. These letters are written to collect money on unpaid bills, but they should also be written to keep a customer.

Therefore, collection letters:

1. insist on payment.
2. emphasize the customer's best interest.

■■■■■■ **PRACTICE CORRESPONDENCE**

For each of the following, prepare a credit or collection letter, as specified in the directions.

A. Mr. Marvin Gold of 1602 Arlington Avenue, Bronx, New York 10477, has had a charge account at Manson's Department Store, 4404 Madison Avenue, New York, New York 10008, for six years. His credit limit is $400. He has always paid his bills on time although he currently has an outstanding balance of $182.54, forty-five days overdue. The National Credit Bureau has contacted Manson's for credit information about Mr. Gold. Write the letter Manson's should send to the National Credit Bureau.

B. The credit references of Ms. Migdalia Ruiz (818 Ocean Parkway, Brooklyn, New York 11202) are all favorable, and so her new charge account with Manson's Department Store has been approved. Write the letter Manson's should send to Ms. Ruiz.

C. Ms. Hiroko Osawa's credit references indicate that, although she has no outstanding debts or record of poor payment, her employment history is unstable. Manson's Department Store, therefore, concludes that she would be a poor credit risk. Write the letter that Manson's should send to Ms. Osawa (6061 Valentine Lane, Yonkers, New York 80301), denying her application for a charge account.

D. Weimar's Furniture Emporium (617 Sherman Road, North Hollywood, California 91605) has owed the Eastgate Furniture Manufacturing Company, Inc., $750 for forty-five days. Eastgate has sent two statements and one letter, which Weimar's has ignored. Write the next letter that Eastgate (305 Bush Street, San Francisco, California 94108) should send to Weimar's.

E. For eight years, Mr. Josef Larsen, of 1 Penny Lane, Summit, Pennsylvania 17214, has been a charge customer of Browne's Department Store (900 Chestnut Street, Philadelphia, Pennsylvania 19107). A "slow pay," he has nevertheless always remitted within sixty days of purchase. However, Mr. Larsen's balance of $269.48 is now ninety days past due. He has not responded to the two statements and two letters Browne's has already sent him. Write the next letter that Browne's should send to Mr. Larsen.

10.
In-House Correspondence

Words to Watch For

accessible (*adj*) understandable
agenda (*n*) list, schedule
dispense (*v*) to give out
motion (*n*) proposal
pertinent (*adj*) relevant
preside (*v*) to act as chairperson, to lead
resolution (*n*) statement of a decision or opinion
transpire (*v*) to take place, to happen
verbatim (*adj*) in the same words

Most of the letters discussed so far were intended to be sent to people outside one's own company. Messages to customers, clients, and other business associates, they emphasized business promotion and goodwill. But business people frequently must communicate in writing with employees of their own company. The main purpose of *in-house correspondence* is to share information.

The Interoffice Memorandum

The ever-growing use of personal computers has reduced the need, within an organization, to communicate on paper, but the need does still exist. Communication may begin on the computer screen or telephone, or even face to face, but "putting it in writing" for the record will prevent future misunderstanding. The format for this written record is known as the interoffice memorandum.

Memorandums, usually called *memos*, are the form commonly used for *short*, relatively *informal* messages between members of the same organization (see Figures 10–1 and 10–2). The memo provides a simplified, standardized format for communicating information *concisely*. The many uses of memos include announcements and instructions, statements of policy, and informal reports.

Because memos are usually used between people who have a regular working relationship, the *tone* of memos tends to be more informal than the tone of other business letters. Expressions and words known only to those employees of the company are permissible in a memo. Similarly, the writer can usually assume that the reader knows the basic facts and so can get to the heart of the message more directly. Note, however, that the level of formality should reflect the relationship between the writer and the reader.

C.P. Dalloway & Sons
Interoffice Memo

TO: Charles Dalloway, Jr.

FROM: Clarissa Woolf

DATE: August 18, [*year*]

SUBJECT: Alternative Methods of Payment to Our New Overseas Suppliers

Because our suppliers have placed us on open account, these are the alternative methods of payment available to us:

1   Check—this method is slow. It requires clearance through the international banking system and will cost some of our suppliers additional bank charges. In some countries, clearance can take as long as a month.

2   Bank draft—our bank will issue a draft drawn on a bank in the supplier's country and currency. Because we send this directly to our suppliers, they receive prompt credit.

3   Electronic transfer—our bank instructs an overseas bank to pay our supplier in either our or their currency. This is the quickest method of payment, but our fees will be the highest.

Please let me know your preference, and I will communicate it to our suppliers.

CW

Figure 10–1
Interoffice Memorandum I

At the same time, a memo, like any piece of written communication, must be prepared with care. It is TYPED neatly and contains COMPLETE, ACCURATE information. It follows the principles of standard English and maintains a COURTEOUS tone no matter how familiar the correspondents may be.

Unlike other types of business letters, the memo is NOT prepared on company letterhead. Nor does it include an inside address, salutation, or complimentary closing. A memo is a streamlined method of communication. Many companies provide printed forms to speed up memo preparation even further.

Goleta Motors, Inc.   Memo
_____

TO: All Sales Representatives

FROM: Peter Koulikourdis

DATE: April 27, [*year*]

SUBJECT: Rescheduling of Monthly Sales Meeting

The May Monthly Sales Meeting has been rescheduled. Instead of Tuesday, May 3, we will meet on

Wednesday, May 4, at 10:30 A.M.

in the Conference Room. Please mark your calendar accordingly.

PK

Figure 10–2
Interoffice Memorandum II

Whether or not a printed form is available, most memos use a standard heading: the company name about one inch from the top followed by the term "Interoffice Memo." Beneath this, four basic subheadings are used:

TO:
FROM:
DATE:
SUBJECT:

(Some companies also include space for such details as office numbers or telephone extensions.)

The TO: line indicates the name of the person to whom the memo is sent. Courtesy titles (such as *Mr.* and *Ms.*) are generally used only to show respect to a superior. Job titles, departments, and room numbers may be included to avoid confusion. When several people will be receiving copies, a CC notation or an inclusive term (such as "TO: All Personnel") may be used.

The FROM: line indicates the name of the person sending the memo. No courtesy title should be used, but a job title, department, or extension number may be included for clarity or convenience.

The DATE: line indicates in standard form the date on which the memo is sent.

The SUBJECT: line serves as a title and should briefly but thoroughly describe the content of the memo.

The body of the memo begins three to four lines below the subject line. Like any piece of writing, it should be logically organized but it should also be CONCISE: the information should be immediately accessible to the reader. For this reason, data are often itemized and paragraphs are numbered. Statistics should be presented in tables, too.

The body of most memos can be divided into three general sections:

1.   An *introduction* states the main idea or purpose.
2.   A *detailed discussion* presents the actual information being conveyed.
3.   A *conclusion* may make recommendations or call for further actions.

> **Note:** Memos are not usually signed. The writer's initials are typed below the message, and if she chooses, she may sign her initials over the typed ones or at the FROM line. Reference initials and enclosure notation are typed below the writer's initials along the left margin.

Minutes

Within most organizations, meetings among members of departments or committees are a regular occurrence. Some meetings are held at fixed intervals (such as weekly or monthly). Others are called for special reasons. *Minutes* (Figure 10–3) are a written record of everything that transpires at a meeting. They are prepared for the company files, for the reference of those in attendance, and for the information of absentees.

Minutes are prepared by a secretary who takes thorough notes during the proceedings. Afterwards, he prepares a *draft* and includes all the pertinent information. (It is usually the secretary's responsibility to decide which statements or actions at a meeting are insignificant and so should be omitted from the minutes.)

In preparing the minutes, the secretary may include complete versions of statements and papers read at the meeting. (Copies are provided by the member involved.) The minutes of *formal* meetings (of, for example, large corporations or government agencies), where legal considerations are involved, are made *verbatim*, that is, they include, word for word, everything that is said or done.

The format used for minutes varies from one organization to another but the minutes of any meeting should contain certain basic facts:

1. the name of the organization
2. the place, date, and time of the meeting
3. whether the meeting is regular (monthly, special, etc.)
4. the name of the person presiding
5. a record of attendance (for small meetings, a list of those present or absent; for large meetings, the number of members in attendance)
6. a reference to the minutes of the previous meeting (a statement that they were read and either accepted or revised, or that the reading was dispensed with)
7. an account of all reports, motions, or resolutions made (including all necessary details and the results of votes taken)
8. the date, time, and place of the next meeting
9. the time of adjournment

Formal minutes would include, in addition to greater detail, the names of all those who make and second motions and resolutions, and the voting record of each person present.

Minutes of the Meeting of the
CAPITOL IMPROVEMENTS COMMITTEE
The Foster Lash Company, Inc.
October 8, [*year*]

Presiding: Patricia Stuart

Present: Mike Negron
              Sheila Gluck
              Ellen Franklin
              Samuel Browne
              Lisa Woo

Absent: Fred Hoffman
              Gina Marino

The weekly meeting of the Capitol Improvements Committee of
the Foster Lash Company was called to order at 11 A.M. in the
conference room by Ms. Stuart. The minutes of the meeting of
October 1 were read by Mr. Negron and approved.

The main discussion of the meeting concerned major equipment
that should be purchased by the end of the year. Among the
proposals were these:

Ms. Woo presented information regarding three varieties of office
copying machines. On the basis of her cost analysis and relative
performance statistics, it was decided, by majority vote, to
recommend the purchase of a CBM X-12 copier.

Mr. Browne presented a request from the secretarial staff for new
typewriters. Several secretaries have complained of major and
frequent breakdowns of their old machines. Ms. Franklin and Mr.
Browne will further investigate the need for new typewriters and
prepare a cost comparison of new equipment versus repairs.

The committee will discuss the advisability of upgrading account
executives' laptop computers. The report will be presented by
Sheila Gluck at the next meeting, to be held on October 15,
[*year*], at 11 A.M. in the conference room.

The meeting was adjourned at 11:45 A.M.

Respectfully submitted,

Ellen Franklin, Secretary

Figure 10–3
Minutes

Summary

Memos are written messages between members of the same organization, therefore, they may be *informal* and *concise*. At the same time, they must be *courteous* and *complete*.

Minutes are the written record of the events at a meeting. They are usually prepared according to a predetermined format. They contain all the information that could be needed by:

1. the people attending the meeting.
2. the people absent from the meeting.
3. the company files and other people in the organization.

■■■■■■■ PRACTICE CORRESPONDENCE

Prepare the in-house correspondence called for in each of the following situations.

A. Your employer, Penelope Louden, requested a schedule of the data processors' planned vacations so that she may decide whether or not to arrange for temporary help during the summer months. The schedule is as follows: Josie Thompkins, July 1–15; Calvin Bell, July 15–29; Stephen James, July 22–August 5; Jennifer Coles, August 12–26. Prepare a memo to Ms. Louden informing her of the schedule and observing that at least three processors will always be present—except during the week of July 22, when both Mr. Bell and Mr. James will be on vacation. Ask if she'd like you to arrange for a temporary processor for that week.

B. As administrative assistant to the president of Conway Products, Inc., it is your responsibility to make reservations at a local restaurant for the annual Christmas party. Because of the high cost per person, you would like to have as accurate a guest list as possible. Write a memo to all the employees requesting that they let you know by December 1 whether they plan to attend.

C. As secretary to the Labor Grievances Committee of the Slate and Johnson Luggage Company, you must prepare the minutes of the monthly meeting held on September 23. At the meeting, you took the following notes:

1. Called to order 4 P.M., employees' cafeteria, by Mr. Falk.
2. Presiding: Mr. Falk; Present: Mr. Baum, Ms. Dulugatz, Mr. Fenster, Ms. Garcia, Ms. Penn; Absent: Mr. Sun.
3. Correction made in minutes of previous meeting (August 21): Ms. Dulugatz, not Ms. Penn, to conduct study of employee washroom in warehouse. Approved as corrected.
4. Mr. Fenster presented results of survey of office employees. Most frequent complaints agreed on. Fenster to arrange to present these complaints to Board of Directors.
5. Report on condition of warehouse employee washrooms presented by Ms. Dulugatz. Accepted with editorial revision.
6. Adjourned 5:15 P.M. Next meeting at same time and place on October 22.

D. As secretary to Alan Warsaw, director of international policy for the U.S. Chamber of Commerce, prepare minutes from the following notes taken at the Special Meeting on American Policy Toward Cuba.

1. Called to order 2 P.M. May 4, [*year*], Sunset Ballroom, Miami Hilton.
2. 102 members present, 13 absent, all officers present.
3. Reading of minutes of last meeting dispensed with.
4. Officers' Reports—
   Aurora Bonilla, U.S.-Cuba Economic Council of Houston, reported on increase in number of American business representatives legally traveling to Cuba—quadrupling over last five years. Also outlined current legal business transactions between U.S. businesses and Cuba (largest is AT&T payment for access to Cuban long-distance telephone market).
   John Ross, PDR Corp., reported on trade show hosted by Fidel Castro and his top ministers for representatives of major U.S. cor-porations. Noted Cuban government's eagerness to do business with American companies. Estimated Cuban market for basic goods and services at $2 billion to $4 billion a year.
   Alan Warsaw, director, outlined advances made by America's trading partners. Companies from 25 countries (including Canada, Italy, and Mexico) have announced deals worth over $5 billion.
5. Motions—
   The director called for committee to draft a resolution advocating a change in American policy. Motion made and carried that existing legal advisory council will constitute committee headed by director. Motion to meet again to vote on committee's draft resolution made and carried.
6. Adjourned 4:10 P.M.

11.
Business Reports and Proposals

Words to Watch For

chronological (*adj*) listed in the order of occurrence
itemize (*v*) to break down into a list
recur (*v*) to happen again
scope (*n*) extent, range
synopsis (*n*) summary
verify (*v*) to confirm, to prove
vital (*adj*) necessary for life
volatile (*adj*) prone to sudden change
voluminous (*adj*) large

Reports

More than ever before, *information* plays a vital role in today's business world. In fact, the latest advances in computers, information-processing systems, and telecommunications have made information itself a commodity. People who process information are valued members of the business community.

The purpose of a *business report* is to communicate essential information in an organized, useful format. Writing a report requires the ability to gather data, organize facts, and compose a readable text.

A well-prepared business report provides COMPLETE, ACCURATE information about an aspect of a company's operations. The subject of a report may vary from expenses to profits, production to sales, marketing trends to customer relations. The information provided by a report is often meant to influence decisions. It may be used in determining changes, improvements, or solutions to problems. Therefore, reports must also be CLEAR, CONCISE, and READABLE.

The *format* of a business report may vary. Brief, *informal reports* are intended for in-house use, while *formal reports* are intended for national public distribution. Some reports consist entirely of prose; others consist of statistics. Still other reports may employ a combination of prose, tables, charts, and graphs.

The *frequency* of reports also varies. Some are unique, submitted one time only as a result of a special project or circumstance. Others are scheduled to be submitted routinely (weekly, monthly, quarterly), often on a preprinted form or in a preestablished format.

The *style* of a report depends upon the audience. An informal report can be worded personally if it will be read by only close associates. In such a report "I" or "we" is acceptable. On the other hand, a formal report must be impersonal and expressed entirely in the third person. Note the difference:

Informal: I recommend that the spring campaign concentrate on newspaper and television advertising.

Formal: It is recommended that the spring campaign concentrate on newspaper and television advertising.

Informal: After discussing the matter with our department managers, we came up with the following information.

Formal: The following report is based upon information provided by the managers of the Accounting, Marketing, Personnel, and Advertising Departments.

Whether formal or informal, the wording of a report should be SIMPLE and DIRECT.

The *type* of report is determined by how the facts are presented and whether the facts are interpreted.

1. *A Record Report* merely states facts, describing the status of a company or a division of a company at a particular point in time.
2. *A Progress Report* also states facts, tracing developments that have occurred over a period of time.
3. *A Statistical Report* presents numerical data, usually in the form of charts, tables, and graphs.
4. *An Investigative Report* is based on a study or investigation of a particular situation or issue. Such a report presents the newly accumulated data. It may also analyze the data.
5. *A Recommendation Report* is an investigative report taken one step further, providing specific recommendations based on the information provided.

There are three important rules to keep in mind when preparing any business report:

1. Cite your sources. *Always* let your reader know where your information comes from so that it may be verified.
2. Date your report. Business is volatile; facts and situations change daily, if not hourly. Your information could become outdated very quickly.
3. *Always* keep a copy of your report for your own reference.

Informal Reports

The informal report is the most common form of business report. It is usually short, five pages or fewer. It is generally written in the form of a memo (Figure 11–1) or a variation of a memo. Sometimes, if it is sent to someone outside the company, an informal report may be written as a letter (Figure 11–2).

The tone and style of an informal report varies according to the subject and audience. But whether friendly or impersonal, a report must always be worded with courtesy and tact.

Informal reports must often be prepared quickly, requiring information to be gathered more casually and unscientifically than for a formal report. Nevertheless, any business report must be THOROUGH and FACTUAL, no matter how minor the topic nor how short the time.

The best approach to gathering data is to begin by defining your *purpose*. If you understand the precise reason for your report, you will know what information to look for.

Once your facts are assembled, the second phase of report writing is *organization*. You must arrange your facts in a logical sequence that can be easily followed.

Finally, the nature of your data and your system of organization will determine your form of *presentation*. If your report calls for prose, organize your paragraphs:

First Paragraph: Present the main idea clearly and concisely.

Middle Paragraphs: Develop the main point with supporting details and information.

Final Paragraph: State an *objective* conclusion. If called for, your own comments and recommendations may be included at the end.

In a short, informal report, it is often a good idea to *itemize* your data. This may simply mean numbering your paragraphs, or it may mean arranging tables of statistics. However you do it, itemization makes a report seem more organized and easier to read.

TO: Mr. Marvin Dawson

FROM: Jim Coates

DATE: February 7, [*year*]

SUBJECT: Report on Secretarial Staff Overtime for January

As you requested, I have computed the number of overtime hours worked by the secretaries of the various departments and the cost of that overtime to the company.

Department	Employee	Hourly Wage	Number of Occasions	Total Hours	Total Cost @ Time and a Half
Executive	Ann Rogers	$15.00	6	15	$337.50
	Wilma Toynbee	15.00	5	14	315.00
Marketing	Maribel Cruz	10.00	8	17	255.00
Accounting	Nicole Foire	10.00	8	18	270.00
Personnel	Judy Hecht	10.00	10	21	315.00
	TOTALS		37	85	$1492.50

The cost of hiring a clerical assistant for 35 hours a week at $7.00 an hour would be $245.00, or $980.00 and 140 hours a month. This would save the company approximately $512.50 yet provide an additional 55 clerical hours.

JC

Figure 11–1
Informal Report (Memo)

International Industries, Inc.
3000 Avenue of the Americas
New York, NY 10019

Dear Shareholder:

Subject: Third Quarter Report

Third-quarter earnings continued at record levels due to a significant increase in International's petroleum operations. Earnings for the first nine months exceeded last year's full-year results.

International Industries' third-quarter income from continuing operations was $42,351,000 or $1.25 per common share, a 40% increase over the income of $30,330,000 or 89 cents per common share for the same period last year.

Operating income for International's petroleum operations increased 53% over the third quarter of last year, contributing over 79% of International's income.

As a result of depressed conditions in the automotive and railroad markets, International's earnings from fabricated metal products continued to decline. International Chemicals' overall quarterly earnings declined although full-year income from International Chemicals should be substantially above last year's levels.

International Industries is a leading manufacturer of petroleum equipment and services, metal products, and chemicals, with annual sales of $2 billion.

Laura M. Carson
Chairperson and Chief Executive Officer

Wayne G. Wagner
President and Chief Operating Officer

November 10, [*year*]

Figure 11–2
Informal Report (Letter)

2

INTERNATIONAL INDUSTRIES, INC.
Consolidated Statement of Income (Unaudited)
(In thousands, except per share)

	For the three months ended September 30	
	1998	1997
Revenues:		
Net Sales	$517,858	$454,866
Income from investments in other companies	8,729	4,046
Other income (loss), net	2,599	990
Total revenues	$529,186	$459,902
Costs and expenses:		
Cost of goods sold	$339,851	$303,893
Selling, general and administrative	111,384	91,597
Interest	9,456	13,001
Minority interest	1,600	705
Total costs and expenses	$462,291	$409,196
Income before items shown below	$66,895	$50,706
Taxes on income	24,544	20,376
Income from continuing operations	$42,351	$30,330
Income from discontinued operations, net of income taxes	—	2,346
Income before cumulative effect of accounting change	$42,351	$32,676
Cumulative effect of accounting change	—	—
Net income	$42,351	$32,676
Income per share of common stock (*):		
Income from continuing operations	$1.25	$.89
Net income per share	$1.25	$.96

NOTE: (*) Income per share of common stock has been calculated
after deduction for preferred stock dividend requirements
of $.03 per share of common stock for the three months
ended September 30.

Figure 11–2 (Continued)
Informal Report (Letter)

TRAVEL EXPENSE REPORT

NAME: _____

DEPARTMENT:_____

DATE: _____

DESTINATION:_____

DATES OF TRAVEL: _____

PURPOSE OF TRIP:_____

                               _____

                               _____

TRANSPORTATION:_____$

HOTEL: _____$

CAR RENTAL: _____$

MEALS:_____$

OTHER (itemize): _____$

                      _____$

                      _____$

TOTAL: $

(For proper reimbursement be sure to attach all receipts.)

Figure 11–3
Informal Report (Preprinted Form)

Formal Reports

A formal report (Figure 11–4) is not only longer, but also more thorough than an informal report. It requires more extensive information gathering and is presented in a more stylized format. It is always presented objectively and relies on extensive details for documentation.

Similar to informal reports, begin preparing your formal report by defining your topic. State the problem to be solved as precisely as you can. Then decide what information is needed to solve that problem and the techniques required to gather that information. Typical methods of information gathering include library research, surveys and interviews, and experimentation.

When your investigation is complete and your data are collected, you must organize and analyze the facts. Your interpretation may or may not be included in the final version of the report. However, before you begin to write, you must understand the data and facts thoroughly.

The formal report consists of the following parts:

1. *Title page:* This page will include the title of the report, the name of the person who prepared the report, the name of the person for whom it was prepared, and the date on which it was completed. The title page, therefore, will contain a great deal of white space.
2. *Table of contents:* This page will be outlined in advance, but it is printed last. It consists of a list of all the headings and subheadings in the report and the number of the pages on which each section begins.
3. *Introduction:* Unlike the introduction to a school research paper, this section is *not* an opening statement leading into your main topic. Rather, it is a statement of three specific items:
   - The purpose of your report (what the report demonstrates or proves)
   - The scope of your report (what the report does and does *not* include)
   - The method by which you gathered your information
4. *Summary:* This section is a concise statement of the main points covered in the report. Think of it as a courtesy for the busy executive who will not have enough time to read your entire report.
5. *Body:* This is the essence of your report. It is the organized presentation of the data you have collected.
6. *Conclusion:* This is an *objective* statement of what the information in the report has demonstrated.
7. *Recommendations:* If required, these should be made on *the basis of the facts* included in the report. They should flow logically from the objective conclusion.
8. *Appendix:* This section consists of supplementary information that does not fit into the body of the report but which is essential to support the data. It is often in the form of charts and graphs.
9. *Bibliography:* A list of references used in preparing the report is required whenever printed material has been consulted. Entries are listed alphabetically by author's last name. Proper format varies

from field to field, so you should consult a manual or style sheet. The following examples, though, will serve as general models:

Book: Toffler, Alvin. *Powershift: Knowledge, Wealth, and Violence at the Edge of the 21st Century*. New York: Bantam, 1990.
Periodical: Rowland, Mary. "Sorting Through the Tax Changes," *The New York Times*, November 4, 1990, section 3, page 17.

RECENT DEVELOPMENTS IN
OFFICE TECHNOLOGY

Prepared by Rachel Orloff
Prepared for Mr. Winston Chin
February 22, [*year*]

Figure 11–4
Formal Report
(Title Page)

TABLE OF CONTENTS

Figure 11–4
Formal Report
(Table of Contents)

INTRODUCTION

The purpose of this report is to examine the latest advances in office machines technology in order to determine what, if any, capital improvements should be made in the office equipment of the ANDMAR Corporation.

This report does not consider security systems or fire detection and control devices.

The information for this report was gathered from information supplied by the National Office Machines Dealers Association as well as from articles in several issues of Secretary's Press, Executive World, and Management Review.

SUMMARY

This report shows that, because of increasing emphasis on the use of very large-scale integrated circuits, major changes are anticipated in office technology during the next decade. These changes will primarily involve:

1. electronic typewriters with memory functions
2. executive, as opposed to central, word-processing stations
3. high-speed and intelligent copiers
4. computers of increased speed, reliability, and memory capacity
5. electronic printing calculators
6. dual-voltage fax with memory

Figure 11–4
**Formal Report
(Introduction and Summary)**

CONCLUSION AND RECOMMENDATIONS

On the basis of the data in this report, it can be concluded that:

1. The installation of electronic typewriters and word-processing stations increases the productivity of secretaries and the efficiency of executives.
2. Medium-speed copiers and fax machines maximize cost-effectiveness when used on a departmental basis.
3. Programmable electronic calculators function at a fraction of the cost of electronic adding machines.

From these conclusions, it is therefore recommended that:

1. An in-depth investigation of currently available electronic typewriters, fax machines, and word-processing systems be conducted to determine the cost and feasibility of installing such equipment.
2. A cost analysis be made to compare the copiers presently in use at ANDMAR to alternatives now on the market.
3. The services of an electronic calculator system sales specialist be engaged to determine the equipment best suited to ANDMAR's particular application.

Figure 11–4
**Formal Report
(Conclusion and Recommendations)**

The most difficult part of a report to prepare, of course, is the body. Since this is where the bulk of your work will be focused, you should proceed systematically:

1. *Research*—Your report will consist of information, and you must determine where to find it. Sources may include your own experience, company files, the Internet and other computer-based data sources, people (by means of interviews and questionnaires), industry and government publications, and other printed literature (such as books and articles).
2. *Organization*—When you have gathered the necessary data, you must arrange it logically. The system you use will be determined by your topic. Some reports require a chronological presentation. In other reports, the purpose will suggest division into categories: Are you comparing, ranking, examining cause and effect? Whatever arrangement you decide on should be emphasized with subtitles and headings.

3. *Illustration*—The body of your report can be substantiated by the use of charts, graphs, tables, diagrams, and photographs. These should be used to present data not easily expressed in prose; they should not be used to repeat data already presented in your text. Each illustration should be labeled and, if many are included, numbered as well.

Finally, you must be sure to cite your sources! When you quote another person's words and ideas, you must give that person credit for the words or ideas. Failure to do this constitutes PLAGIARISM, which is essentially information theft. If you interview people, give their names. If you refer to books or articles, footnote them (see #6 below). You lose no credit when you acknowledge the source of your information, but you lose all credibility (and maybe even your job) if you are caught presenting another person's ideas as your own.

When your report is complete and ready to be printed, keep in mind these guidelines for preparing the manuscript:

1. Use *standard manuscript form*—double space on one side of 8½ × 11" paper.
2. *Number every page*—except the title page—in the upper right-hand corner.
3. Leave lots of *white space*—allow ample margins as well as space between subtopics.
4. Use lots of *headings and subheadings*—make your report logical by giving headings of equal weight parallel wording; surround headings with white space.
5. Pay attention to *paragraphing*—try to keep your paragraphs more or less equal in length. (A paragraph of 15 lines should not be followed by one of 6 lines; on the other hand, paragraphs of 15 and 11 lines, although unequal, would not be too unbalanced.) Also, give each paragraph, like the report as a whole, a logical structure; start with a topic sentence and follow with supporting details.
6. Be sure to *footnote* information that you take from other sources—quotations should be followed by a raised number[1] and at the bottom of the page a notation should be made:

   [1]Helen J. McLane, *Selecting, Developing and Retaining Women Executives* (New York: Van Nostrand Reinhold, 1980), pp. 71–73.

7. *Proofread* your report for errors in grammar, spelling, capitalization, and punctuation.
8. Bind the finished manuscript securely.

Proposals

A proposal is a sales pitch for an idea. Its purpose is to persuade someone to accept your idea and put it into action.

Proposals are required in a variety of situations. For example, you may want to:

- suggest an idea to your employer to change a company procedure, hire an additional employee, purchase new equipment, and so on.
- recommend an idea or project to a committee or board.
- apply for a grant to fund a project.
- solicit financial backing from investors for a new business or project.
- solicit a contract from a potential customer or client.

The information you include and the format you choose for your proposal will vary with the purpose of the proposal. Some proposals, particularly grant applications, require the completion of extensive application forms and must follow a format prescribed by the organization offering the grant. In any case, all proposals must:

1. *Define the idea*. Early in the proposal you must state CLEARLY your actual idea. You must define its purpose, as well as its scope and limitations. If you are presenting the idea to people unfamiliar with the background for the idea, you must inform them, creating a context in which the idea fits logically.
2. *Be persuasive*. Offer specific reasons for your idea, including the benefits or advantages to be gained from it. Present these reasons logically, not just as a list, but as an organized progression. You want to gradually build an irrefutable case for your idea.
3. *Anticipate objections*. Provide answers to questions or doubts before they occur. This may include credentials of people involved, justification of costs or expenditures, or arguments against alternative ideas.
4. *Explain how to proceed*. What must be done to implement your idea? What would you like your reader to do? Is there a deadline by which a decision must be made?

The size of your idea will determine the length of your proposal. If you are proposing the purchase of an extra computer terminal for your secretarial staff, you will need a briefer argument than you would for a proposal for a bank loan to start up a new business. Still, all proposals contain:

- TITLE: This identifies your idea clearly. It should be short.
- HEADINGS: Divide your persuasive argument into subtitled sections. You will make your proposal easier to read and your argument easier to follow.

A long proposal may also include:

- SUMMARY: At the beginning, you will provide the busy executive with a synopsis of your idea and main supporting points.

PARMA REFRIGERATOR & STOVE CO., INC.   Sales & Service
_____

1500 Wellman Square   PHONE   718-428-1800
Bronx, New York 10481   FAX   718-428-1810

PROPOSAL
Bid to Provide Appliances Under HUD Guidelines

TO: Federation of Latino Communities, Inc.
       Bedford Paraiso SRO Program
       50 Bedford Park Row
       Bronx, New York 10492

ATT: Fernando Lebron

FROM: Angela Parma Stern
       Vice President

DATE: April 18, [*year*]

Based on a bulk order, single delivery and all installations being completed in one day, we can provide the appliances you specified at the following discount:

- 22 Federal Electric all-electric stoves, Mod. No. ES02V delivered and installed @ $420 each $9,240.00
- 48 Federal Electric 30" ductless range hoods, Mod. No. RH32 delivered and installed @ $66 each $3,168.00
- Parts for Federal Electric cooktop, Mod. No. CT201B
  44 6" burners @ $20 each, delivered only ....$ 880.00
  44 8" burners @ $25 each, delivered only $1,100.00
  22 burner receptacles @ $9.50 each, delivered only $ 209.00

TOTAL: $14,597.00

TERMS: • 20% ($2,919.40) retainer due upon signing of contract (certified check)
       • Balance ($11,677.60) due upon delivery (certified check)

ADDITIONAL CRITERIA: (1) All merchandise is covered by a manufacturer's one-full-year warranty
                      (2) We carry $2 million liability insurance
                      (3) All members of our crew are union members with prior experience on HUD projects
                      (4) We conform to all regulations of the Davis-Bacon Act regarding hiring practices

All items are available for immediate shipment. We can process your order as soon as we hear from you.

Figure 11–5
Proposal I

A PROPOSAL TO SPEED COVERAGE
FOR ABSENT EMPLOYEES

This is a proposal to provide the employees of Shoji International with a means of reporting anticipated absences during nonworking hours. The purpose is to enable the Personnel Department to assign temporary coverage for absent employees by 9 A.M.

WHAT WE PROPOSE TO DO

We would install an answering machine in the Personnel Department, enabling employees throughout the company to call in sick any time between 5 P.M. the previous day and 8:30 A.M. the day of the absence. An assistant from Personnel will be rescheduled to work from 8:30 to 4:30 (instead of the present 9 to 5) to listen to the messages left on the machine, schedule the temporary assignments, and notify the substitute employees, who should be in place at their temporary workstations between 9 and 9:15 A.M.

WHAT WE WOULD LIKE TO SOLVE

Under the present system, an employee must report an absence to his/her supervisor. The majority of these calls, therefore, come in between 9 and 9:15 A.M., after the work day has begun. Next, the various department managers notify the Personnel Department, where temporary coverage is then arranged. The substitute employees may not arrive at their workstations before 10 A.M. An hour of down time, particularly in such departments as Sales and Customer Relations, can result in backlogs that last all day and may ultimately result in lost sales.

WHAT BENEFITS WE WILL ACHIEVE

The benefits will occur at four levels:

1. Employees will benefit by being able to report an expected absence at any time. They will be relieved of the need to rise from a sick bed at exactly 9 A.M. to call their office. They will experience enhanced self-esteem by not having to report their illness to their supervisor. We anticipate improved employee morale.

2. Supervisors and managers will benefit by no longer having to relay messages to Personnel about absent employees, a process that has taken time when a department was already short-handed. They will also benefit by having absentees' positions filled at the start of the work day, avoiding delays within their departments as well as added burdens on other employees. They will, further, be relieved of the need to discuss an employee's reasons for being absent until the employee returns to work (thereby losing no authority but reserving the authority to be used with those employees whose attendance records are questionable).

3. The Personnel Department will benefit by knowing early in the morning what rescheduling will be required that day. We will be relieved of the 9 A.M. rush of calls from managers that has until now slowed the process of assigning "temps." With adequate time, we will be able to make the most appropriate reassignment to cover each absence, and we will be finished earlier, allowing more time to be devoted to our other responsibilities.

Figure 11–6
Proposal II

4. Finally, Shoji International will benefit. There will be reduced risk of lost sales or business due to the delays that, until now, have taken place in the morning. There will be the advantages of enhanced employee morale and more efficient morning operations throughout the company. (We anticipate that there might even be a reduction in absenteeism as a result of improved morale. This can be monitored as part of a follow-up study of the proposed change.)

WHAT THIS WILL COST

The only cost of the proposed change is the price of a telephone answering machine. We have investigated a few models, all of which cost less than $60. With approval, we would like to buy the ANSO #229 at $49.95.

WHAT HAPPENS NEXT

With approval of the proposal, we will purchase and install the answering machine. On the day before it is installed, we will hold a brief managers' meeting to inform them of the change. On the next day, a memo will go out to all employees, explaining the new procedure for reporting absences. Finally, on the first day of full operation of the answering machine, Maribel Acevedo, Personnel Assistant, will begin working her new hours, 8:30–4:30.

We are ready to institute the proposal as soon as we receive an executive decision.

Figure 11–6 (Continued)
Proposal II

- APPENDICES: Supporting data can be attached at the end. Appendices may include resumes of the people involved in the project, tables and charts of financial figures or other relevant statistics, and any other information that may interrupt the flow of your persuasive argument, but is, nonetheless, essential to the proposal.
- COVER: A long proposal should be bound in a plastic or cardboard cover.

Finally, you must consider the tone of your proposal. You want your argument to be based on the *logic* of your idea, supported by specific facts and information, but you must also convey your own enthusiasm for the idea. You must communicate a sense of urgency if you want your reader to act. A proposal is a sales pitch, but you will not successfully promise an idea you do not believe in.

Summary

A report is a presentation of information in an organized format. A well-written report contains:

1. a well-defined topic
2. complete, accurate, well-researched information
3. a clear, logical, well-organized presentation

Some reports are informal, others formal. But all reports are based on facts.

A proposal is a presentation of an idea. Its purpose is to persuade. Therefore, a proposal contains more than facts and information. It offers reasons for accepting the idea.

■■■■■■ PRACTICE CORRESPONDENCE

The following activities require that you prepare either a formal or an informal report. Be sure to employ an appropriate format.

A. Your employer has requested the latest closing prices on the following stocks (both preferred and common):

AT&T	General Motors
Microsoft	IBM
Exxon	ITT

Consult a newspaper for the necessary information and present the data in an informal report.

B. A strike of the local transit workers union is anticipated in your community. In order to be prepared, your employer has asked you to investigate the cost of renting hotel rooms for the chief executives of the company. Contact a number of local hotels to find out their daily and weekly rates. Then present this information in an informal report. Include your recommendation for the most economical and convenient place to stay.

C. The budget for your department in the coming fiscal quarter includes funds for the purchase of a fax machine. Your supervisor plans to purchase a machine that is both state-of-the-art and appropriate to department needs. Prepare a formal report on at least six different fax machines currently on the market. Consider such features as memory, resolution, half-tones, and speed, as well as other available options.

D. Your local school board is seeking to raise funds to expand the high school library. It has turned to the business community for fund-raising ideas. As a local business owner, you would like to suggest a town fair to be held in the school yard on a Saturday. Because local businesses as well as private citizens could rent space from the school board to run booths or games, the entire community could be involved in such a fund-raising activity. Write a proposal to the school board suggesting your idea for a town fair. When you present your plan of action, be sure to include persuasive reasons for your idea. Also be sure to anticipate possible objections.

E. Imagine that you are the assistant casting director of a major film production company; the company is planning to produce a film version of a popular novel. Using a novel that you have recently read, write a formal report describing all the characters in the book and the actors to be considered for each role. Discuss at least two actors for each part.

12.
Employment Correspondence

Words to Watch For

affiliation (*n*) association, relationship
erratic (*adj*) inconsistent, unstable
extracurricular (*adj*) non-school-related
personnel (*n*) group of employed people
prospective (*adj*) possible
sporadic (*adj*) occasional, infrequent
trendy (*adj*) very fashionable
vouch (*v*) to verify, to guarantee

Of all the different kinds of business letters, perhaps the most important for your personal career are the letters you write to apply for a job. Your letter of application and accompanying resume can help you get the job of your choice if they are well planned and written.

Before you write your resume or cover letter, you must think about yourself because your employment correspondence must give a prospective employer a positive—and desirable—picture of your personality, background, and experiences.

A good way to start is to make a list. In any order, as you think of them, list such facts as:

- jobs held
- schools attended
- areas majored in
- special courses you have taken
- extracurricular activities you have participated in
- memberships you have held
- awards or honors you have received
- sports you enjoy
- languages you speak
- special interests you have
- special skills you have

Try to include on your list any FACT that could help an employer see your value as an employee.

After you are satisfied with your list, rewrite it, arranging the facts into categories. This will serve as your worksheet when you are ready to write your resume and letter of application.

The Resume

The resume is sometimes called a data sheet or vita. It is an OUTLINE of all you have to offer a new employer (see Figures 12–1, 12–2, and 12–3). It presents your qualifications, background, and experiences in a way that will convince a business person to grant you an interview.

Your resume, with its cover letter, is the first impression you make on an employer. It promotes those traits you want the employer to know you possess. For that reason, it must look PROFESSIONAL.

First of all, a resume *must* be PRINTED on business-size bond. It is acceptable to send photocopies, but these must be PERFECT and look like originals. This can be accomplished by using the services of a quick print shop where your resume can be professionally copied on bond paper. When your resume is updated and you add new experiences, you must REPRINT the whole thing. *Never* send a resume with handwritten, or even typed, additions squeezed in. This looks careless, unorganized, and lazy.

The resume must have an overall NEAT appearance: margins are wide and balanced. Headings should stand out (for example, be underlined, capitalized, or printed in boldface type) and should be PARALLEL.

The information contained on your resume must be ACCURATE and COMPLETE. It should consist of FACTS. (You will be able to *interpret* the facts in your application letter.) Because you are presenting these facts in *outline form*, the information is expressed in short phrases rather than whole sentences.

Nowadays, it is preferable to keep a resume to *one page*. Therefore, you must be efficient in selecting the facts to include and clever in arranging them.

Working from your casual list, decide which facts you would like an employer to know. (Eliminate those you would rather he not know.) Also, consider what the employer would like to know about you. (Eliminate those facts that he would probably consider irrelevant.) Unless relevant to the job, omit your religious or political affiliations. Definitely exclude negative information such as lawsuits. DO NOT offer reasons for leaving previous jobs. DO NOT make critical comments about a previous employer (on your resume or at an interview)! And, of course, do NOT lie!

In making these decisions, keep in mind the specific job for which you are applying. What facts on your list best qualify you for the job? *These* are the facts to emphasize on your resume.

Having narrowed down your list, recopy it again—arrange the facts into logical order.

Olga Godunov
2500 North Fruitridge Road
Terre Haute, Indiana 47811
(519) 772-1248

CAREER OBJECTIVE:
To obtain a position as an executive secretary with a large corporation.

WORK EXPERIENCE:

March 1993 to Present	Secretary, the Benlow Corporation. 620 West Second Street, Terre Haute, Indiana. Responsible for general running of the office of a small private firm; duties included typing, filing, billing, answering telephones, scheduling appointments, etc.
October 1991 to March 1993	Receptionist, Dr. Mark Roan, 702 South Fulton Street, Berne, Indiana.
January 1991 to October 1991	File Clerk, Ajax Insurance Company, 277 Westgate Avenue, Berne, Indiana.

EDUCATION:

Judson Secretarial School, Berne, Indiana. September 1990–January 1991. Courses in typing, filing, Gregg shorthand, and business machines operation.

Central High School, Berne, Indiana. Diploma, June 1990.

SPECIAL SKILLS:

Typing—70 w.p.m.
Shorthand—120 w.p.m.
Languages—French
Computers—IBM WordPerfect, Microsoft Word, QYX Level IV

REFERENCES:

Ms. Alba Jenkins, Owner
The Benlow Corporation
620 West Second Street
Terre Haute, Indiana 47814
(519) 793-8686

Dr. Mark Roan
702 South Fulton Street
Berne, Indiana 46711
(777) 803-9171

Ms. Sarah Cohen, Instructor
Judson Secretarial School
141 River Road
Berne, Indiana 46781

Figure 12–1
Resume I

Arnold Stevens • 25-92 Queens Boulevard, Bayside, NY 11202 • (212) 884-7788

Career Objective
An entry-level position in the travel industry

Education
The Bowker Business Institute, 600 Fifth Avenue, New York, New York 10011
       Associate degree, June 1997
       Major: Travel and Tourism
       Courses included: The World of Travel
                        Reservations and Ticketing
                        World Geography
                        Salesmanship
                        Business Management
                        Accounting 1
                        Travel Sales and Services
                        Travel Industry Organization

Bayside High School, Bayside, New York
       Diploma, June 1995
       Technical courses included: Typing
                                    Bookkeeping

Work Experience
Sales Assistant   M & M Shoe Store, 70-19 Lefferts Boulevard, Bayside, New York 11202
                      September 1995 to present

Stock Clerk   Same as above
                      September 1994 to September 1995

Skills
 Typing: 50 w.p.m.
 Language: Spanish
 Computer: Sabre

References
References will be furnished on request.

Figure 12–2
Resume II

Nicolas Balaj
201 New Oak Street
Newark, New Jersey 07555
(201) 885-8855

CAREER OBJECTIVE

Sales Management: a position utilizing experience in sales and
supervision

SKILLS

- Over 11 years in sales and sales management
- Documented success developing both leads and long-term
  business relationships
- Experience developing "team" environment, training, and
  motivating sales staff

WORK EXPERIENCE

Summit & Storch   Sales Supervisor
Newark, New Jersey   1991–present
- Supervise staff of 12 salespeople: hire and train new
  representatives, set quotas, assign leads, manage budgets, plan
  presentations
- Increased sales from $350,000 to $1,100,000; directed opening
  of southern office (Atlanta, GA); established relationships with
  major manufacturers (including Whirlpool, Maytag, and General
  Electric)

S.G. Walters   Sales Representative
Trenton, New Jersey   1986–1991
- Conducted sales of wide product line to major distributors in
  tri-state region
- Participated in product development and presentation planning
- Increased territory sales by 75%

EDUCATION

Rutgers University   B.A.—Marketing
Rutgers, New Jersey   1986

MISCELLANEOUS

- Fluent in Spanish
- Member SRBA since 1987
- Willing to travel or relocate

Figure 12–3
Resume III

Now you are ready to set up your resume. At the top, type your name, address, and telephone number (including your area code). This information can be centered or blocked along the left margin. In either case, it provides a sufficient heading. (The word *resume* is unnecessary.)

The rest of the resume consists of the facts from your list, categorized and typed under headings. Some recommended headings are:

Employment (or Career) Objective
Education and/or Training
Awards and Honors
Work Experience
Related or Extracurricular Activities
Special Skills
Personal Data
References

You do not need to use all of these categories. Use, of course, only those that relate to facts on your list. Also, the order in which you list the categories is flexible. You may list your strongest sections first, or you may list first the section that is most relevant to the job in question.

For example, if you have had little business experience but are thoroughly trained, list EDUCATION first. On the other hand, if your college education was in an unrelated field but you have had relevant part-time jobs, list WORK EXPERIENCE first.

Note: It has become trendy to arrange your entire resume around employment skills. The FUNCTIONAL RESUME lists your employment skills in order of relevance to the job at hand, filling out in a brief paragraph what you have done to acquire or demonstrate that skill. BE AWARE that many employers are suspicious of such resumes for they do not present your career chronologically and may thus conceal an erratic or sporadic work history.

Let's look at some of these headings in greater detail.

EMPLOYMENT OBJECTIVE: Many career counselors recommend that this be included and listed first, immediately after your name and address. Mentioning a clearly defined job goal creates the favorable impression that you are a well-directed, motivated individual. On the other hand, many businesspeople prefer applicants with flexible objectives. Thus, you might consider under this heading a general statement such as, "Acceptance in a management training program" or "Entry-level position in an accounting environment."

EDUCATION: List, in reverse chronological order (that is, most recent first), the schools you have attended. Include school names, dates of attendance, and degrees or diplomas awarded. (If you have gone to college, you may omit high school unless your high school experiences are relevant to the job being applied for.) You should list, as well, any job-related courses you have taken. (If you attended a school but did not graduate, include it but be sure to list special courses taken there.)

WORK EXPERIENCE: Between WORK EXPERIENCE and EDUCATION, you must account for *all* your time since high school. Part-time and summer jobs, as well as volunteer work, should be included. (You needn't have gotten paid to have developed a valuable and marketable skill.)

Each job experience should be listed (the most recent jobs listed first) with your position or title, employer's name and address (and preferably telephone number), dates of employment, and a brief description of your responsibilities.

EXTRACURRICULAR ACTIVITIES and SPECIAL SKILLS: Under these headings you may list any facts that don't fit under EDUCATION or WORK EXPERIENCE but that demonstrate your value to an employer. For example, if you can type and take dictation but have never held a secretarial position, here is the place to list your speeds. If you can operate specialized machinery or speak several languages, note these facts as well.

PERSONAL DATA: Essential FACTS, such as any licenses or certifications you hold, should be included; however, it is not necessary to list such facts as age, height, weight, health, and marital status. Indeed, FEDERAL and many STATE LAWS prohibit employers from asking about race, religion, or sex; therefore some career counselors advise omitting this category altogether.

However, if a personal fact is particularly relevant to the job you are seeking, mention it. For example, a family member employed in the field could indicate that you have a thorough understanding of the responsibilities of the job. Or being in perfect health could be important on a job that requires a great deal of physical activity.

REFERENCES: The *last* section of your resume is a list of those people willing to vouch for your ability and experience. Former employers and teachers (especially teachers of job-related courses) are the best references. Friends or members of the clergy may be used as *character* references, but their word regarding your skills will have little influence.

Each reference should be listed by name, position or title, business address, and telephone number. A minimum of three names is recommended. Alternatively, under this heading, you may simply state, "References furnished on request," if you prefer to give a prospective employer photostated copies of previously prepared letters of reference.

> **Note:** Be sure to ask permission of each individual before you list anyone as a reference. Also, while some employers prefer to contact your references directly, it is a good idea to get a general letter of reference from each to keep for your own files. (Businesses move or go bankrupt; people move, retire, or die; and, after many years, you may simply have been forgotten!)

A WORD OF CAUTION

Recent years have seen the rise of professional resume services. These services will, for a fee, prepare your resume and cover letter. Services range from simply formatting and then printing a resume you have composed yourself to interviewing you in depth, analyzing your skills, and then composing and printing your resume for you. Some services will even do a mass mailing.

These services are valuable if you have difficulty organizing your career data. If the service includes an interview, it can help you begin thinking of your skills in new and creative ways. However, when you use a professional resume preparer, your resume will look just that—professionally prepared! It will be obvious that you paid someone else to prepare your resume. This can create doubts in a prospective employer's mind about your own skills, particularly if your target job calls for organizational, communication, clerical, or computer skills.

An alternative could be to prepare your resume on a computer yourself. Software packages are now available that provide models, allowing you to insert your own data using a variety of formats. This simplifies the process of arranging your information and printing perfect copies.

Letters of Application

A *letter of application* is a *sales letter* in which you are both salesperson and product. Its purpose is to *attract* an employer's attention and *persuade* her to grant you an interview. To do this, the letter presents what you can offer the employer, rather than what you want from the job.

A letter of application serves as the COVER LETTER of your resume. Like a resume, it is a *sample of your work*. It is also an opportunity to *demonstrate* your skills and personality. To be successful, it should be written with flair, understanding, and professional care.

There are two types of application letters. A SOLICITED letter is sent in response to a help-wanted ad (see, for example, Figure 12–4). Because this letter will compete with many others, it must be composed with distinction. At the same time, it must refer to the ad and the specific advertised job.

An UNSOLICITED letter (Figure 12–5) is sent to a company for which you would like to work even though you know of no particular opening. The advantage of this type of application is that there will be little competition. You can personally define the position you would like to apply for. Also, you can send out as many of these letters as you wish, to as many companies as you are aware of. It is a good idea, though, to find out the name of a specific person to whom you can send the letter. This makes the letter more effective than simply addressing a letter to "Personnel."

Your letter of application should *look* as good as your resume, prepared with the same care on plain business-size bond. Here, again, the services of a quick-print shop can be useful.

2500 North Fruitridge Road
Terre Haute, Indiana 47811
March 1, [*year*]

Mr. Ikuo Saito, Vice-President
Indiana Gas and Electric Company
1114 Broad Street
Terre Haute, Indiana 47815

Dear Mr. Saito:

Having served for the past several years as the sole secretary of a private business, I would like to apply for the position of executive secretary that you advertised in the Terre Haute Gazette of Sunday, February 28, [*year*].

As secretary to the Benlow Corporation here in Terre Haute, I was directly responsible to Ms. Alba Jenkins, the company's owner. My services were generally those of an administrative assistant. In addition to the usual typing, filing, and taking dictation, I was responsible for scheduling all of Ms. Jenkins' appointments, screening her telephone calls and visitors, and organizing her paperwork and correspondence.

Essentially, I did everything I could to make Ms. Jenkins' heavy responsibilities easier. Thus, I am familiar with the duties of an executive secretary and believe I am prepared to anticipate and meet all your expectations. I am confident, too, that, with enthusiasm and sincere effort, I can make the transition from a small business to a large corporation smoothly.

I would appreciate your giving me the opportunity to discuss my qualifications in person. I would be happy to come for an interview at your convenience, and I can be reached after 5:00 P.M. at 772-1248.

Sincerely yours,

Figure 12–4
Letter of Application I

Because a letter of application must sell your qualifications, it must do more than simply restate your resume in paragraph form. While the resume must be factual, objective, and brief, the letter is your chance to interpret and expand. It explains how your background relates to the specific job, and it emphasizes your strongest and most pertinent characteristics. The letter should demonstrate that you know both yourself and the company.

A letter of application must communicate your ambition and enthusiasm. Yet it must, at the same time, be *modest*. It should be neither aggressive nor meek. Neither boast nor ask for sympathy. It should *never* express dissatisfaction with a present or former job or employer. And you should avoid discussing your reasons for leaving your last job. (If

---

25-92 Queens Boulevard
Bayside, New York 11202
June 15, [*year*]

Ms. Loretta Vasquez
The Vasquez Travel Agency
1402 Broadway
New York, New York 10032

Dear Ms. Vasquez:

This month I completed a two-year course of study in Travel and Tourism at the Bowker Business Institute, and my placement counselor, Mr. Robert Feiner, suggested I apply to you for a position as assistant travel agent.

As you will see from my enclosed resume, I have taken courses in nearly every aspect of the travel industry. I have participated in workshops simulating computer and telephone operations, and I have had extensive practice in ticketing and reservations.

My work experience, moreover, has helped me develop an ability to deal with the public, a valuable asset for a travel agency. Not only as a sales assistant, but even as a stock clerk, I have learned to be customer oriented; I have found that courtesy and a smile keep business flowing smoothly.

I would like very much, Ms. Vasquez, to put my skills to work for your travel agency. I am available for an interview Monday through Friday during business hours. You can reach me at (718) 884-7788.

Yours truly,

Figure 12–5
Letter of Application II

asked this question at an interview, your answer, though honest, should be positive and as favorable to yourself as you can make it.)

When you begin to write your letter of application, keep in mind the principles of writing sales letters:

1. *Start by attracting attention.* You must say, of course, that you are applying and mention both the specific job and how you heard about it (or, in an unsolicited letter, why you are interested in the particular company). But try to avoid a mundane opening. Instead of:

---

201 New Oak Street
Newark, New Jersey 07555
May 1, [*year*]

Mr. Noah Dylan
Personnel Manager
Greenwich Corporation
87-91 Partition Street
Hattiesburg, Mississippi 39411

Dear Mr. Dylan:

To explore the possibility of joining your company, I am enclosing my resume for your consideration. Gina Bassano of your Marketing Division suggested I contact you.

Several years as Sales Supervisor at Summit & Storch have afforded me management skills that would prove highly valuable to an industry leader such as Greenwich Corporation. I am willing to relocate and, through my experience establishing a sales office in Atlanta, I am familiar with the southern market.

I would be happy to travel to Hattiesburg for an interview and so will call you at the end of the month. Please feel free to call me before then should you have any questions about my qualifications.

Sincerely yours,

Nicolas Balaj

Figure 12–6
Letter of Application III

> I would like to apply for the position of legal secretary which you advertised in the *Los Angeles Times* of Sunday, August 10, {*year*}.

try something a *bit* more original:

> I believe you will find that my experiences in the Alameda District Attorney's office have prepared me well for the position of legal secretary which you advertised in the *Los Angeles Times* of Sunday, August 10, [*year*].

2. *Continue by describing your qualifications.* Highlight your strengths and achievements and *say* how they suit you for the job at hand. Provide details and explanations not found on your resume, and refer the reader to the resume for the remaining, less pertinent facts.
3. *Assure the employer that you are the person for the job.* List verifiable facts that prove you are not exaggerating or lying. Mention the names of any familiar or prominent references you may have. In some way distinguish yourself from all the other qualified applicants.
4. *Conclude by requesting an interview.* Make it easy to contact you. Mention your telephone number (even though it is on your resume) and the best hours to reach you, or state that you will call the employer within a few days. (Keep in mind that some employers consider a follow-up call admirably ambitious, but others consider it pushy and annoying. Use your judgment.)

A complete application should contain both a letter of application and a resume.

Do NOT include copies of your letters of reference or of your school transcripts. These can be provided later if you are granted an interview. Do NOT include a photograph of yourself. The briefer the application, the better.

A final word about salary: Basically, unless instructed by the want ad, it is best that you not mention the subject. Indeed, even if an ad requires that you state your salary requirements, it is advisable simply to call them "negotiable." However, when you go on an interview, you should be prepared to mention a salary range (such as, $20,000–$25,000). For this reason, you should investigate both your field and, if possible, the particular company. You don't want to ask for less than you deserve or more than is reasonable.

Follow-Up Letters

Few people nowadays send a *follow-up letter* (Figure 12–7) after an interview. For this reason alone, it can be highly effective.

A follow-up letter should be *courteous* and *brief*. It should merely thank the employer for the interview and restate your interest in the job. A reference to a successful moment at the interview is a good, personalizing touch.

25-92 Queens Boulevard
Bayside, New York 11202
June 25, [*year*]

Ms. Loretta Vasquez
The Vasquez Travel Agency
1402 Broadway
New York, New York 10032

Dear Ms. Vasquez:

Thank you for allowing me to discuss my travel qualifications in person.

Having met you and Mrs. DeLoia, and seen your agency in operation, I sincerely hope I will have the chance to put my training to work for you.

Enclosed is a copy of my transcript from the Bowker Business Institute, along with the letters of reference you requested. I can be reached at (718) 884-7788 during regular business hours.

Sincerely yours,

Figure 12–7
Follow-Up Letter

Letters of Reference and Recommendation

The difference between letters of reference and recommendation is slim. A *recommendation* (Figure 12–9) is an endorsement while a *reference* (Figure 12–8) is simply a report. A recommendation is persuasive while a reference verifies facts.

Both types of letters start out the same. Each should include:

1. a statement of the letter's purpose
2. an account of the duties performed by the applicant or of the applicant's general qualifications

A letter of recommendation would add a third item—a concluding statement specifically *recommending* the applicant for the particular position.

---

m&m shoe store
70-19 Lefferts Boulevard
Bayside, New York 11202

June 17, [*year*]

Ms. Loretta Vasquez
The Vasquez Travel Agency
1402 Broadway
New York, New York 10032

Dear Ms. Vasquez:

I am happy to provide the information you requested regarding Arnold Stevens, with the understanding that this information will be kept confidential.

Mr. Stevens has been a stock clerk and then a sales assistant in my store since September 1994. He has always been willing to work odd hours, including weekends and holidays, and has proven to be a hardworking and trustworthy employee.

Sincerely yours,

Otto Munson
Proprietor

Figure 12–8
Letter of Reference

BBI The Bowker Business Institute, 600 Fifth Avenue New York, N Y 10011

June 17, [*year*]

Ms. Loretta Vasquez
The Vasquez Travel Agency
1402 Broadway
New York, New York 10032

Dear Ms. Vasquez:

Arnold Stevens was a student in three of my travel courses during the 1996–97 school year. He was always an outstanding student.

Mr. Stevens demonstrated his thorough grasp of the subject matter in his class performance as well as written work. His assignments were always executed with conscientiousness and punctuality. Moreover, he was an enthusiastic participant in class discussions and helped to make the courses rewarding experiences for everyone else involved.

Therefore, I can recommend Mr. Stevens, without hesitation, for the position of assistant in your travel agency.

Yours truly,

Jack Adler
Instructor

Figure 12–9
Letter of Recommendation

Note: Before you write a reference or recommendation, be sure your company has no policy forbidding them so you can avoid possible lawsuits or complaints. If you do write such a letter, it is advisable to mark both the envelope and letter "Confidential" to protect yourself and the applicant.

Declining a Job Offer

You may find yourself in the fortunate position of choosing from several job offers. Or you may be offered a job that does not meet your needs or expectations. In such situations, you should send a courteous, discreet letter declining the job. By doing so, you will preserve a potentially valuable business contact and leave open the possibility of future employment.

25-92 Queens Boulevard
Bayside, New York 11202
July 1, [*year*]

Mr. Paul Nguyen
Nguyen Travel Associates
1133 Third Avenue
Flushing, New York 11217

Dear Mr. Nguyen:

Thank you for taking time to discuss with me both my career goals and the needs of your organization. I appreciate your offering me a position as receptionist.

Unfortunately, I must decline your offer at this time. As I mentioned when we met, I am eager to put my newly acquired travel agent skills to work and would like to begin as an assistant travel agent.

I am, nevertheless, disappointed that we will not be working together. I hope you will understand my decision.

Yours truly,

Figure 12–10
Letter Declining a Job Offer

Rejecting a Job Applicant

Every employer must face the unpleasant task of rejecting job applicants. When the search for a new employee has been properly conducted, there will be one successful candidate but several unsuccessful candidates. A personal letter explaining specific reasons for an applicant's rejection is professional and preferable, but a form letter is more often used to reject, in general terms, all the unsuccessful candidates.

Ahmed Abudan Travel, Inc.
312 Lexington Avenue
New York, NY 10021

July 2, [*year*]

Dear

    I am sorry to inform you that we have filled the position of assistant travel agent for which you recently applied.

    Please be assured that your qualifications were thoroughly reviewed, and it was only after careful consideration that we offered the position to the candidate whose experience and career goals were most compatible with the direction of our organization.

    Thank you for your interest in Abudan Travel. We wish you success in your career.

Yours truly,

Figure 12–11
Applicant Rejection Letter

Letters of Resignation

Landing a new job usually means resigning from an old one. Speaking personally to your current employer is appropriate, but putting the resignation in writing is also advisable.

As with refusals, resignations must convey a negative message as positively as possible. You may be delighted to be leaving or feel hostile toward your former boss, but your letter of resignation should express regrets, not anger. Be sure to:

1. state that the letter is your resignation, mentioning the date on which you would like to leave.
2. express appreciation for your old job and/or regret at leaving.
3. offer assistance with any work that you will be leaving undone or with helping the person who will replace you.

---

201 New Oak Street
Newark, New Jersey 07555
June 12, [*year*]

Mr. Seamus O'Toole
President
Summit & Storch
875 Davidson Street
Newark, New Jersey 07501

Dear Mr. O'Toole:

My eleven years at Summit & Storch have been rewarding, so it is with regret that I must submit my resignation, effective June 26, [*year*].

A management opportunity has arisen, and I feel I must pursue it. Still, I shall always appreciate the support and encouragement you have shown me.

I am prepared to remain at my duties for the next two weeks to ease the transition for my successor. Please let me know if this is acceptable.

Sincerely yours,

Nicolas Balaj

Figure 12–12
Letter of Resignation

You may mention a reason for leaving, such as an opportunity for advancement, but doing so is optional.

Remember, leaving a job on good terms is in your best interest. Even if you plan never to return, you may need references in a future job search. (It is even possible that your supervisor may also leave the company and you could find yourselves working together again some day!) So keep the resignation letter positive and brief.

Letters of Introduction

Letters of introduction (Figure 12–13) are written to a business associate on behalf of a third person, such as an employee, customer, or client. They are written when a person you know would like to establish a busi-

The Vasquez Travel Agency

1402 Broadway

New York, New York 10032

May 20, [*year*]

Mr. Jonathan Vecchio
Alpine Leisure Village
Aurora, Colorado 80707

Dear Jonathan:

Arnold Stevens has been my assistant for the past year, and he is currently touring the Denver-Aurora area.

So that he may knowledgeably inform our clients of the many delights of Alpine Leisure Village, I would greatly appreciate your giving him a tour of your facilities when he visits.

With much appreciation,

Loretta Vasquez

Figure 12–13
Letter of Introduction

ness relationship with another person whom you also know and the two businesspeople have never met.

In such a situation, the letter of introduction you write explains three points:

1. the relationship between you and the person being "introduced"
2. your reason for introducing him to your reader
3. what you (or he) would like the reader to do for him

The letter of introduction is a combination of request and reference. It should be worded with *courtesy*.

Generally, the letter of introduction is given to the individual being introduced, who then in turn delivers it in person. However, it is customary to forward a copy of the letter, along with an explanatory (and less formal) cover letter, so that your reader will anticipate the visit.

Summary

Together, your resume and letter of application advertise your career qualifications to potential employers.

- The RESUME is an outline about you. It is objective, based on facts and organized to show your value as an employee. It documents your educational and work history.
- The LETTER OF APPLICATION is a cover letter for your resume. It is persuasive, expanding and explaining the facts on your resume. It illustrates your ambition and job knowledge.

Other employment letters include:

- *Follow-Up Letter:* A thank-you note written after an interview
- *Reference Letter:* A verification of someone's employment
- *Recommendation Letter:* An endorsement based on someone's past job performance
- *Job-Declining Letter:* A letter saying "no" to a job offer
- *Rejection Letter:* A letter saying "no" to a job applicant
- *Letter of Resignation:* A written statement of the intention to leave a job
- *Letter of Introduction:* A letter that introduces two business acquaintances to each other

PRACTICE CORRESPONDENCE

Prepare your own employment correspondence according to the following instructions.

A. List all the facts that you can think of about your personality, background, and experiences. Then arrange the list in a logical order and decide on categories under which to group the facts. From this worksheet, prepare your resume.

B. Imagine the ideal job for which you would like to apply. With this job in mind, write an unsolicited letter of application to a prospective employer and ask for an interview.

C. Now imagine that you have been offered your ideal job. Write a letter of resignation to your current employer.

Part Two

USAGE

13.
The Basic Sentence

When we speak, we use words to express ideas. But we can give extra structure to our ideas by means of pauses, facial expressions, and body movements. In writing, we have none of these tools. We must depend almost totally on the words we choose in order to get our meaning across.

When mastering a new language, we often focus on learning the meaning of individual words. When we know what "apple" means, it will signify to us what it signifies to all English-speaking people. We agree on the meanings of words so that we can communicate.

Similarly, we agree on a standard form of grammar. In English, the *order* in which we use words contributes as much meaning to a sentence as do the definitions of individual words. For example, the sentence "Sam sees the tree" conveys a different meaning from "The tree sees Sam." In fact, the first sentence makes sense. The second one does not.

The reason for this is the first principle of English sentence structure:

EVERY SENTENCE MUST HAVE AT LEAST TWO PARTS,
A SUBJECT AND A VERB.

In both of the sentences above, *sees* is the verb. But in the first sentence *Sam* is the subject, while in the second sentence *The Tree* is the subject. So the sentences mean two different things.

Recognizing Verbs

The VERB is the part of the sentence that indicates what someone or something DOES or IS or HAS:

My accountant *filled* out my income tax return.
His method *is* more efficient than mine.
He *has* a lot of information to save me money.

Often, the VERB is the word that shows action. In the following sentences, the verbs are underlined:

A cashier <u>sells</u>.
A bricklayer <u>builds</u>.
A teacher <u>instructs</u>.
A gymnast <u>jumps</u>.
Mechanics <u>repair</u>.
Tailors <u>sew</u>.
Farmers <u>plant</u>.
Philosophers <u>think</u>.

The VERB in the last example is different from the others. It expresses action, but not the kind of action you can see or hear. "Think" shows mental activity, something that happens in a person's mind.

ACTION VERBS CAN BE DIVIDED INTO VERBS OF PHYSICAL ACTION AND VERBS OF MENTAL ACTION.

The VERBS in the following sentences express mental action:

Ruth *believes* in equal pay for equal work.
Her boss *agrees* with her.
She *chooses* to pay female employees as much as males.
Ruth *considers* this quite fair.
She *hopes* to stay on this job for many years.

Many verbs consist of more than one word. Consider these examples:

John *is learning* data processing.
I *am studying* DOS.
Rose *has taken* computer courses in the past.
She *will graduate* before us.

You will notice that in these sentences the verbs contained two words. But a verb may consist of three or four words, too:

Alex *has been working* for five years.
He *may be promoted* next month.
Then he *will be running* the credit department.
Roger *will have been transferred* by that time.
He *should have been promoted* long ago.

Another difficulty with verbs is that a sentence may contain more than one:

Enzo *cooks* and *waits* on tables.
He *works* hard but *earns* little money.
He *wants* to quit his job and *look* for another.

Recognizing Subjects

The SUBJECT of a sentence is the word doing the action of the verb.
The SUBJECT must always be a NOUN or a PRONOUN. A noun is the name of a person, place, thing, or idea. A pronoun is a substitute for a noun used to avoid repetition.

> **Remember:** Not every noun in a sentence is a subject. The SUBJECT is only the noun performing the action of the VERB.

In the following sentences, all the subjects have been underlined:

A <u>woman</u> sat at a computer.
<u>She</u> keyed in her password.
The <u>screen</u> went blank.
A <u>virus</u> had attacked.

If you first identify the VERB in a sentence, you can then find the SUBJECT by asking WHO or WHAT is doing the action of the VERB.

April sings with a band.
VERB? Sings
Who sings with a band?
SUBJECT? April

EXERCISE 1

In these sentences, underline the verb and then circle the subject.

1. John is a computer programmer.
2. He likes his job.
3. He had planned to become a teacher.
4. But computer science is a fascinating field.
5. His plans had to be changed.
6. Marie is a bookkeeper.
7. She enjoys her job a great deal.
8. Mathematics always had been her strong subject.
9. So she went to school and developed her specialty.
10. The atmosphere and salary of her job are satisfying to her.

As you probably noticed, there are two subjects in the last sentence of the previous exercise. Just as a sentence may have more than one verb, so *a verb may have more than one subject.*

Here are some examples (the subjects have been underlined):

Word processing and shorthand are two highly marketable skills.
Study, hard work, and patience are necessary to master them.
A pleasant job and a good salary can be the rewards for a diligent student.

EXERCISE 2

In these sentences, underline the verbs and circle the subjects.

1. Mr. and Mrs. Price are buying a house.
2. Their real estate agent and their banker are helping to arrange the mortgage.
3. The agent and the Prices' lawyer disagree over the terms of the sale.
4. The Prices and the banker are eager about the deal.
5. The agent, the banker, the lawyer, and the Prices all will be happy after the settlement of the purchase.
6. Regina and her boss were discussing her salary.
7. Accuracy, thoroughness, and conscientiousness were her reasons for a raise.
8. Poor sales and high expenses were his justification for low salaries.
9. Regina and her employer met frequently to discuss her salary.
10. Her raise will begin on the first of the month.

In this letter, underline the verbs and circle the subjects.

Dear Madam:

We would like to introduce you to Dark Lady, a new fragrance by Leonard of London.

Dark Lady is named for William Shakespeare's mysterious love. Its bouquet is steeped in the poetry and romance of the Bard's greatest heroines. One drop mingles all the flowers of Ophelia's garland. Rosemary, violets, and pansies evoke remembrance, faithfulness, and thought. The greatest loves and lyrics of 400 years blend in a crystal vial.

Dark Lady perfume and cologne are now available at all our fine stores. For a limited time, we are offering a special bonus. A half-ounce purse-atomizer and a floral silken pouch are yours with any Dark Lady purchase of $10 or more.

Of course, this and all your purchases can be charged and ordered by phone.

Yours truly,

Principal Parts of the Verb

Before we begin to study longer sentences, we must make one more point about verbs.

Every VERB has FIVE PRINCIPAL PARTS. These are the INFINITIVE, the PRESENT TENSE, the PAST TENSE, and the TWO PARTICIPLES.

A Model Verb

Infinitive:	to go
Present Tense:	go
Past Tense:	went
Present Participle:	going
Past Participle:	gone

Of these five parts, only the PRESENT TENSE and the PAST TENSE can be the VERB of a sentence. The other parts can only act as the verb in a sentence when they are accompanied by a helping verb (like *to be* or *to have*).

The bill *was paid.*
The paid bill *was entered* on the books.

In the first sentence, *was paid* is the verb. In the second sentence, *paid* is not the verb; *was entered* is the verb and *bill* is its subject. In the second sentence, *paid* is a PAST PARTICIPLE (with *no* helping verb) describing *bill*.

▌Remember: PARTICIPLES are words that look like verbs but aren't.

Thus PRESENT PARTICIPLES and PAST PARTICIPLES can be used to describe, or modify, nouns. When a PRESENT PARTICIPLE is used without a helping verb (and so is *not* the main verb in a sentence), it can also be used as a SUBJECT. For example:

Walking is good exercise.
Typing ninety words per minute is remarkable.

The INFINITIVE of a verb is also used this way. Without a helping verb, the INFINITIVE can be a SUBJECT:

To get a good job requires a good skill.
To pay bills promptly is a good policy.

EXERCISE 4

In these sentences, underline all verbs and circle all subjects.

1. Bicycling to my job keeps me healthy.
2. Writing checks makes me frugal.
3. Balancing my checkbook makes me proud.
4. To answer the treasurer's mail is the responsibility of his assistant.
5. To admit one's errors indicates maturity.
6. To lose one's job is a traumatic experience.
7. Waiting on lines infuriates me.
8. Smoking cigarettes is hazardous to your health.
9. To find a good job demands perseverance.
10. To operate this computer requires special training.

EXERCISE 5

Using each of the following present participles, write three sentences. In one, use the participle as the verb (with a helping verb); in another, use the participle as the subject; and in the last, use the participle to describe the subject.

EXAMPLE:

Answering
a. Verb: *I have been answering the telephones all morning.*
b. Subject: *Answering telephones bores me.*
c. Describing word: *The answering machine was disconnected.*

1. Selling
   a. Verb: _____
   b. Subject: _____
   c. Describing word: _____

2. Speaking
   a. Verb: _____
   b. Subject: _____
   c. Describing word: _____

3. Paying
   a. Verb: _____
   b. Subject: _____
   c. Describing word: _____

4. Writing
   a. Verb: _____
   b. Subject: _____
   c. Describing word: _____

5. Looking
   a. Verb: _____
   b. Subject: _____
   c. Describing word: _____

EXERCISE 6

Using each of the past participles given, write two sentences. In one, use the participle as a verb (with a helping verb); in the other, use the participle to describe the subject.

EXAMPLE:
   Elected
   a. Verb: *The attorney was elected to the town council.*
   b. Describing word: *Elected officials have a responsibility to the public.*

1. Lost
   a. Verb: _____
   b. Describing word: _____

2. Tried
   a. Verb: _____
   b. Describing word: _____

3. Printed
   a. Verb: _____
   b. Describing word: _____

4. Opened
   a. Verb: _____
   b. Describing word: _____

5. Advertised
   a. Verb: _____
   b. Describing word: _____

Adjectives

As we have just seen, a participle can be used to describe another word.

The **exhausted** <u>stenographer</u> <u>dropped</u> her pad.
    PARTICIPLE   SUBJECT   VERB

The **answering** <u>machine</u> <u>was</u> out of order.
    PARTICIPLE   SUBJECT   VERB

In these examples, the participles are describing (or adding information to) the subjects. This means that the participles here are acting as ADJECTIVES.

> AN ADJECTIVE IS ANY WORD (OR GROUP OF WORDS) THAT ADDS INFORMATION TO A NOUN OR PRONOUN.

You will remember that not all nouns are subjects. Therefore, an adjective may describe a noun even if the noun is *not* the subject in a sentence.

The <u>executive</u> <u>fired</u> the **exhausted** stenographer.
      S   V

In this example, <u>stenographer</u> is NOT the subject. But it is being described (or modified) by the adjective/participle *exhausted*.

EXERCISE 7

In these sentences, underline each adjective and circle the noun it is describing.

1. A roving reporter phoned in her story.
2. It concerned a growing controversy.
3. The demanding editor wanted the details.
4. The reporter interviewed a politician accused of graft.
5. She asked provoking questions.
6. The alleged criminal did not evade the questions.
7. He had been offered a tempting bribe.
8. Refusing, he called the FBI.
9. They had been investigating the suspected politician.
10. He claimed to be an honest man.

You probably noticed that the adjective in the last sentence was not a participle. Participles are only one type of adjective.

There are many words in English that are ADJECTIVES BY DEFINITION. They have no other function.

The *big* boss
The *small* chair
The *slow* driver
The *bleak* weather

EXERCISE 8

Underline each adjective and circle the noun it is modifying.

1. A difficult job can be challenging.
2. But a good boss is an inspiration.
3. Sheila has a quiet boss.
4. He keeps a low profile.
5. Gary has a dynamic boss.
6. She keeps long hours.
7. Both employers earn high salaries.
8. This is a fair situation.
9. They are smart individuals.
10. Sheila and Gary appreciate their rare positions.

Still other adjectives can be formed by adding a word ending (or SUFFIX) to another word.

The *reasonable* employer (reason + able)
The *tactful* salesperson (tact + ful)
The *friendly* receptionist (friend + ly)
The *tireless* file clerk (tire + less)

Below is a list of ADJECTIVE-SUFFIXES. If you memorize them, you will be able to recognize them when they appear in your own writing.

ADJECTIVE-SUFFIXES

-able	understandable	-il	civil
-ac	demoniac	-ile	senile
-al	musical	-ish	foolish
-an	American	-ite	erudite
-ant	expectant	-ive	active
-ar	molecular	-less	helpless
-ary	revolutionary	-ly	lonely
-ate	fortunate	-ory	transitory
-ent	confident	-ose	bellicose
-ful	beautiful	-ous	glamorous
-ible	sensible	-ulent	fraudulent
-ic	economic	-y	angry
-ical	whimsical		

EXERCISE 9

Turn each of these words into an adjective by providing an appropriate suffix. Then use each new adjective in a sentence.

1. care →

_____

2. express →

_____

3. love →

_____

4. luck →

_____

5. boast →
_____

6. photograph →
_____

7. sense →
_____

8. magic →
_____

9. mood →
_____

10. planet →
_____

Another type of adjective must be mentioned here. It consists of more than one word and is called a PREPOSITIONAL PHRASE.

> The book *on my desk* belongs to Roger.
> The office *across the hall* is the President's suite.
> The flowers *in that vase* are dying.

First of all, you will notice that a PREPOSITIONAL PHRASE comes *after* the noun it describes. In the three examples, the modified nouns are *book, office*, and *flowers*.

The second important fact about prepositional phrases is that they always *begin with a preposition*. In the three examples, the prepositions are *on, across*, and *in*.

A PREPOSITION is a connecting word that shows the relationship between a noun and another word in the sentence. Sometimes this is a space relationship:

> The book *on* the desk
> The worm *under* the rock

Sometimes this is a time relationship:

> The day *before* yesterday
> The week *after* next

Here is a list of some of the more frequently used prepositions:

aboard	beside	off
about	between	on
above	by	outside
after	except	over
among	for	to
around	from	under
at	in	up
before	inside	upon
behind	into	until
below	like	with
beneath	of	within

The third thing you must know about a prepositional phrase concerns its NOUN.

A NOUN THAT FOLLOWS A PREPOSITION IS <u>NEVER</u> THE SUBJECT OF A SENTENCE.

Consider this sentence:

The rug on the floor is blue.

As you know, the verb is *is*; the subject is *rug*. *Floor* is a noun, but it is NOT the subject of the verb *is*. The meaning of the sentence supports this: the rug is blue, not the floor! *On the floor* is just a three-word adjective describing *rug*.

Technically, the noun that follows a preposition is called the OBJECT of the preposition. A noun cannot be an object and a subject at the same time.

EXERCISE 10

Fill in the blank in each sentence with an appropriate preposition.

1. The woman _____ charge is Ms. Skelton.
2. She is the president _____ the company.
3. The suite _____ the sixth floor is her office.
4. The telephones _____ her office never stop ringing.
5. The people _____ her work hard.
6. The man _____ her side is her partner.
7. He is chairman _____ the board.
8. They work very closely _____ the office.
9. The success _____ her career took much effort.
10. She is a woman _____ determination.

Adverbs

Verbs can be modified in much the same way as nouns are. For example, consider this sentence:

Margaret types slowly.

In this case, the verb is *types*, and the subject is *Margaret*. The adverb *slowly* explains *how* she types; it does not describe Margaret herself.

AN ADVERB IS ANY WORD (OR GROUP OF WORDS) THAT ADDS INFORMATION TO A VERB.

In the following sentences, the ADVERBS are underlined:

Ben speaks <u>well</u>.
He looks <u>confidently</u> at his listeners.
He expresses his ideas <u>smoothly</u>.
He <u>clearly</u> articulates each word.

Notice that three of the four ADVERBS used end in *-ly*. In fact, most adverbs in English do end in *-ly*; they are formed by adding the *-ly* to an adjective.

slow	→	slowly
happy	→	happily
quiet	→	quietly
strong	→	strongly

Even many adjectives that are participles can be used as adverbs by adding an *-ly* ending:

exhausted	→	exhaustedly
alleged	→	allegedly
haunting	→	hauntingly
laughing	→	laughingly

EXERCISE 11

First change these adjectives into adverbs. Then use each new adverb in a sentence.

1. silent →

_____

2. excited →

_____

3. merry →

_____

4. horrible →

_____

5. weary →

_____

6. patient →

_____

7. studious →

_____

8. correct →

_____

9. joyful →

_____

10. boasting →

_____

You should also know that PREPOSITIONAL PHRASES can be used as ADVERBS, not just as ADJECTIVES.

I walked across the room.

In this sentence, the verb is *walked*, and the subject is *I*. You already know that *across the room* is a prepositional phrase; it consists of a preposition (*across*) followed by a noun (*the room*). But this time, the prepositional phrase is not adding information to another noun in the sentence. Instead, it is modifying the verb; it explains *where* or *how* I walked.

Here are some other examples of PREPOSITIONAL PHRASES being used as ADVERBS:

> The treasurer signed *on the dotted line*.
> The comet streaked *through the sky*.
> The witness squirmed *in his chair*.
> The manuscript slipped *from my hands*.

You are probably familiar with words like *not* and *never*. But did you know that they are ADVERBS?

> Gwen *never* leaves work early.

In this sentence, the verb is *leaves*, and the subject is *Gwen*. The word *never* is changing the verb in such a way as to make it NEGATIVE. *Never* is an ADVERB, not part of the verb.

> Ken did *not* answer the telephone.

This time, the verb is a two-word verb: *did answer*. The subject is *Ken*. Here, the word *not* also makes the verb negative; it comes between the two words of the verb, but it is still an ADVERB, not part of the verb itself.

Not all adverbs that work this way are negative. Here are some other examples:

> Norma *always* works hard.
> Alice *sometimes* goofs off.
> She can *also* concentrate on her job.

Notice that in the last of these examples the verb is *can concentrate*, split up by an adverb.

One last point must be made about adverbs. Consider this sentence:

> The terribly exhausted stenographer dropped her pad.

We've already seen that *dropped* is the verb; *stenographer* is the subject, and *exhausted* is an adjective describing the subject. But what is *terribly*?

From the *-ly* ending, we can tell that *terribly* is an ADVERB. But it does not seem to be modifying a verb. In fact, the only verb in this sentence is *dropped*, which is not connected to *terribly* at all.

In this case, *terribly* is adding information to *exhausted*. That is, the adverb is modifying an adjective.

Similarly, an adverb can modify another adverb:

> Mercedes reads very slowly.

Here, *slowly* is an adverb describing the verb *reads*. But *very* is another adverb describing the main adverb *slowly*.

Therefore, we must expand our definition of the adverb:

AN ADVERB IS ANY WORD (OR GROUP OF WORDS) THAT ADDS INFORMATION TO A VERB, AN ADJECTIVE, OR ANOTHER ADVERB.

Direct Objects

As you've probably noticed, many of the sentences we've studied contained more than one noun. But not all of these nouns acted as the subject in its sentence.

For example, when we first discussed prepositional phrases, we said that <u>the noun that follows a preposition is called the OBJECT of the proposition</u>.

In the sentence:

> The rug on the floor is blue.

we said that the *floor* is the object of the preposition *on*. Together, the prepositional phrase *on the floor* is acting as a three-word adjective describing *rug*.

Another important kind of OBJECT is called the DIRECT OBJECT. This is a noun or pronoun that *receives* the action of the verb.

Consider this example:

> Amina wrote the letter.

Here, the verb is *wrote*, and the subject is *Amina*. We find the subject by asking a question: Who or what *wrote the letter?*

To find the DIRECT OBJECT, we ask a different question: *Amina wrote what?* The answer (in this case the *letter*) is the direct object.

In the following sentences, the objects are underlined:

> The lawyers argued the <u>case</u>.
> The jury delivered its <u>verdict</u>.
> The judge conferred the <u>sentence</u>.

EXERCISE 12

In each sentence, underline the direct object.

1. Greg was writing a memo.
2. He made it short and clear.
3. It concerned a specific topic.
4. It transmitted the necessary information.
5. He carefully retained a copy.
6. Greg's boss answered his memo.
7. She asked several questions.
8. Greg examined his copy.
9. He had omitted some details.
10. He quickly wrote another memo.

Predicate Nominatives and Adjectives

There is one more type of sentence completer we must discuss here. Sometimes a noun that comes after a verb is not an OBJECT.

> Janice is a dentist.

In this sentence, the verb is *is*, and the subject is *Janice*. But *dentist* is not an object. Janice isn't doing something to a dentist; Janice and a dentist are one and the same. In other words, the sentence:

> Janice is a dentist.

can be written as an equation:

> Janice = a dentist

When a noun after a verb is the equivalent of the subject, it is called a PREDICATE NOMINATIVE. (*Predicate* simply means *verb; nominative* simply means *noun*. So this difficult label actually makes sense.)

In the following sentences, the PREDICATE NOMINATIVES are underlined:

> Juanita was a <u>secretary</u>.
> Now she is an <u>administrator</u>.
> She may be the next company <u>president</u>.

Adjectives can also be used this way:

> Janice is skillful.

As in our earlier example, *is* is the verb, and *Janice* is the subject. But this time, they are followed by an adjective, not a noun.

Still, we can set up an equation:

> Janice = skillful

When an adjective after a verb is the equivalent of the subject, it is called a PREDICATE ADJECTIVE.

In the following sentences, the PREDICATE ADJECTIVES are underlined:

> Juanita is <u>ambitious</u>.
> She appears <u>inexhaustible</u>.
> She will be <u>successful</u>.

■■■ REVIEW EXERCISES

Fill in the blanks in the following letters, choosing from the list of words to the left of each letter.

A.

appreciate
arrived
cost
credit
enclose
is
listed
received
ordered
was

Dear Sir:

On April 12, I _____ a microwave oven from your store. The model number _____ 129-C. According to your spring catalog, it _____ $425.95. I _____ the oven on April 25.

However, on May 1, your bill _____. It _____ the oven at $460.95. This _____ $35 more than the original price.

I _____ a check for $425.95. Please _____ my account for the $35 discrepancy. I _____ your attention to this matter.

Sincerely yours,

B.

Americans
article
consideration
I
it
places
prices
readers
restaurants
you

Dear Mr. Morris:

With the value of the dollar fluctuating abroad, many _____ are reconsidering that long-saved-for trip to Paris. _____ am submitting a copy of my article, "Paris on a Budget," for your consideration. The _____ of *Tourist* magazine may find it helpful.

Based on my own recent experiences, the _____ is a guide for the tourist on a tight budget. _____ suggests moderately priced but comfortable hotels and boarding houses. Inexpensive but delightful _____ are recommended. Free or nearly free _____ to go are listed also. All details and _____ have been researched carefully.

Your _____ of my article is appreciated greatly. _____ are welcome to make any necessary editorial revisions.

Sincerely yours,

C.

current
delayed
great
high
outstanding
overdue
personal
prompt
sound
troublesome

Dear Mrs. Cochran:

Paying bills on time can save you money! _____ interest rates accumulate quickly on _____ accounts. So why not send us a _____ check today to clear your _____ balance of $264.84.

Your _____ bill is now 60 days overdue. Two months are not a _____ lapse of time. But you have always been a _____ customer. And _____ payments have a _____ way of being forgotten.

We look forward to hearing from you soon and keeping your _____ credit rating in tact.

Yours truly,

D.

belatedly
carefully
daily
efficiently
immediately
improperly
initially
later
promptly
slowly

TO: Mr. Frank Doolittle, Supervisor

FROM: Liza Higgins, Assistant

DATE: October 12, [year]

SUBJECT: Mailroom Delays

At your request, I have looked _____ into the problem of mailroom delays. Departments are receiving mail _____ for a number of reasons:

1. Some mail is addressed _____. So it is sent _____ to the wrong department and must _____ be forwarded.

2. The mailroom is understaffed. The clerks handle mail as _____ as possible. But they get to each department _____. They cannot cover all the departments _____.

This problem must be dealt with _____. Complaints are mounting _____.

LH

14.
Building Sentences

Basic Sentence Patterns

One of the first things we discussed at the beginning of this section was that THE CORE OF AN ENGLISH SENTENCE CONSISTS OF A SUBJECT AND A VERB:

> <u>Sam</u> <u>sees</u> the tree.

We have also examined sentences with one subject performing two verbs:

> <u>Sam</u> <u>sees</u> the tree and <u>hears</u> the birds.

And we have seen sentences with two subjects both of which perform the same verb:

> <u>Sam</u> and <u>Willy</u> <u>talk</u>.

It is even possible for a sentence to have two subjects each of which performs two verbs:

> <u>Sam</u> and <u>Willy</u> <u>talk</u> and <u>laugh</u>.

Thus, we have already identified the FOUR BASIC SENTENCE PATTERNS. If we use *S* to mean *subject* and *V* to mean *verb,* we can make a chart:

> S V.
> S V and V.
> S and S V.
> S and S V and V.

Based on these patterns, we can start to define a *sentence*. For now, let us say that

> A SENTENCE IS A GROUP OF WORDS CONTAINING A SUBJECT AND A VERB.

More Complicated Sentences

To write even simple business letters, you will certainly need longer sentences than the four basic ones listed above.

One of the easiest ways to write a longer sentence is to take two basic sentences:

> Sam sees the tree.
> Willy hears the birds.

and combine them.

First of all, they can be combined with punctuation. Instead of keeping them as two separate sentences with a period between them, we can attach them with a SEMICOLON:

> Sam sees the tree; Willy hears the birds.

A semicolon, we might say, is used much the way the period is used. It gets a subject-verb core on either side.

But a semicolon doesn't add much meaning. It suggests that the two parts are closely related, but it doesn't say how. A more meaningful way to combine sentences is to use a word.

There is a group of words you are already familiar with, called COORDINATORS, also known as CONJUNCTIONS. Coordinators are another easy way to combine two short sentences into one longer one:

> Sam sees the tree, *and* Willy hears the birds.

Here, *and* is a COORDINATOR. It is used with a comma (*before* it) to combine two short sentences into one. There is a subject-verb core (<u>Sam sees</u>) to the left of the comma (and) and there is a subject-verb core (<u>Willy hears</u>) to the right of <u>and</u>.

There are seven coordinators that work just like <u>and</u>:

and	or	so	
but	nor	yet	for

Obviously, the difference between the COORDINATORS is in their meanings, but grammatically, they all function the same way. Therefore, we can add two more sentence patterns to our chart:

> S V ; S V .
> S V , [coordinator] S V .

The patterns hold up, too, if you want to attach any combination of the original four basic sentence patterns, for example:

> S V and V, [coordinator] S V.

> Sam sees and hears the birds, but Willy sleeps.

EXERCISE 1

Combine these pairs of sentences, using one of the seven coordinators.

1. Peter would like to be an accountant. He would like to be a computer programmer.
2. He wants an interesting job. He hopes for a good salary.
3. He has planned his career carefully. He will probably reach his goal.
4. Sometimes he gets discouraged. He never gives up.
5. Megan didn't like her job. She simply quit.
6. At first she felt relieved. She hadn't considered her alternatives.
7. Now she is unemployed. She doesn't know what to do.
8. She hasn't found a new job. She has very little experience.
9. She could ask for her old job back. She could return to school.
10. Pam is a diligent lawyer. She hasn't received a promotion.
11. She is eager to advance. She thrives on new challenges.
12. She should speak to her boss. He may not be aware of her ambitions.
13. He may discourage her plans. She will be disappointed.
14. He may also encourage her. She should try the direct approach.
15. Women and men must take charge of their own careers. Nothing will happen.
16. They must prepare for their chosen jobs. They must accumulate experience.
17. They must be patient. They must also assert themselves.
18. Some companies are very large. You will have to attract your boss's attention.
19. Employers regard good workers. First they must be aware of the workers' merits.
20. Do your best. You will succeed.

Still More Complicated Sentences

There is yet another way to combine two short sentences to form one longer one. This requires a different kind of conjunction called a SUBORDINATOR.

> SENTENCE: Sam saw the tree.
> SENTENCE: Willy heard the birds.
> LONGER SENTENCE: Sam saw the tree *before* Willy heard the birds.

In this example, *before* is a SUBORDINATOR. It is used much as COORDINATORS are. It has a subject-verb core to the left and a subject-verb core to the right.

We can now add another pattern to our chart:

S V │subordinator│ S V .

Notice that no comma is used before the SUBORDINATOR in this sentence pattern.

Here is a list of additional subordinators:

> as, after, although
> before, because
> how
> if
> once
> since, so that
> than, that, though
> unless, until
> who, what, where, when, why, which, whether, while

EXERCISE 2

Combine the pairs of sentences by using a subordinator between them.

1. Many people invest in gold. They are fiscal conservatives.
2. They keep a large portion of their investment portfolio in gold. Its average annual return in the 1990s was less than 1 percent.
3. Some gold investors buy futures and mutual funds. Others buy physical gold such as coins and bars.
4. They want to amass physical gold. A social disaster takes place.
5. They consider gold a haven in a crisis. It has often soared in value during war.
6. Gold historically has held its value. Inflation has been high.
7. People invest heavily in gold. They want safety.
8. Investment experts advise caution. Gold is not always a profitable investment.
9. Gold offers a very small return. The stock market is strong.
10. Gold can decrease safety. You invest too much of your portfolio in it.

EXERCISE 3

Combine the pairs of sentences by using a subordinator between them.

1. You should plan your wardrobe. You go on a job interview.
2. Your outfit deserves careful thought. First impressions are important.
3. Conservative garments are best. You want to appear competent and sensible.
4. They should also be comfortable. You don't want to be distracted.
5. For a woman, a simple skirt and blouse are a good choice. A dress is also acceptable.
6. Pants are not a good idea. They are appropriate to the particular job.
7. A man should wear a jacket and tie. The position is an office job or not.
8. Unpolished shoes or excessive makeup could ruin your chances. You answer any questions.
9. You should scrutinize yourself in a mirror. You leave for the interview.
10. You want to look your best. You can be your best.

SUBORDINATORS are a bit more flexible than COORDINATORS. We can use them in an additional way. We can use a SUBORDINATOR at the beginning of the first of two sentences we wish to combine.

SENTENCE: Sam saw the tree.
SENTENCE: Willy heard the birds.
LONGER SENTENCE: *After* Sam saw the tree, Willy heard the birds.

Thus, our fourth sentence pattern can be charted like this:

subordinator S V , S V .

Notice that when a subordinator comes at the beginning of a sentence, a comma is used between the two subject-verb cores.

EXERCISE 4

Combine the pairs of sentences by using a subordinator at the beginning.

1. James did not intend to look for a job immediately. He set up his resume before graduation.
2. He did not want to risk being forgotten. He asked three teachers for letters of reference.
3. He could get practice. He went on a few job interviews.
4. He was ready to look for a job. He was prepared.
5. Judy wanted to start work right after school. She contacted the placement office a month before graduation.
6. That gave her several weeks. She knew she needed as much time as possible to look for a job.
7. She went on more and more interviews. She learned to relax.
8. The ideal job came along. She handled the interview impressively.
9. She had had practice. Nervousness didn't get in her way.
10. James and Judy planned ahead. Their job hunts were successful.

EXERCISE 5

Combine the pairs of sentences by using a subordinator at the beginning.

1. Some people get a great deal done in a given amount of time. Others do not.
2. You want to get more done. Effective scheduling is essential.
3. You set aside some time each day for planning. You will have trouble getting organized.
4. You allow time for planning. You should cross all other committed time off your calendar.
5. You set deadlines. You will be more likely to achieve your goals.
6. You schedule an activity. You should estimate its required time.
7. You schedule time for relaxation. You will not be as effective on the job.
8. Overcommitment is one of the major causes of ineffectiveness. You must decide what not to do.
9. You work best in the morning. Schedule important tasks for that time of day.
10. You capitalize on your time. You can become a more effective person.

Words of Transition

> **WARNING:** There is a group of words that look a lot like subordinators and often have the same meanings. They are called WORDS OF TRANSITION.

But words of transition may not be used to combine two short sentences into one long one.

I felt sick. I stayed home.
I felt sick. Therefore I stayed home.

OR

I felt sick; therefore I stayed home.

Therefore is NOT a subordinator or coordinator, so it CANNOT be used to combine two sentences into one. When *therefore* is used, a period or a semicolon is still required between the two subject-verb cores.

If you have memorized the coordinators and subordinators, there should be no problem. But here is a list of WORDS OF TRANSITION so that you'll know them when you see them.

WORDS OF TRANSITION

accordingly	henceforth	nevertheless
also	however	on the contrary
anyhow	in addition	on the other hand
as a result	indeed	otherwise
at the same time	in fact	still
besides	in other words	that is
consequently	instead	then
for example	likewise	therefore
furthermore	meanwhile	thus
hence	moreover	

Summary

SENTENCE STRUCTURE

Basic Sentences	*More Complicated Sentences*
S V.	S V; S V.
S V and V.	S V, coordinator S V.
S and S V.	S V subordinator S V.
S and S V and V.	subordinator S V, S V.

On a separate sheet of paper, rewrite these groups of words as a single paragraph. To do this, decide whether a period, comma, or no punctuation at all is needed at the end of each line. Do not change the order of the lines, and remember to capitalize the first word of your new sentences.

A. You must prepare carefully
    before you go on a job interview
    you should anticipate questions
    that you may be asked
    about items on your resume
    you should dress conservatively
    but feel comfortable about your appearance
    you should take with you a pen, a pad, and your resume
    also you should be sure to arrive on time
    to make a good impression

B. Some businesses grow substantially
    even when the economy as a whole suffers from recession
    they prosper
    because they benefit from the recessionary situation
    employment agencies are busy
    when more unemployed people are looking for jobs
    repair services do well
    whether the stock market goes up or down
    people try to repair their old possessions
    before they spend money on new ones
    discount stores show increased sales
    although department store sales drop
    when people are worried about the future
    they want to get more for their money now
    clever entrepreneurs discover
    that recession can work to their advantage
    they provide goods and services
    that people in a recessionary economy demand
    these business persons use a difficult situation
    while other people complain and wait.

C. Even before the American revolution
    the American labor movement had begun
    the first unions were associations of skilled artisans
    whose aim was to provide each other with mutual help
    in the event of misfortune
    as unions grew in the early nineteenth century
    small locals were isolated within their communities
    but gradually began to unite
    forming national associations
    more than thirty-two national unions were formed

by the end of the Civil War
some of them are still in existence
their original purpose
which was to improve working conditions and wages
continues to exist as well

D. Public relations letters
a highly specialized mode of business communication
are written to influence public opinion
a public relations writer prepares news releases
as well as advertisements, speeches
and other written forms
that promote an organization's positive image
to become a public relations writer
one must be clever with words
but knowledge of sales technique
and a sense of timing
are further requirements
a persistent competitive spirit will also help
for public relations is a difficult field
to break into

E. Experiencing rapid growth in the past decade
the paralegal profession offers many opportunities
to become a paralegal can take
as little as three months
in one of the hundreds of paralegal training programs
across the country
paralegals are legal assistants
who work with lawyers and other legal professionals
the paralegal's duties include legal research
as well as drafting and indexing legal documents
and assisting in trial preparation
employed by local, state, and federal governments
by private law firms
and by corporations
there are over 80,000 paralegals in the United States
nearly 80 percent of them are women

15.
Advanced Sentence Structure

Parallelism

A PARALLEL SENTENCE is one in which elements of equal (or "parallel") weight are expressed in equal (or "parallel") grammatical forms.

This principle of sentence structure can be illustrated most easily with a LIST. PARALLELISM dictates that items in a list (whether they are verbs, nouns, or any other part of speech) must be expressed in *parallel grammatical forms*. Consider this example:

> Rosemary *types, files*, and *takes* dictation.

This sentence lists three things that Rosemary, the subject, can do. Each of Rosemary's skills is listed as a verb. (The basic sentence pattern here is S V, V, and V.) And because all three skills are given equal weight (or importance) in the sentence, all are expressed in the same verb form, the simple PRESENT TENSE.

Not all lists, of course, consist of verbs. Look at this example:

> *Typing, filing*, and *taking* dictation are Rosemary's strongest skills.

This time, Rosemary's skills are listed as subjects of the verb *are*. (Sentence pattern: S, S, and S V.) Again, all three are of equal importance, so all are expressed in the same form: the PRESENT PARTICIPLE.

Sometimes, the parallelism of a sentence is begun but not carried through.

> This project is tedious, difficult, and makes me very tired.

In this sentence (verb: *is*; subject: *project*), a list of adjectives is begun: *tedious, difficult*, and _____. But after the *and*, when the reader expects a third and final adjective, there is a new *verb* instead! This sentence, therefore, demonstrates *faulty parallelism* and must be corrected:

> This project is tedious, difficult, and tiring.

This time, the list is completed with a third adjective, not a verb. The long section "makes me very tired" is replaced with one word: *tiring*.

EXERCISE 1

Rewrite the underlined parts of these sentences to correct parallelism.

1. Finding a job in today's economy requires ingenuity, perseverance, and <u>it helps to be flexible</u>.

   _____

   _____

2. Traditional ways to get a job included mailing resumes, using a school placement counselor, or <u>employment agencies</u>.

   _____

   _____

3. These methods don't always work in the face of a weak economy, high unemployment, and <u>lots of people are competing with you</u>.

   _____

   _____

4. With experience in sales, public relations, and <u>the ability to supervise others</u>, Lewis sought a position as a store sales manager.

   _____

   _____

5. Instead of using resumes, agencies, or even <u>answering help-wanted ads</u>, he personally visited every major store in his community.

   _____

   _____

6. One store owner was impressed by Lewis's assertiveness, determination, and <u>she liked his personality</u>.

   _____

   _____

7. Due to her present business volume, staff size, and <u>the costs of her overhead</u>, she didn't need a sales manager.

   _____

   _____

8. Instead, she offered Lewis a job as salesperson, with a reasonable starting salary, commission structure, and <u>the benefits were also good</u>.

   _____

   _____

9. Lewis was concerned about income, security, and <u>to be able to advance on the job</u>.

   _____

   _____

10. He accepted the job, confident he could impress his employer, increase her sales, and <u>achieving his own career goals would come in time</u>.

    _____

    _____

Sometimes parallel sentence structure involves more than single parts of speech. Longer sections of a sentence must also be set up in parallel forms when the meaning of those sections is balanced. The following sentence contains faulty parallelism:

> Reading an annual report is not as laborious as to write one.

The correct version of this sentence should express the two activities (*reading* and *to write*) in parallel forms, for the two activities are being "balanced," held up for comparison. Therefore, there are two solutions. We may use a present participle for both activities:

> *Reading* an annual report is not as laborious as *writing* one.

Or we may use infinitives:

> *To read* an annual report is not as laborious as *to write* one.

Parallelism may also be disrupted by the slightest change in wording:

> Paul got his information reading books and by talking to people.

In this example, parallel verb forms are used (*reading* and *talking*). However, the second present participle is preceded by a preposition (*by*), which unbalances the sentence. This can be corrected in a number of ways. First of all, the *by* may be omitted:

> Paul got his information *reading* books and *talking* to people.

Or, *by* may be used before both verb forms:

> Paul got his information *by reading* books and *by talking* to people.

Finally, the *by* may be inserted before the first participle but omitted before the second:

> Paul got his information by *reading* books and *talking* to people.

In this last solution, the *by* is not actually part of the parallel sections, but rather commences them.

Consider yet another example:

> Mrs. Grey is a boss whom employees respect but is a little frightening.

The solution here depends upon where we see the parallelism beginning. If we see the parallelism as including *whom*:

> Mrs. Grey is a boss *whom employees respect* but *is a little frightening*.

we may correct the error by inserting another pronoun:

> Mrs. Grey is a boss whom employees respect but *who* is a little frightening.

On the other hand, if we see the parallelism as beginning after *whom*, we must completely rewrite the second section:

> Mrs. Grey is a boss whom employees respect but *fear*.

By balancing the verb *respect* with another verb, *fear*, we not only restore the parallelism; we have also made the sentence more concise without changing the meaning.

EXERCISE 2

These sentences contain instances of faulty parallelism. Correct the errors and write your revised sentences in the space provided.

1. Having started a family and able to finish school at the same time, Beth was prepared for the pressures of her new job.

   _____

   _____

2. Still, holding a job and to try to raise her family were difficult.

   _____

   _____

3. Her ambitions were to nurture her children, her career, and remain sensitive to her husband's needs.

   _____

   _____

4. Beth succeeded because of her children's understanding, her husband's support, and due to the fact that the family respected what she was doing.

   _____

   _____

5. Sometimes Beth's husband was the housekeeper, dishwasher, baby-sitter, and he also cooked the meals.

   _____

   _____

6. Beth reciprocated by doing the shopping, the laundry, and made time to be alone with her husband.

   _____

   _____

7. The children learned to clean their own room, make their own lunch, and the value of independence.

   _____

   _____

8. On weekends, they all made a point of spending time together and to discuss their feelings.

   _____

   _____

9. Beth had explained her hopes for the family, her goals for her career, and why she had wanted to work in the first place.

   _____

   _____

10. As a result of Beth's working, the family has benefited socially, financially, and they feel better about each other, too.

   _____

   _____

A number of idiomatic expressions also demand parallel sentence structure. Consider this example using the expression "_____ than _____":

He was more willing *to make* his boss coffee than *to run* errands for him.

The word *than*, here, is both preceded and followed by an infinitive (*to make* and *to run*). Similarly, the expression "_____ rather than _____" requires parallel structure:

I decided to *get* a job after high school rather than *begin* college immediately.

Although *rather than* is preceded and followed by an infinitive (*to get* and *to begin*), we may omit the second *to* with the understanding that the parallelism begins with the word *get*.

Another idiom that requires parallel structure is found in the following example:

Maria is *not only* clever *but* efficient.

With the expression "not only _____ but _____," we must use parallel forms to fill in the blanks. Therefore, we may rewrite this sentence in a variety of ways:

Maria not only *is clever* but *is efficient*.

or:

Not only *is Maria clever*, but *she is efficient*.

The more words we include between *not only* and *but*, the more words we must insert after *but*.

> **Note:** In the preceding examples, use of the word *also* would NOT disrupt the parallelism:
> Maria not only *is clever* but also *is efficient*.

"Both _____ and _____" works in a similar way:

My boss explained *both* how to operate the computer *and* how to process orders.

By moving the *both*, we can eliminate repeating the words *how to*:

My boss explained how to *both* operate the computer and process orders.

Finally, "either _____ or _____" and "neither _____ nor _____" require parallel structure:

Raises were given *neither* to the secretaries *nor* to the junior executives.
Either we work together, *or* we fail separately.

Again, each of these can be revised to avoid repetition as long as the parallelism is maintained:

Raises were given **to** *neither* the secretaries *nor* the junior executives.
We *either* work together *or* fail separately.

EXERCISE 3

In the space provided, rewrite the sentences, correcting any faulty parallelism.

1. Many small investors would rather save their money than risking it in the stock market.

_____

_____

2. They are more interested in financial security than to make a large profit.

_____

_____

3. They think they must either jeopardize all they own in the stock market or must settle for 3½ percent interest.

_____

_____

4. Actually, small investors can afford neither low interest rates nor to risk all their money in the stock market.

_____

_____

5. So, both recession and the fact that savings accounts yield low interest have led many people to other areas of investment.

_____

_____

6. These people are looking not only for security but a high return.

_____

_____

7. Many, therefore, have put their money into mutual funds rather than depositing it in a savings account.

_____

_____

8. Mutual funds not only provide high yield but they offer reasonable security.

_____

_____

9. They provide the investor not only with professional management but also diversification.

_____

_____

10. Thus, the investor is taking neither an enormous risk nor giving up to recession.

_____

_____

Misplaced Modifiers

A modifier should be placed as close as possible to the word it modifies. A MISPLACED MODIFIER, as you would expect, is one that has been incorrectly placed in the sentence. The following sentence contains an example:

> When only a small child, my mother inspired me to become a nurse.

The expression "When only a small child" is clearly not modifying *mother* (a woman is not a mother at the same time that she is a small child). It is intended to modify *me*, yet it is placed closer to *mother* than to *me*. The sentence may be revised by moving the expression closer to the word actually being modified:

> My mother inspired me, when only a small child, to become a nurse.

Sometimes, as in the preceding example, a reader will know anyway which word a misplaced modifier is actually modifying. But more often, a misplaced modifier will make a sentence ridiculous, confusing, or both.

> I bought the gift at a large department store which cost only $10.99.

Clearly, an entire department store cannot cost $10.99. But according to the principles of sentence structure, the modifier "which cost only $10.99" is modifying *store*, the nearest noun. Revised, this sentence should read:

> I bought the gift, which cost only $10.99, at a large department store.

Consider the meaning of this sentence:

> Curtis found a memo inserted in a file that had been prepared by his boss.

If it was indeed the file that was prepared by Curtis's boss, then this sentence is correct. But if the boss actually prepared the memo, not the file, revision is called for:

> Curtis found, inserted in a file, a memo that had been prepared by his boss.

Even more unclear is this example:

> People who ride the subway on a daily basis witness its continuing deterioration.

The problem here is that the adverb, *on a daily basis*, is placed between two verbs, *ride* and *witness*. The reader has no way of knowing which verb is in fact being modified. If the writer intended to modify *ride*, the modifier must be placed *before* the verb:

> People who, on a daily basis, ride the subway witness its continuing deterioration.

On the other hand, if the modifier is meant for *witness*, it must come *after* the verb:

> People who ride the subway witness on a daily basis its continuing deterioration.

EXERCISE 4

In the space provided, rewrite each of these sentences, correcting any misplaced modifiers.

1. Employees were curious about the executive board meeting all through the company.

_____

_____

2. Secretaries could not figure out why the president had been so nervous around the water cooler.

_____

_____

3. He had explained to his assistant why the company was in trouble on Monday.

_____

_____

4. He began the meeting by saying, "Customers who buy our products frequently are discovering defects."

_____

_____

5. The meeting was attended by all executive personnel that stretched on for hours.

_____

_____

6. An assistant delivered cold dinners to hungry board members in cardboard boxes.

_____

_____

7. After much discussion, they pinpointed the source of the problem behind locked doors.

_____

_____

8. They agreed on the following day to institute new procedures.

_____

_____

9. After going through the assembly line, the board decided that each product would be inspected by an expert.

_____

_____

10. They are trying to devise a set of standards for employees that are foolproof.

_____

_____

EXERCISE 5

Some of these sentences are fine; others contain misplaced modifiers. If the sentence is correct, write a C in the space provided. If it is incorrect, rewrite the sentence.

1. Acme Computer Repair provides prompt service, which greatly pleases its customers.

_____

_____

2. All one must do is call their number, which is listed in the Yellow Pages.

_____

_____

3. They fixed the terminal in our reception area, which is only six months old but already unreliable.

_____

_____

4. We had called them Monday morning, and their service technician arrived before noon.

_____

_____

5. The precision of this man greatly impressed our office manager, who seemed to know exactly what he was doing.

_____

_____

6. In less than ten minutes, we watched as he returned the machine to perfect working order.

_____

_____

7. So, due to a damaged computer, little company time was lost.

_____

_____

8. The receptionist was back at her workstation by 12:15 P.M.

_____

_____

9. Of course, Acme is as prompt in its billing as in its service.

_____

_____

10. Tuesday, their bill was on our office manager's desk, which was very reasonable.

_____

_____

Dangling Modifiers

While a modifier may be placed too far from the word it modifies, a modifier will also be incorrect if there is *no* word at all being modified in the sentence. Such a modifier is called a DANGLING MODIFIER; it has no word to attach itself to and so is not in fact properly part of the sentence. Consider this example:

Walking down the street, a limousine caught my attention.

"Walking down the street" should be modifying a noun somewhere else in the sentence. However, the rest of the sentence follows a simple pattern (Subject-Verb-Object) and contains only two nouns (*limousine* and *attention*). Neither of these nouns can walk.

The problem is that the modifier is describing a pronoun (*I*) that does not actually appear in the sentence. To correct the error, the pronoun must be inserted:

While I was walking down the street, a limousine caught my attention.

or:

Walking down the street, *I noticed* a limousine.

Present participles, like *walking* in the preceding example, are frequent causes of dangling modifiers. Infinitives are similar culprits.

To get the order out on time, temporary help had to be hired.

Again, "to get the order out on time" should be modifying a noun. But the only noun elsewhere in the sentence is *temporary help*. But who had to get the order out on time? Certainly not the new employee, but the boss or the company itself, neither of which is mentioned in the sentence. To correct the error, an appropriate noun must be inserted:

For the company to get the order out on time, temporary help had to be hired.

or:

To get the order out on time, *Mr. Guzman had to hire* temporary help.

Dangling modifiers are a particular danger in writing instructions or making general statements about human behavior, when the doer of an action is left unspecified. For instance:

To become a successful entrepreneur, self-confidence is essential.

"To become a successful entrepreneur" cannot be modifying *self-confidence*, the only noun in the rest of the sentence. Indeed, only a human being can become an entrepreneur, yet none is mentioned. A number of revisions are possible:

For a person to become a successful entrepreneur, self-confidence is essential.

or:

To become a successful entrepreneur, *one needs* self-confidence.

EXERCISE 6

In the space provided, rewrite these sentences, correcting any dangling modifiers.

1. Settling down at my desk, the day started.

_____

_____

2. The morning passed quietly, preparing reports and filing them away.

_____

_____

3. When nearly finished with the last report, the telephone rang.

_____

_____

4. Answering it promptly, a salesman walked in.

_____

_____

5. To run an office smoothly, tact is often necessary.

_____

_____

6. Asking the salesman to have a seat, the caller left a message.

_____

_____

7. About to give his sales pitch, two customers arrived.

_____

_____

8. Listening to one customer's complaint, the salesman continued pushing his products.

_____

_____

9. Wandering around the showroom, I tried to keep an eye on the second customer.

_____

_____

10. Finally handling each in turn, the day resumed its leisurely pace.

_____

_____

EXERCISE 7

Some of these sentences contain dangling modifiers; other sentences are correct. Rewrite, in the space provided, those sentences in need of revision; indicate with a C those that are correct.

1. At the grand opening of his boutique, Al seemed relaxed and self-assured.

   _____

   _____

2. Walking in and out all day long, Al served dozens of customers single-handedly.

   _____

   _____

3. Though he intended to hire a salesperson, he knew that for now he could manage alone.

   _____

   _____

4. However, when first starting up the business, help was required.

   _____

   _____

5. Without any help, Al did all the buying.

   _____

   _____

6. Also, pricing and displaying the merchandise himself, the boutique was set up for opening day.

   _____

   _____

7. But, to incorporate the operation, legal assistance was necessary.

   _____

   _____

8. To set up his system of record keeping, an accountant's advice was relied on, too.

   _____

   _____

9. Even the layout of the store needed the work of a professional architect and designer.

   _____

   _____

10. To get a business going, the expense of a team of professionals should not be avoided.

    _____

    _____

Indirect Discourse

INDIRECT DISCOURSE refers to a sentence that relates, without the use of quotation marks, what another person has said or asked. (Thus, when quotation marks *are* used, and the speaker is quoted word for word, the mode is called DIRECT DISCOURSE; see page 259 for a discussion of quotation marks.) Indirect discourse falls into two subdivisions, INDIRECT QUOTATIONS and INDIRECT QUESTIONS.

Indirect Quotations

For the purpose of accuracy, it is often wise, when quoting another person's remarks, to cite those remarks word for word and put them in quotation marks. However, there are times when a full quotation is not necessary. Only part of the quotation may be relevant to your own subject. Or an exact repetition of the speaker's words may disrupt the flow of your own writing. For such reasons, it is important to know how to transpose a direct quotation into an indirect quotation.

For example, suppose your boss, Ms. Fein, tells you, "I am angry." If you want to report her remark to someone else, you have a number of options. You may use direct quotation:

> Ms. Fein says, "I am angry."

To avoid direct quotation, though, you may alter her remark slightly without becoming inaccurate.

1. First, you eliminate the quotation marks and the comma that precedes the quotation.
2. Then, you insert the subordinator *that* before the quotation.
3. Finally, you may have to change the pronouns and verb forms in the quotation.

Therefore, our example could become:

> Ms. Fein says *that she is* angry.

We have replaced the quotation marks with *that*; since only Ms. Fein would refer to herself as *I*, we have replaced *I* with *she*; and to agree with *she*, we have changed the verb to *is*.

One of the difficulties with indirect quotations involves the verb tense. The tense of the verb in the indirect quotation depends upon the tense of the original statement.

When the original statement is in the present tense (as in our example), then the tense of the verb in the indirect quotation should match the tense of the verb of saying:

> Ms. Fein says, "I am angry."
> Ms. Fein *says* that she *is* angry.
>
> Ms. Fein said, "I am angry."
> Ms. Fein *said* that she *was* angry.

When the verb in the original statement is in the past tense, it must be taken a step back on our tense "time line" (see Chapter 17) when quoted indirectly.

EXERCISE 8

In the space provided, rewrite as an indirect quotation each of these direct quotations.

EXAMPLE:

Herb told me, "You are the smartest person I have ever known."
Herb told me that I was the smartest person he had ever known.

1. Pat told the personnel officer, "I am applying for a position as an administrative assistant."

   _____

   _____

2. The personnel officer replied, "We have no such opening at this time."

   _____

   _____

3. Pat said, "I would like to make out an application for your waiting list anyway."

   _____

   _____

4. While she was writing, the man said, "We are looking for an executive secretary."

   _____

   _____

5. He explained, "The position is with the assistant vice president of marketing."

   _____

   _____

6. Pat said, "I am willing to begin as a secretary if there are opportunities for advancement."

   _____

   _____

7. The personnel officer assured her, "We fill most higher positions from within the company."

   _____

   _____

8. Then he added, "If your skills are appropriate, I will arrange an interview for you."

   _____

   _____

9. Pat informed him, "I can type 80 words a minute and take dictation at 120."

   _____

   _____

10. Now, she tells people, "Within an hour, I had the job."

    _____

    _____

Indirect Questions

When one is not asking a question but relating that someone else has asked a question, it is not always necessary to repeat the question word for word. That is, like any statement, the question may be repeated indirectly.

For instance, suppose your boss asks, "Are you angry?" If you repeat the question to a third person, you may do so directly:

> Ms. Fein asks, "Are you angry?"

The process of transforming this DIRECT QUESTION into an INDIRECT QUESTION is fourfold:

1. Eliminate the punctuation: quotation marks, question mark, and comma before the question. *End the whole sentence with a period.*
2. Insert the word *if* or *whether* before the question. Or, if the original question already contains a subordinator, retain it. For example—

> Ms. Fein asks, "*What* are you doing?"
> Ms. Fein asks *what* you are doing.

3. Adjust all necessary tenses and pronouns.
4. Invert the subject and verb in the question back to normal sentence order—first subject, then verb.

Thus, our example becomes:

> Ms. Fein asks if you are angry.

Note that the indirect questions ends with a period, not a question mark, because it is not actually a question but a statement.

The third step in the process requires further explanation, for the pronouns in the question itself will depend upon to whom the question is being put. For example, Ms. Fein may be questioning you yourself:

> Ms. Fein asks me, "<u>Are you</u> angry?"
> Ms. Fein asks me if <u>I am</u> angry.

On the other hand, she may be directing the question to the same person to whom you are speaking:

> Ms. Fein asks you, "<u>Are you</u> angry?"
> Ms. Fein asks you if <u>you are</u> angry.

Or, Ms. Fein may be questioning one person, and you are repeating it to yet another:

> Ms. Fein asks her, "<u>Are you</u> angry?"
> Ms. Fein asks her if <u>she is</u> angry.

The matter of tenses for indirect questions is the same as for indirect quotations. When the question is in the present tense, then the tense of the verb in the indirect question should match the tense of the verb of asking:

Ms. Fein asks, "Are you angry?"
Ms. Fein *asks* if you *are* angry.

Ms. Fein asked, "Are you angry?"
Ms. Fein *asked* if you *were* angry.

If the original question is in the past tense, then the verbs should *not* match when an indirect question is used:

Ms. Fein asks, "Were you angry?"
Ms. Fein *asks* if you *were* angry.

Ms. Fein asked, "Were you angry?"
Ms. Fein *asked* if you *had been* angry.

As with indirect quotations, when the original direct question is in the past tense, the verb in the indirect question must be more in the past than the verb of asking.

EXERCISE 9

In the space provided, rewrite as an indirect question each of these direct questions.

EXAMPLE:

My mother asked me, "What questions did the panel pose at the interview?"
My mother asked me what questions the panel had posed at the interview.

1. The program director began by asking me, "Have you had any previous experience in an old age home?"

   _____

   _____

2. Then she asked, "Can you tell us about your relevant education?"

   _____

   _____

3. The director's assistant wanted to know, "How did you find working with people much older than yourself?"

   _____

   _____

4. A third person queried, "What special approaches are necessary when working with an elderly population?"

   _____

   _____

5. Next, the director again asked, "What would you do if you thought someone were having a heart attack?"

   _____

   _____

6. Another member of the panel inquired, "What musical instruments do you play?

_____

_____

7. Then the assistant asked, "Do you feel you can work on your own?"

_____

_____

8. She further questioned, "Are you willing to work long hours?"

_____

_____

9. The director then asked, "What salary range would you consider acceptable?"

_____

_____

10. Finally, she inquired, "When can you start?"

_____

_____

▆▆▆▆ REVIEW EXERCISES

Proofread these letters for faulty parallelism, misplaced modifiers, and dangling modifiers. Where direct discourse is used, determine whether indirect discourse would be more appropriate. Then, rewrite each letter, making all necessary changes.

A.

October 8, [*year*]

Trumbel's Furniture Center
4069 Lexington Avenue
New York, New York 10077

Dear Sirs:

As advertised in your fall catalog, I would like to order a desk. The model number is 15C-2J, solid oak, priced at $495.

Please send the desk to the following address and charge it to my account number, 7651-38-801, immediately:

   96 Lakeview Drive
   Riverdale, New York 11232

Thank you.

Yours truly,

B.

April 28, [*year*]

Highpoint Tenants' Association
7272 Cliffside Drive
Baltimore, Maryland 12991

Dear Apartment Owner:

It is with great pleasure that your executive council has contracted our refrigeration and stove repair services. It is our intention to provide each apartment in Highpoint with the most prompt and efficient repair service possible.

For an annual fee of $150 per apartment, we have agreed to assume responsibility for all malfunctions of refrigerators, freezers, and gas ranges. There will be no additional charge for repairs to you, even if the cost of these services should exceed $150.

This contract is on an apartment-by-apartment basis. Therefore, please let us know, "Are you interested in securing our Kitchen Insurance for your home?" We have enclosed a handy, self-addressed reply card for your convenience. Or you may call us at 824-5200 during business hours.

We look forward to serving you.

Very truly yours,

C.

Dear Mrs. Poirot:

Thank you for your letter of April 10 regarding the portable television you wish to return. In checking our records, you have indeed owned the set for only six weeks.

We can clearly understand your anger at having a television purchased so recently break down; however, our terms of sale do not permit the return of merchandise beyond seven days of purchase.

Nevertheless, your set is under warranty with the manufacturer for twelve months. We have contacted the factory repair service for you, who informed us, "We will get in touch with Mrs. Poirot immediately to arrange for the free repair of her set."

Thank you for understanding our position, Mrs. Poirot. We hope that we have been of some help in this matter and that you will enjoy your television for many years to come.

Sincerely yours,

D.

Dear Ms. MacIntosh:

Thank you for requesting credit privileges at Degnan's Department Store.

A standard review of credit applications includes checking accounts, savings accounts, and any debts that you may have outstanding. Having investigated your ability to assume such credit, it appears that your current obligations are substantial. We therefore feel that the extension of further credit would endanger your financial reputation.

We hope you will continue with Degnan's as a cash customer. Please be assured that our decision in no way reflects your integrity and that, should your current obligations be reduced, we will gladly reconsider your application in the future.

Cordially yours,

E.

TO: Mr. Buckheim

FROM: Ms. Brandes

DATE: October 18, [*year*]

SUBJECT: Telephone-Answering Machines

On Tuesday, October 12, you instructed me, "Find out which telephone-answering equipment will best suit our office needs." You asked me, "What are the three top models?" Here is the information I discovered:

1. Dictaphone, model 108B—equipped with 30-second announcement cartridge, 90-minute message cassette, and remote control message receiver; available at Berkeley's Office Equipment, Inc., for $165

2. Ansaphone, model 26-60, comes equipped with 30-second announcement cartridge, 60-minute message cassette, fast-forward device, and remote control message receiver and is available at Audrey's Audio for $100

3. Quadraphone, model number XJ9, equipped with 20-second announcement cartridge, 90-minute message cassette, message length switch, and remote control message receiver; at all Taylor Discount Stores, for $125

All three models use standard leaderless C-type cassettes, and all operate only on 110 AC electrical outlets.

Please let me know if you require additional information.

RB

16.
Subject-Verb Agreement

The rules of SUBJECT-VERB AGREEMENT are all based on the use of S-endings.

The S-ending does *not* always make a word plural. Actually, the S-ending has several uses, depending upon the kind of word it is attached to.

The Noun S

This is the PLURAL S. By adding an S to the end of a singular noun, the noun becomes plural:

| 1 book | 2 book<u>s</u> |
| 1 hat | several hat<u>s</u> |

By adding this S-ending, we go from one to more than one.

However, if a noun already ends in S, we add an ES-ending to make it plural:

| 1 kiss | 10 kiss<u>es</u> |
| 1 bus | many bus<u>es</u> |

ES is also used if a noun ends in CH, SH, X, or Z:

watch	watches
dish	dishes
tax	taxes
quiz	quizzes

Also, nouns that end in Y form plurals in one of two ways:

1. If the letter before the Y is a consonant, the plural is formed by changing the Y to I and adding ES.

| company | companies |
| secretary | secretaries |

2. If the letter before the Y is a vowel, just add an S.

| attorney | attorneys |
| essay | essays |

Since there are so many irregular nouns in English, it is difficult to formulate other rules. For example, some nouns that end in F or FE become plural by changing the F to V and adding ES:

| half | halves |
| wife | wives |

But others become plural by simply adding an S:

chief	chiefs
proof	proofs

Similarly, some nouns that end in O are made plural with an S:

radio	radios
piano	pianos

But other nouns that end in O need an ES to become plural:

tomato	tomatoes
hero	heroes

Special kinds of irregular nouns will be discussed later in this chapter. But you should always consult a dictionary whenever you aren't sure of a plural form.

EXERCISE 1

This chart should contain both the singular and plural form of each noun. Fill in the blanks.

SINGULAR	PLURAL	SINGULAR	PLURAL
cost			factories
journey		safe	
	buzzes	life	
	inquiries		foxes
	holidays	banana	
anniversary		loss	
	requests		cargoes
	finances		trustees
success			phonies
ax		banjo	

The Possessive S ('s *or* s')

This S-ending is also attached to nouns. But it does *not* turn a singular noun into a plural noun. In fact, the POSSESSIVE S turns a noun into a kind of adjective!

One girl has a pen
The girl's pen is green.
(The pen of the girl is green.)

In the first sentence, the verb is *has*, and the subject is *girl*. Therefore, *girl* is being used as a noun.

But in the second sentence, the verb is *is*, and the subject is *pen*. The word *girl's* is describing the word *pen*. That means that by adding the *'s*, we turned an ordinary noun into an adjective.

As you can see, the difference between the NOUN S and the POSSESSIVE S is the use of a punctuation mark. This mark is called an APOSTROPHE.

> **Note:** To make a *plural noun* possessive, *do not* add *'s*. Just add an apostrophe. (The S is already there!)
> The girls' pens are blue.
> (The pens of the girls are blue.)

For other uses of the APOSTROPHE, see page 256.

For other uses of the APOSTROPHE, see page 256.

EXERCISE 2

Rephrase each of these by using a possessive S-ending.

EXAMPLE:

The responsibilities of the supervisors are distributed equally.
The supervisors' responsibilities are distributed equally.

1. The policy of this company is to review salaries every six months.

_____

_____

2. The salaries of all employees are evaluated carefully.

_____

3. The performance of an employee, of course, is most important.

_____

4. The opinion of an immediate superior is also a major consideration.

_____

5. The objectivity of the administration is reasonably high.

_____

6. The loyal service of an employee is usually recognized.

_____

7. The merit of a raise is usually acknowledged.

_____

8. A reward often follows the outstanding performance of someone.

_____

9. The employees of this company find the system fair.

_____

10. The bosses know how to maintain the satisfaction of their workers.

_____

_____

The Verb S

This is the difficult S-ending. It is added to VERBS, not nouns, making them, in a sense, SINGULAR!

The basic rule is this: When the subject of a PRESENT TENSE VERB is a SINGULAR noun, the verb needs an S-ending.

> The stenographer takes dictation.
> The secretary types the letter.

> **Note:** The VERB *S* is only used in the PRESENT TENSE. That means the verb must be happening RIGHT NOW.

If the PRESENT TENSE VERB has a PLURAL noun for a subject, the verb gets NO S-ending.

> Stenographers take dictation.
> Secretaries type letters.

Notice that this means that between a verb and its subject there is really only one S-ending to go around. Either there is an S on the verb, *or* there is an S on the subject.

> My vacation seems short.
> Our vacations seem short.

A singular noun that ends in S doesn't really have an S-*ending*. So its verb would still need an S-ending:

> The boss yells.
> The bosses yell.

EXERCISE 3

In each sentence, if the subject is singular, make it plural. If the subject is plural, make it singular. Then change the verb to agree with the new subject.

EXAMPLE:

The new file clerk appears to be doing well.
The new file clerks appear to be doing well.

1. An airport employs many people.

_____

2. The pilot flies jets all over the world.

_____

3. The navigator keeps track of direction.

_____

4. The flight attendants take care of the passengers.

_____

5. The ground crew checks the plane's condition.

_____

6. The baggage handlers toss the luggage.

_____

7. The ticket agents arrange the seating.

_____

8. The customs official opens bags.

_____

9. Tower controls direct the planes.

_____

10. The security agents watch for terrorists.

_____

EXERCISE 4

In these sentences, find the subjects. Then decide whether the verb should have an S-ending or not. Circle the correct verb form.

1. Local government (offer, offers) many job opportunities.
2. Cities (hire, hires) policemen.
3. Citizens (need, needs) fire protection.
4. Sanitation workers (clean, cleans) the streets.
5. Town Hall (employ, employs) many clerks and secretaries.
6. Politicians (have, has) government jobs, too.
7. The mayor's salary (come, comes) from the government.
8. Taxes (pay, pays) all these wages.
9. So taxpayers really (employ, employs) all these people.
10. Each citizen (are, is) actually an employer.

In the last sentence of the preceding exercise, the verbs were a bit different from the others. Yet *is* and *are* are verbs that you have already seen. You know that they are part of the verb TO BE. You may not know that TO BE presents special problems in subject-verb agreement.

First of all, TO BE is irregular. So we can't just add an S-ending or not. The S-forms and the non-S-forms are completely different words (as in the case of *is* and *are*).

Also, unlike any other verb in English, TO BE has an S-form and a non-S-form in the PAST TENSE, too.

	PRESENT	PAST
SINGULAR	is	was
PLURAL	are	were

Here are a few examples:

One bookkeeper is not enough.
Two bookkeepers are enough.

One executive was working on the deal.
Several executives were working on the deal.

Am, the fifth form of the verb TO BE, is of course used only when the subject is *I*.

I am busy.

EXERCISE 5

In each sentence, find the subject. Then circle the correct form of the verb.

1. Recession (is, are) a serious economic problem.
2. Because of it, companies (is, are) closing down.
3. Workers (is, are) being laid off.
4. Consumers (is, are) buying fewer goods and services.
5. As a result, stores (is, are) going out of business.
6. Homeowners (is, are) having difficulty meeting mortgage payments.
7. Real estate prices (was, were) high.
8. Now, however, real estate values (is, are) falling.
9. Banks (was, were) paying higher interest rates than they are now.
10. Americans (is, are) worried about the future.

Using *am* when the subject is *I* introduces another important point about SUBJECT-VERB AGREEMENT. What happens to the verb when its subject is a pronoun?

Since pronouns don't get S-endings to make them plural, and since some pronouns (like *you*) can be used as either singular or plural, the rules we have learned so far will not help us when a pronoun is the subject of a present tense verb.

But the problem is not difficult:

WHEN THE SUBJECT IS *HE, SHE, IT, THIS,* OR *THAT,* THE VERB NEEDS AN S-ENDING. WHEN THE SUBJECT IS *I, YOU, WE, THEY, THESE* OR *THOSE,* THE VERB GETS NO S-ENDING.

For example:

He travel<u>s</u> on business quite often.
They travel on business occasionally.

This idea i<u>s</u> interesting.
Those are not interesting.

EXERCISE 6

Identify the subject of each sentence; then circle the correct form of the verb.

1. It (are, is) easy to get to our office.
2. We (travel, travels) by various means.
3. I (take, takes) the bus to work every day.
4. You usually (drive, drives).
5. She (have, has) to take a bus and then a train.
6. They (walk, walks) together.
7. When it (rain, rains), they don't walk.
8. Then they (take, takes) a cab.
9. It (are, is) most expensive to drive to work.
10. You (have, has) to pay for gas as well as parking.

Although the basic rules of subject-verb agreement are straightforward, there are situations in which the rules are not easy to apply. Looking for an S-ending on the subject to decide whether the verb needs an S-ending will not always work.

Compound Subjects

As you remember, one of our basic sentence patterns included a COM-POUND SUBJECT:

S and S V.
<u>Sam and Willy</u> <u>talk</u>.

That is, the whole subject consists of two nouns (at least) connected by the word *and*.

In terms of subject-verb agreement, compound subjects (nouns connected by *and*) are considered plural. That means their present tense verbs *do not* take S-endings.

The desk *is* mine.
The chair *is* mine.
    BUT
The desk and chair *are* mine.

In this example, neither noun in the subject has an S-ending on it. Still, we give the verb no S-ending either. By connecting the nouns with *and*, we are in effect adding them together; the subject is now two things.

Of course, sometimes one or more nouns in a compound subject will have an S-ending.

The treasurer and her two assistant<u>s</u> work hard.
The typewriter<u>s</u> and adding machine need repair.
All sales representative<u>s</u> and their famili<u>es</u> are invited to the company picnic.

But these S-endings are just an extra clue. The *and* alone requires us *not* to put an S-ending on the verb.

EXERCISE 7

After finding the subject (Watch out for compounds!), circle the correct verb in each of these sentences.

1. My salary and benefits (satisfy, satisfies) me.
2. Ten vacation days and twelve holidays (are, is) allowed off.
3. My insurance (cover, covers) all kinds of emergencies.
4. Medical bills and dental expenses (are, is) included.
5. I even (have, has) life insurance.
6. Profit sharing and incentives (augment, augments) my income.
7. A pension plan and savings program (help, helps) me prepare for retirement.
8. My expense account (meet, meets) my business needs.
9. Business trips and conventions occasionally (break, breaks) the routine.
10. My work and its returns (are, is) quite rewarding.

Or and Nor

When the nouns in a subject are connected by *or*, the rules change. Let's look at some variations:

> My secretary or my assistant *screens* my calls.
> My secretaries or my assistant *screens* my calls.
>   BUT
> My secretary or my assistants *screen* my calls.
> My secretaries or my assistants *screen* my calls.

The word *secretary* has no effect on the verb; whether it has an S-ending or not doesn't matter.

The word *assistant* is what counts here. When *assistant* has no S-ending (the first two examples), the verb gets an S-ending. When *assistants* is used with an S-ending (the second two examples), the verb gets *no* S-ending.

This is because *assistant* is the noun closest to the verb.

WHEN THE NOUNS IN A SUBJECT ARE CONNECTED BY <u>OR</u>, OR THE NOUN CLOSEST TO THE VERB DETERMINES WHETHER THE VERB GETS AN S-ENDING.

This rule also applies with the expression "either . . . or . . .":

> Either your bill or our records *are* in error.

The noun *records* is closest to the verb; because *records* has an S-ending, we use a verb with no S-ending, *are*.

The rule holds true, as well, with *nor* and the expression "neither . . . nor . . .":

> Neither I nor my partner *recalls* your order.

Here, *partner* is closest to the verb, so *recalls* gets an S-ending.

EXERCISE 8

In each sentence, examine the subject; then circle the correct form of the verb.

1. Neither good connections nor a wealthy father (are, is) enough to get ahead.
2. Friends or parents (are, is) of course helpful.
3. But your career choice or specialization (do, does) not necessarily coincide with theirs.
4. An ambitious self-starter (make, makes) his or her own contacts.
5. A liberal arts college or vocational training (provide, provides) a good start.
6. Either a sound education or solid work experience (are, is) essential.
7. Related courses or apprentice work (prepare, prepares) you for your first real job.
8. Good grades or favorable references (say, says) much about your work habits.
9. Summertime or after-school jobs (help, helps) build up resumes.
10. Your own ambition and determination (are, is) what ultimately count.

Indefinite Pronouns

INDEFINITE PRONOUNS are a group of pronouns that do not point out a specific person or thing. When used as the subject of a present tense verb, an INDEFINITE PRONOUN presents a problem because it doesn't have an S-ending to let us know whether it is singular or plural.

Fortunately, INDEFINITE PRONOUNS can be divided into three smaller groups, according to whether they are singular or plural.

1. Singular Indefinite Pronouns

Singular indefinite pronouns require an S-ending on their verbs.

another	little	every
each	much	

These words (except *every*) can be used alone:

Little <u>remains</u> to be done.

Or they may be used with a real noun right after them:

Little work <u>remains</u> to be done.

(Of course, in the second situation, the S-ending on the verb is obviously needed because *work* has no S-ending. Right?)

Some of these words *seem* to mean something plural. For instance, when we say "every person in the room" we are referring to a lot of people. However, what we *mean* is "every single person in the room considered individually." The same thing is true of *each*: it implies "each *one*."

Much is similar. It suggests a large quantity of something. But think of it as a single quantity, very big but only one. "Much money" could mean many dollars, but it is *one* amount altogether.

There is also a group of "combination" indefinite pronouns that are singular, too (and so need an S-ending on their verbs). These can be learned by studying a chart. Attach any one word on the left to any one word on the right, and you come up with a SINGULAR INDEFINITE PRONOUN.

some	
	one
every	
	body
any	
	thing
no	

For example:

Someone ha<u>s</u> borrowed my slide rule.
Nothing i<u>s</u> impossible.

Some of these combinations seem to be plural, like the other singular indefinite pronouns mentioned before. Here, though, *one, body*, and *thing* are all singular. Neither has an S-ending. So their verbs (in the present tense) must take an S-ending.

EXERCISE 9

Examine the subject in each sentence. Then circle the correct form of the verb.

1. Everyone (want, wants) to join the committee.
2. Each (pay, pays) a membership fee.
3. Much (are, is) collected.
4. Another problem (remain, remains).
5. Somebody (have, has) to be elected chairperson.
6. No one (seem, seems) willing to take the post.
7. Finally, two members (volunteer, volunteers).
8. Little (are, is) said before the vote.
9. Someone (move, moves) to end the meeting.
10. Another (are, is) scheduled before adjournment.

2. Plural Indefinite Pronouns

Five indefinite pronouns are always plural. Therefore, when used as a subject of a present tense verb, they require *no* S-ending on the verb.

both   few   many   several   others

For example:

Few <u>recognize</u> the importance of perseverance.
Many <u>give</u> up too readily.

Notice that the *meaning* of these words is plural, which should help when you memorize them.

EXERCISE 10

Circle the correct verb for each sentence.

1. Many (have, has) applied for the job.
2. Several (are, is) being interviewed.
3. Few actually (qualify, qualifies).
4. Two applicants (seem, seems) most experienced.
5. Both (have, has) done similar work in the past.
6. Each (are, is) well trained.
7. Many questions (are, is) put to them.
8. Several points (contribute, contributes) to the final decision.
9. Both (are, is) eventually hired.
10. The others (are, is) turned away.

3. Variable Indefinite Pronouns

The last group of indefinite pronouns is tricky because they are variable.

all   most   none   some

These pronouns can be singular or plural depending upon the "real" noun to which they refer.

When the "real" noun is used, this is clear:

Some coffee *is* left.
Some employees *are* leaving.

Because *coffee* has no S-ending, we know to use *is*; because *employees* has an S-ending, we know to use *are*.

But it is possible to have a sentence in which the "real" noun is omitted—in response to a question, for example, or in a paragraph when the noun has been mentioned previously:

> The responsibility is all yours.
> None <u>is</u> mine.

> These books belong to you.
> None <u>are</u> mine.

It is essential, therefore, that when you use a variable indefinite pronoun, you keep in mind the "real" noun it is referring to.

Here is a method you can use to help you decide whether or not the verb gets an S-ending:

—If you can *count* the real noun that an indefinite pronoun is referring to, it is plural: DO *NOT* give the verb an S-ending.
—If you must *measure* the real noun, it is singular: DO give the verb an S-ending.

Look back at our first example. *Coffee* must be measured, so it is singular and requires an S-ending on its verb. But *employees* can be counted, so the subject is plural and the verb needs no S-ending.

Similarly, we must measure *responsibility*, but we can count *books*.

EXERCISE 11

In each sentence, circle the correct verb form after considering the subject.

1. Some of the ink (have, has) spilled.
2. Some of the letters (were, was) ruined.
3. None of the blotters (are, is) helping.
4. None of the work (are, is) salvageable.
5. Most of the mess (have, has) been cleaned up.
6. Most of the papers (are, is) being retyped.
7. All of the damage (were, was) unnecessary.
8. All of us (need, needs) to be more careful.
9. One of us (are, is) responsible.
10. Some (are, is) still angry.

"There"

The important point to remember about *there* is that, although it may be the first word of a sentence, it is *not* the subject.

> There goes my boss.

You may have recognized that *there* is actually an adverb. In the above example, the verb is *goes*; the subject (who goes?) is *my boss*.

Sentences that begin with *there* are called INVERTED SENTENCES because in such situations the subject is the noun *after* the verb. Many inverted sentences can be reversed and put back into normal subject-verb order:

There <u>is</u> <u>a calculator</u> on the desk.
<u>A calculator</u> <u>is</u> on the desk

There <u>are</u> <u>four documents</u> relevant to this case.
<u>Four documents</u> <u>are</u> relevant to this case.

Reversing an inverted sentence (at least mentally) can help you decide if the verb needs an S-ending.

In any case, remember: When a sentence begins with *there*, the subject comes *after* the verb. So you have to look or think ahead when deciding whether or not to put an S-ending on the verb.

EXERCISE 12

Find the subject in each of these sentences. Then circle the correct verb form.

1. There (seem, seems) to be a lack of organization in this office.
2. There (are, is) papers strewn all about.
3. There (are, is) an excess of noise.
4. There (appear, appears) to be no one answering the telephones.
5. There (are, is) too many people taking coffee breaks at once.
6. There (are, is) coffee spilled on the floor.
7. There (have, has) been an audit done by the company.
8. There (seem, seems) to be no solution.
9. There (are, is) no recommendations.
10. There (are, is) too much work getting done.

Irregular Nouns

Many English nouns are irregular; that is, they don't form their plural by the addition of an S-ending. Therefore, when an irregular noun is the subject of a present tense verb, the decision whether to put an S-ending on the verb is not simple to make.

For example, look at these three "people" nouns:

man
woman
child

Each noun is used to refer to a single individual.

The man seem<u>s</u> tired.
The woman <u>is</u> concerned.
The child sleep<u>s</u>.

There is no S at the end of the noun, so when it is the subject of a present tense verb, we use an S-ending on the verb.

But think of the plural forms of these nouns:

man   men
woman   women
child   children

All three plurals end in EN. (By the way, this should make them easier to remember.) So, when used as a subject of a present tense verb, there is no plural S-ending to remind us *not* to use an S-ending on the verb.

The men work hard.
The women contribute equally.
The children learn.

What you must remember (and this is true for all irregular nouns) is that A PRESENT TENSE VERB GETS NO S-ENDING WHEN ITS SUBJECT IS A PLURAL NOUN.

Another group of irregular nouns forms the plural with a vowel change:

foot   feet
mouse   mice

Thus,

My tooth aches. (singular)
My teeth ache.   (plural)

Some words are difficult for the opposite reason; these are nouns that indicate fields of study or branches of knowledge. For example:

mathematics
linguistics
economics

These words have S-endings but are the names of *single* subjects. So the verb must get an S-ending, too.

Economics confuses me.

The names of several diseases work this way. They end in S, but they are still *one* disease:

Tuberculosis has become a worldwide problem.

Notice that some words that fall into this category are actually variable. When used to indicate a subject area, they are considered singular; when used in some other sense, they are considered plural:

Politics *is* a fascinating subject.
A person's politics *change* as circumstances change.

In the second sentence, *politics* is used to mean "political views."

Then there are words that end in S and are usually considered plural, although their *meaning* is actually singular.

Pants are acceptable office wear for women nowadays.
The scissors are in my desk drawer.

Finally, you must keep in mind that many English words are borrowed from other languages. While most such words are anglicized (that is, adapted to English grammatical forms), some retain their "foreign" plural form. Again, this means that a final S may not be a guide to whether or not the verb needs an S-ending.

The following list illustrates some typical "foreign" endings to watch out for:

SINGULAR	PLURAL
crisis	crises
analysis	analyses
stimulus	stimuli
cactus	cacti
medium	media
datum	data
criterion	criteria
phenomenon	phenomena
larva	larvae
vertebra	vertebrae

As pointed out earlier in this chapter, always consult a dictionary whenever you are unsure of a noun's plural form.

EXERCISE 13

In each of these sentences, decide whether the subject is singular or plural. (Don't be fooled by final S-endings!) Then circle the required verb form.

1. Five women (have, has) conducted a scientific experiment.
2. The data (were, was) collected in a laboratory.
3. Mice (were, was) used in the experiment.
4. Measles (were, was) the main topic of the scientists' investigation.
5. Their thesis (appear, appears) in the introduction of their report.
6. Their analysis (have, has) sparked a controversy.
7. Their research tactics (are, is) being questioned.
8. The phenomenon (are, is) not unusual in the scientific community.
9. The media (are, is) not covering the story.
10. News (have, has) to be more earthshaking.

Collective Nouns

COLLECTIVE NOUNS are words that refer to a *group* of things or people but that act as a single unit.

For instance, a *class* may contain 25 students, but there is only one class.

Therefore, collective nouns are singular; used as the subject of a present tense verb, they require an S-ending on the verb.

The class listens attentively.

There are many such nouns in English; here are a few examples.

army	family	orchestra
committee	group	series
crowd	jury	team

Or course, a collective noun can be made plural when referring to two or more such units.

> The football teams confront each other in the stadium.

Also, a collective noun may occasionally be used to refer, not to the group, but to the individual members of the group. In this special case, the collective noun would be considered plural, and the verb would get no S-ending.

> The team remove their uniforms right after each game.

Team here implies "the members of the team," which is plural, with an S-ending on *members*.

This may be a good place to raise the problem of the word *number*. Sometimes *number* is a kind of collective noun:

> The number of desks in this office is inadequate.

The number, considered as a single unit or figure, requires an S-ending on the verb.

At other times, *number* is plural:

> A number of new desks have been ordered.

A number, considered as a total, is plural and requires *no* S-ending on the verb.

EXERCISE 14

Find the subject in each of these sentences; consider whether it is a collective noun. Then circle the correct form of the verb.

1. Our program director believes that the Navy (offer, offers) good opportunity.
2. Many (feel, feels) that military training is good experience for anyone.
3. Her staff (disagree, disagrees) with her.
4. A series of opinions (have, has) been expressed.
5. Some (feel, feels) that military training is good experience.
6. The majority (are, is) less certain.
7. Sometimes, a team (provide, provides) important support for an individual.
8. Other times, a group (obstruct, obstructs) individual growth.
9. Nevertheless, the director (want, wants) to find a new career.
10. Military life (are, is) one of her options.

Prepositional Phrases

As you have already learned, a PREPOSITIONAL PHRASE that is attached to a subject is actually a long adjective. It adds information to the subject, but it does not change whether the noun is singular or plural.

> The engineer is working hard.
> The engineer *at the controls* is working hard.

In the first sentence, *engineer* is the subject, so *is* (a verb with an S-ending) is needed. In the second sentence, *engineer* is still the subject, so *is* is still the correct verb form. *Controls* is plural, but because it is not the subject, its S-ending doesn't affect the verb.

In the following examples, the opposite occurs:

> The secretaries do a lot of typing.
> The secretaries *in that office* do a lot of typing.

In the first sentence, the verb *do* (with no S-ending) is used because the subject *secretaries* is plural (with an S-ending). In the second sentence, the verb remains *do* because the subject has remained *secretaries*. *Office* is part of the prepositional phrase; it is not the subject and so has no effect on the form of the verb.

Let's look at this matter another way:

> These ledgers are inaccurate.
> One *of these ledgers* is inaccurate.

In the first sentence, the verb *are* has no S-ending because the subject *ledgers* does have an S-ending. But in the second sentence, the verb *is*, with an S-ending, is needed because *ledgers* is no longer the subject; this time, *one* is the subject and *ledgers* is part of a prepositional phrase.

Similarly, words like *kind, part, portion,* and *type* are always singular, even when followed by a prepositional phrase containing a plural noun:

> A portion of the responsibilities is mine.

EXERCISE 15

Circle the correct form of the verb after identifying the subject. (Watch out for prepositional phrases.)

1. The effects of corporate policies on the environment (have, has) come under close scrutiny in recent years.
2. Paper recycling in the office (are, is) being encouraged.
3. The use of styrofoam by fast food chains (have, has) come under vocal attack.
4. Excessive layers of packaging (induce, induces) consumers to buy another company's products.
5. Guidelines for the safe disposal of industrial waste (are, is) being more carefully enforced.
6. However, more work in this area (need, needs) to be done.
7. Not surprisingly, most companies in America (put, puts) financial concerns ahead of the environment.
8. Fear of increased production costs (lead, leads) to reluctance to comply with environmental regulations.
9. Shortages of enforcement staff (encourage, encourages) scofflaws.
10. The survival of our planet (depend, depends) on the willingness of consumers to insist that companies become environmentally responsible.

Parenthetical Expressions

PARENTHESES are punctuation marks used to set off extra or interrupting comments in a sentence. For example:

> Knowledge of office machines (especially the fax and word processor) is valuable nowadays.

A PARENTHETICAL EXPRESSION, like a comment enclosed in parentheses, is an extra bit of information inserted into a sentence.

A parenthetical expression may be used to describe the subject of a sentence. Much like prepositional phrases, therefore, parenthetical expressions act as adjectives and do not affect whether the subject is singular or plural.

Examples:

> The cordless telephone and the answering machine *cost* $400.
> The cordless telephone including the answering machine *costs* $400.

In the first sentence, the verb *cost* needs no S-ending because the subject is compound (*the cordless telephone AND the answering machine*). In the second sentence, the verb *costs* does need an S-ending because the subject is simply *the cordless telephone. Including the answering machine* is a parenthetical expression, an adjective describing the subject but not part of the subject itself.

Sometimes a parenthetical expression is set off by two commas:

> My boss, *like her predecessor,* is hard to please.

Often, parenthetical expressions are introduced by words such as:

as well as	like
in addition to	together with
including	with

EXERCISE 16

In each sentence, identify the subject. (Be sure to eliminate parenthetical expressions.) Then circle the correct form of the verb.

1. Social work, including case work, group work, and community organization, (are, is) a twentieth-century development.
2. Churches along with philanthropic groups (were, was) the original sources of public relief.
3. The availability of government resources, in addition to private funds, (have, has) added greatly to the number of jobs for social workers.
4. Psychology, along with sociology, (are, is) an important requirement for the would-be social worker to study.
5. College departments as well as specialized graduate schools (provide, provides) training for social workers.
6. A troubled economy with its accompanying social problems (increase, increases) the need for social work.
7. Social ills including unemployment, drug addiction, alcoholism, and broken families (grow, grows) in hard times.

8. Individuals along with their families (require, requires) greater help in adjusting to society.
9. Social workers, with the aid of other professionals like physicians and psychiatrists, (are, is) trained to help these people.
10. Social work, together with other kinds of counseling, (make, makes) a good career choice for the future.

Who, Which, and That

When the subordinators *who, which*, and *that* are used in one of our basic sentence patterns,

S V | subordinator | S V.

they often serve both as the SUBORDINATOR *and* as the SUBJECT of a verb.

> I am studying accounting, which I find difficult.
> I am studying accounting, which is difficult for me.

In the first sentence, *which* is connecting two subject-verb cores, I <u>am</u> <u>studying</u> and I <u>find</u>. But look carefully at the second sentence. We still have I <u>am studying</u> to the left of *which*, yet to the right we have only the verb <u>is</u>. This is because <u>which</u> is the subject of <u>is</u> as well as the subordinator. It is a kind of PRONOUN standing for *accounting*.

Now, the point to remember for subject-verb agreement is that *which, who*, and *that* are neither singular nor plural. When they are the subject of a present tense verb, the S-ending depends upon the "real" noun to which the SUBORDINATOR/PRONOUN refers. Therefore, in our example, we need *is* with an S-ending because *which* is referring to a singular noun, *accounting*, with no S-ending.

Sometimes our basic sentence patterns can be rearranged. The first subject and verb can be split up by the subordinator and the second subject and verb.

S <u>V</u> | subordinator | S V.
S | subordinator | S V <u>V</u>.

It is basically the same sentence pattern, but with a slightly rearranged order.

> The receptionist whom I hired expresses herself clearly.

Here, *receptionist* is the subject of the verb *expresses*. *I* is the subject of the verb *hired*. They are connected by the subordinator *whom*.

Now look at this example:

> A receptionist who expresses herself clearly pleases the customer.

This time, *receptionist* is the subject of the verb *pleases*; the other verb *expresses* has the subordinator *who* for its subject. Because *who* is standing for *receptionist*, we need an S-ending on the verb *expresses*.

Again, the rule to follow is this: when *who, which*, or *that* is used as the subject of a present tense verb, check the real noun the subordinator is standing for before you decide whether or not the verb needs an S-ending.

EXERCISE 17

In each sentence, circle the correct form of the verb in parentheses.

1. Accounting is one of the major fields that (offer, offers) many opportunities.
2. The many factors that have led to the growth of accounting (include, includes) the expansion of corporate activity and the complex tax structure.
3. Accounting, which (were, was) developed in the nineteenth century, involves the classification and analysis of financial records.
4. The professional who (supply, supplies) these services is called an accountant.
5. She evaluates bookkeeping records, which (show, shows) the progress or decline of a business.
6. She also establishes the financial records and chooses the system of accounts that best (provide, provides) the needed information.
7. Individuals who meet educational and experiential requirements (are, is) eligible for the title Certified Public Accountant.
8. Such certification, which (are, is) government controlled, requires the passing of an examination.
9. People who (meet, meets) the requirements join such organizations as the American Institute of Accountants and the American Accounting Association.
10. A career in accounting (are, is) challenging and rewarding.

REVIEW EXERCISES

A. Circle the correct form of the verb in each sentence.

1. Two-thirds of total U.S. economic activity (consist, consists) of consumer spending.
2. There (are, is) a direct correlation between a strong economy and what consumers spend.
3. Bleak news reports, along with local talk of sagging business, (frighten, frightens) consumers.
4. Similarly, high unemployment statistics and the fear of losing one's own job (discourage, discourages) a person from spending.
5. People (prefer, prefers) to buy expensive items when they are hopeful about the future.
6. Neither optimistic government reports nor stock market gains (are, is) enough to convince people to spend.
7. Few (make, makes) purchases when they see neighbors losing their jobs.
8. Everyone (worry, worries) when local businesses close.
9. Most (wait, waits) for signs that the economy is looking up.
10. Much (depend, depends) on sales in major industries.
11. A steady rise in auto sales (are, is) one encouraging factor.
12. Another sign that consumers can look for (are, is) improved real estate sales.

13. Stable wholesale prices (have, has) an effect on the economy, too, by minimizing inflation.
14. American industry (realize, realizes) that the American consumer is the key to the economy.
15. Economics (are, is) a fascinating subject to explore.

B. For each of these, underline the correct verb form.

1. Preparing for retirement (is, are) an important aspect of personal finance.
2. Financial goals and the means to achieve them (is, are) necessary considerations when planning a successful retirement.
3. Individuals who plan early (is, are) likely to enjoy a secure and satisfying retirement.
4. Yet many (puts, put) off planning for retirement until relatively late in life.
5. There (is, are) several concerns when planning for retirement.
6. For example, upon retirement, income from salary or wages (ceases, cease).
7. Usually, neither Social Security benefits nor a pension plan (provides, provide) equivalent income.
8. Therefore, the accumulation of income-producing resources (is, are) an important long-range goal.
9. Moreover, living on a fixed income, together with the effects of inflation, (reduces, reduce) an individual's purchasing power after retirement.
10. Thus, an emotional crisis sometimes (compounds, compound) financial difficulties.
11. A wise individual (plans, plan) for both the additional leisure time and the reduced income brought about by retirement.
12. On the one hand, regular savings and thoughtful investment (alleviates, alleviate) the financial difficulties of retirement.
13. On the other hand, developing hobbies and interests (enriches, enrich) the retirement years with rewarding experiences.
14. Retirement (does, do) not have to be a dreaded time of financial deprivation.
15. With forethought and effort, it (becomes, become) a well-earned and pleasurable rest.

C. There are a number of S-ending errors in this letter. Find and correct them.

Dear Mr. Hyman:

As you know, job hunting in this day and age are a difficult proposition. With the economy down and competition up, we need all the help we can get to land that dream job.

Now, Integrity Careers, Inc., have the help you need. Our career guidance kit, "Know Thyself," provide the answers to your biggest questions: What job do I really want? What are my most marketable skill? What factors has kept me from reaching my goals up to now? What do I do to finally land the job of my dream?

This kit, including job lists and model resumes, are not available in any store. You can get it only through Integrity Careers, Inc. That's right! Only those who receives this letter even know the kit exist.

So why not send us $50 postage paid to receives your Integrity Career Guidance Kit? Start today toward a successful tomorrow.

Yours truly,

D. This invitation contains a number of S-ending errors. Find and correct them.

Corro Communications are pleased to announce the promotion of Augusta Samuels to assistant vice president of marketing. The former advertising director of our South and Midwest divisions bring to her new job a wealth of dedication and experience.

Ms. Samuels new office will be located in the New York headquarters building at 1 Sixth Avenue.

To mark the occasion, Corro request the pleasure of your company at a reception honoring Ms. Samuel. The reception will be held on May 24 at 4:30 P.M. in the Executive Lounge of the headquarters building.

R.S.V.P.   David Nathan, Ext. 222

E. Proofread the letter for S-ending errors.

Dear Mr. Mitchell:

Thank you for submitting your resume and application to the DuRite Corporation. We appreciate your interests in a position with our company.

Although we received over 200 responseses to our advertisement for an administrative assistant, we have given each applicants resume careful consideration. Because your background and experience meets our companys criteria, we would like to invite you to come in for an interview.

Interviews will be held the week of September 4. Please call us at (921) 664-0932 for an appointment.

Sincerely yours,

17.
Verb Forms

The last chapter focused on the use of S-endings on verbs, and the use of the present tense. In this chapter, we will look at the other verb tenses—how to form them and use them. Verbs are the most changeable part of speech in English.

In Chapter 13 we mentioned the PRINCIPAL PARTS OF THE VERB. We stressed that the simple present and the simple past are the only parts that act as verbs on their own. The other parts need helping verbs.

INFINITIVE:	to sing
PRESENT TENSE:	sing, sings
PAST TENSE:	sang
PRESENT PARTICIPLE:	singing
PAST PARTICIPLE	sung

Basically, the other tenses in English are formed by using one of the participles with a helping verb. For instance, the PRESENT PARTICIPLE (the -ING part) is often used with parts of the verb *to be*, and the PAST PARTICIPLE is often used with parts of the verb *to have*. Different combinations of helping verbs and participles result in different tenses. Consider some examples:

have sung
had sung
will have sung
are singing
were singing
will be singing

Tense Formation

Notice that *have sung* and *had sung* are in two different tenses. Each used the PAST PARTICIPLE *sung* (from the verb *to sing*), but the first uses the PRESENT TENSE of *to have* (*have*) while the second uses the PAST TENSE of *to have* (*had*). Therefore, the "combination" tenses mark important differences in meaning.

This takes us to the second point about verb tenses. Like other verbs, the two major helping verbs have five principal parts. That is what allows us so many different combinations of helping verbs and participles.

INFINITIVE:	to be	to have
PRESENT TENSE:	are, is, am	have, has
PAST TENSE:	were, was	had
PRESENT PARTICIPLE:	being	having
PAST PARTICIPLE:	been	had

Let's look at our model verb *to sing*. The past participle *sung* may be used with the present and past tenses of *to have*:

has sung
have sung
had sung

All three are perfectly good two-word verbs and may be used with a subject to form a sentence:

The soprano has sung that aria many times.

Similarly, the present participle of to sing (singing) may be used with the present or past tense of to be:

are singing
is singing
am singing
were singing
was singing

All five of these two-word verbs may be used with a subject to form a complete sentence:

Today, she is singing with the Metropolitan Opera.

The present participle may also be used with the past participle of to be:

been singing

However, as you know, a participle cannot be used with a subject unless it has a helping verb. Although *singing* has a helping verb (*been*), *been* itself needs to have a helping verb. Since *been* is a past participle, we need part of the verb to have:

has been singing
have been singing
had been singing

All of these three-word verbs may now be used with a subject to form a complete sentence:

She has been singing with the Met for six years.

On the basis of these various combinations, we can form a little chart:

VERB FORMATION

$$\left.\begin{array}{l}\text{has}\\\text{have}\\\text{had}\end{array}\right\} \text{sung} \qquad \left.\begin{array}{l}\text{are}\\\text{is}\\\text{am}\\\text{were}\\\text{was}\\\left.\begin{array}{l}\text{has}\\\text{have}\\\text{had}\end{array}\right\}\text{been}\end{array}\right\}\text{singing}$$

EXERCISE 1

A verb form has been omitted from each of these sentences. Following each sentence is a list of verbs, some of which will correctly fill in the blank in the sentence. First, decide which of the principal parts of the verb is needed. Then, put a check next to each verb that can be correctly inserted into the sentence.

1. My employer had _____.

spoken ____	went ____	forgotten ____
say ____	done ____	take ____
written ____	did ____	go ____
been ____	took ____	gone ____
do ____	said ____	taken ____

2. Right now, his assistant _____.

laughed ____	typing ____	argues ____
types ____	laughs ____	speaks ____
speaking ____	spoke ____	worked ____
works ____	argue ____	said ____
says ____	knows ____	known ____

3. He is _____.

types ____	typing ____	speaking ____
answering ____	spoke ____	laughed ____
works ____	filing ____	wastes ____
laughing ____	try ____	working ____
filed ____	loafs ____	trying ____

4. Yesterday, he _____.

typed ____	rests ____	transcribes ____
filed ____	worked ____	correcting ____
forgot ____	typing ____	transcribed ____
resting ____	decided ____	files ____
works ____	work ____	corrected ____

5. For years, they have _____.

work ____	argue ____	cooperated ____
fought ____	argued ____	conferring ____
bicker ____	confides ____	disagreed ____
disagree ____	fighting ____	conferred ____
arguing ____	bickered ____	cooperate ____

Irregular Verbs

Just as nouns can be irregular in the way they form the plural, so verbs can be irregular in the way they form the PAST TENSE and the PAST PARTICIPLE. Consider these two model verbs:

INFINITIVE:	to talk	to sing
PRESENT TENSE:	talk, talks	sing, sings
PAST TENSE:	talked	sang
PRESENT PARTICIPLE:	talking	singing
PAST PARTICIPLE:	talked	sung

The PRESENT TENSE and the PRESENT PARTICIPLE are easily understood. We have already studied the rules for using S-endings on present tense verbs. And the present participle is formed by simply adding an ING-ending to the infinitive without the *to*.

With REGULAR VERBS, the PAST TENSE and the PAST PARTICIPLE are rather simple, too. In fact, both are formed by adding an ED-ending to the infinitive without the *to*. This means that for regular verbs the past tense and the past participle are spelled exactly alike. One of our model verbs, *to talk*, is an example of this.

Problems arise, though, with IRREGULAR VERBS. First of all, the PAST TENSE and the PAST PARTICIPLE of irregular verbs are *not* formed by adding an ED-ending to the infinitive. Secondly, the PAST TENSE and the PAST PARTICIPLE of many irregular verbs are two completely different words. Our other model verb, *to speak*, is an example of this.

To make matters worse, there are no rules to help us determine the past tense and past participle of irregular verbs. (That, logically enough, is why they are called "irregular.") However, they do fall into groups from which we can see *spelling patterns*. These are of some help.

I. For example, there is a group of verbs whose past tense and past participle are the same as the present tense. That is, the verb undergoes *no* change. Here is a partial list of them:

Present Tense	Past Tense	Past Participle
cast	cast	cast
cost	cost	cost
cut	cut	cut
hit	hit	hit
quit	quit	quit
split	split	split
bet	bet	bet
let	let	let
set	set	set
bid	bid	bid
rid	rid	rid
shed	shed	shed
spread	spread	spread
burst	burst	burst
hurt	hurt	hurt
put	put	put

Thus, no matter what tense you wish to form, the "meaning" verb is always the same:

I <u>hit</u> my head on that shelf quite often.
I <u>hit</u> my head on it yesterday.
I <u>have hit</u> my head on it every day this week.

II. A second group of verbs has only two forms; almost like regular verbs, the PAST TENSE and the PAST PARTICIPLE are alike:

Present Tense	Past Tense	Past Participle
have	had	had
make	made	made
build	built	built
bend	bent	bent
lend	lent	lent
send	sent	sent
spend	spent	spent

For example:

Sue <u>spends</u> too much money on shoes.
Last Friday, she <u>spent</u> her whole paycheck on shoes.
She <u>had spent</u> the check before that on shoes, too.

III. Then there is a group of verbs that, again, share the same past tense and past participle form. But what makes them unique is that the past forms are constructed by changing a vowel in the present tense:

Present Tense	Past Tense	Past Participle
bleed	bled	bled
feed	fed	fed
lead	led	led
read*	read	read
speed	sped	sped
meet	met	met
win	won	won
dig	dug	dug
stick	stuck	stuck
sit	sat	sat
hold	held	held
shoot	shot	shot
hang	hung	hung
swing	swung	swung
slide	slid	slid
light	lit	lit
shine	shone	shone
bind	bound	bound
fight	fought	fought
find	found	found
wind	wound	wound

*Notice that, although *read* is spelled the same in all three parts, it is pronounced as if a vowel has been changed.

For example:

> David <u>reads</u> a book every week.
> Last week, he <u>read</u> *The Sun Also Rises* by Ernest Hemingway.
> He <u>has read</u> all of Hemingway's other novels, too.

IV. In yet another group of verbs, the past tense and past participles are alike. But this time there is the addition of a T- or D-ending as well as a vowel change:

Present Tense	Past Tense	Past Participle
feel	felt	felt
creep	crept	crept
keep	kept	kept
sleep	slept	slept
sweep	swept	swept
weep	wept	wept
tell	told	told
sell	sold	sold
lose*	lost	lost
hear*	heard	heard
mean*	meant	meant
say	said	said
flee	fled	fled
stand	stood	stood
think	thought	thought
seek	sought	sought
buy	bought	bought
bring	brought	brought
catch	caught	caught
teach	taught	taught

For example:

> I <u>stand</u> on the bus every morning.
> I <u>stood</u> all the way to work today.
> I <u>have stood</u> the whole way each morning this week.

V. As we have seen, some irregular verbs are different in all three parts:

Present Tense	Past Tense	Past Participle
is, are, am	was, were	been
go	went	gone
do	did	done

We have already seen examples of these verbs in use; here are a few more:

> I <u>go</u> to the movies at least once a week.
> I <u>went</u> to the movies last Saturday.
> I <u>have gone</u> to the movies every Saturday this month.

---

*Notice that the vowel sound changes, although its spelling does not.

VI. Some verbs are different in all three parts as a result of two separate vowel changes:

Present Tense	Past Tense	Past Participle
begin	began	begun
drink	drank	drunk
ring	rang	rung
sing	sang	sung
swim	swam	swum
come	came	come
run	ran	run

Notice that the last two of these verbs (*come* and *run*) have a past participle that is just like the present tense:

> For exercise, I <u>run</u> every afternoon.
> I <u>ran</u> yesterday for one hour.
> I <u>have run</u> in several marathons.

VII. Some verbs form the past tense by changing the vowel in the present and form the past participle by adding an N to the present:

Present Tense	Past Tense	Past Participle
arise	arose	arisen
drive	drove	driven
ride	rode	ridden
rise	rose	risen
take	took	taken
write	wrote	written
give	gave	given
shake	shook	shaken
blow	blew	blown
know	knew	known
grow	grew	grown
throw	threw	thrown
draw	drew	drawn
eat	ate	eaten
see	saw	seen

For example:

> I usually <u>take</u> the train to work.
> But yesterday I <u>took</u> the bus.
> I <u>have taken</u> the bus twice this week.

VIII. A similar group of words forms the past tense by changing the vowel in the present and forms the past participle by adding an N to the past tense:

Present Tense	Past Tense	Past Participle
bear	bore	born
tear	tore	torn
swear	swore	sworn
get	got	gotten
break	broke	broken
choose	chose	chosen
speak	spoke	spoken
steal	stole	stolen

For example:

Mandy <u>tears</u> her stockings too often.
She <u>tore</u> a pair this morning.
She <u>has torn</u> three pairs this week.

Also in this last category is an especially troublesome verb *to lie*, meaning *to recline*. It is often confused with *to lie*, meaning *to tell a falsehood*, and *to lay*, meaning *to set out* (as in "laying out a picnic blanket"). But each verb has its own distinct set of verb forms:

Present Tense	Past Tense	Past Participle
lie (to tell a falsehood)	lied	lied
lie (to recline)	lay	lain
lay (to set out)	laid	laid

The first verb, you'll notice, is REGULAR; it simply needs an ED-ending for both the past tense and the past participle. The last verb is almost regular, but instead of an ED-ending, the Y is changed to I and just a D is added. This is patterned just like the verb *to pay*:

pay   paid   paid

The difficult verb is the middle one, and there's nothing to do but memorize it. (Notice that *not one* of its parts has a *D* in it!)

EXERCISE 2

Referring to the preceding pages as little as possible, fill in the blanks in this chart. When it is complete, you will be able to use the chart as a quick reference.

Present Tense	Past Tense	Past Participle
arise		
		born
	began	
	bent	
bet		
bid		
		bound
	bled	
		blown
break		
bring		
	burst	
		bought
	cast	
catch		
		chosen
come		
cost		
	crept	
		cut
dig		
	did	
		drawn
drink		
	drove	
	ate	
		fed
feel		
fight		
	found	
		fled
		flown
forget		
get		
		given

Present Tense	Past Tense	Past Participle
	went	
grow		
hang		
	had	
		heard
	hit	
hold		
		hurt
		kept
	knew	
lay		
	led	
	lent	
		lain
	lied	
light		
		lost
make		
mean		
	met	
pay		
		put
		quit
	read	
		rid
	rode	
ring		
rise		
	ran	
say		
	saw	
		sought
		sold
		sent
	set	
	shook	
shed		

Present Tense	Past Tense	Past Participle
shine		
shoot		
	sang	
		sat
sleep		
	slid	
	spoke	
	sped	
spend		
	split	
		spread
stand		
steal		
stick		
		sworn
	swept	
swim		
swing		
	took	
		taught
		torn
tell		
throw		
	won	
	wound	
		written

EXERCISE 3

In each sentence, there is an infinitive in parentheses. On the line at the right, fill in the correct form of the verb.

1. All her life, Audrey has (to want) to become a nurse.   _____

2. As a child, she (to love) to play nurse with her dolls.   _____

3. She also (to read) all the *Cherry Ames* books.   _____

4. Whenever she went to the doctor, she (to ask) the nurse dozens of questions.   _____

5. When Audrey started college, she naturally (to major) in nursing.   _____

6. But as she studied, she realized her enthusiasm had (to change).   _____

7. Audrey's career goal was not what she thought it had (to be).   _____

8. When she finished college, she immediately (to continue) her education.   _____

9. Audrey now (to attend) medical school.   _____

10. She is (to study) to become a doctor.   _____

The Future Tense

You may have noticed that one category of tenses has not been discussed yet. All of the verbs that we've looked at so far are variations of the present tense or variations of the past tense. But what about the FUTURE TENSE?

The future tense is formed a bit differently. In English, we indicate an action that has not yet happened by using the helping verb *will*. But unlike the other helping verbs, *will* is NOT used with a participle.

Will is a special kind of helping verb called a MODAL, which is used with an infinitive to form a whole verb. To do this, take the infinitive of the verb that signifies the action:

to sing

Then, drop the *to* and replace it with the modal:

~~to~~ sing
will sing

The resulting combination verb may be used with a subject to form a complete sentence:

The soprano *will sing* the aria tonight.

The future tense, of course, gets as complicated as the past and present tenses. The future modal *will* may be used along with the other helping verbs and the participles of the verb you use for meaning. For instance, if you use *singing* (the present participle), you'll need a form of *to be* in front of it:

will (to be) singing

The use of *will* requires the infinitive without the *to*, so the correct verb form is:

will be singing.

Or, we may use the past participle *sung*, which will need a form of *to have* in front of it:

will (to have) sung

Again, the modal *will* requires an infinitive without the *to*, so the correct verb form is:

will have sung

Finally, we may use the present participle *singing* with the past participle of *to be* (*been*), which needs part of *to have* in front of it:

will (to have) been singing

And this time, too, *will* requires the infinitive without the *to*. The correct verb form is:

will have been singing

Naturally, all of these variations of the future tense may be used with a subject to form a complete sentence:

By the time the opera ends, she *will have been singing* for three hours.

Note that, like *will*, other helping verbs fall into the category of modals. The most common modals are:

can	could
may	should
might	would
must	would rather
shall	had better

When used as helping verbs, the modals alter the meaning of the main verb:

I *should type* this letter before I make any phone calls.
I *may leave* early today if my boss permits me to.

EXERCISE 4

A verb form has been omitted from each of these sentences. Following each sentence is a list of verbs, some of which will correctly fill in the blank in the sentence. Put a check next to each verb that can be correctly inserted into the sentence.

1. Tomorrow, they _____.

    work _____   tries _____   studying _____
    apologizing _____   meet _____   prepare _____
    rest _____   study _____   rested _____
    try _____   thought _____   apologize _____
    prepared _____   working _____   met _____

2. I will be _____ when you arrive.

    sleeping _____   works _____   planned _____
    study _____   typing _____   worked _____
    types _____   slept _____   writing _____
    planning _____   cooking _____   studying _____
    cooked _____   written _____   working _____

3. She will have _____ by next Sunday.

    resting _____   finished _____   try _____
    gone _____   graduating _____   recovering _____
    tried _____   goes _____   graduated _____
    learning _____   learned _____   rested _____
    recovered _____   went _____   finishes _____

4. By one o'clock, he will have been _____ for an hour.

    talking _____   studies _____   writing _____
    works _____   walking _____   typed _____
    typing _____   slept _____   studying _____
    sleeping _____   written _____   talked _____
    walked _____   working _____   trying _____

EXERCISE 5

For each of these sentences, fill in the blank with one of the modals listed on page 231. (There may be more than one possible answer for each sentence.)

1. With sufficient self-confidence and capital, you _____ start your own business.

2. Without these two crucial ingredients, you _____ be better off working for someone else.

3. A business-owner _____ be completely self-assured, about his personality as well as his goods or services.

4. A business-owner _____ also be optimistic and genuinely believe in his business's potential.

5. If you are at all hesitant about starting a business, you _____ keep your present job.

6. In addition, to start a business, you _____ have at least a year's expenses in addition to start-up costs.

7. In all likelihood, your business _____ not show a profit the first year.

8. At the beginning, a successful business _____ barely break even.

9. But you _____ not give up.

10. If your business survives its first few years, yours _____ be a true success story.

Tense Use

Up to now, we have discussed only tense FORMATION; we have said nothing about how to USE the tenses. Although there are so many tenses in English, their use is not as tricky as it may at first seem.

Essentially, VERB TENSES are used to express ideas about TIME. Tenses enable us to communicate information about things that happen in time. But, of course, tense and time are not the same thing; a verb tense won't tell us the hour of day it is or the day of the week.

Still, because tense is used to talk about time, the relationship between the tenses is temporal (that is, based on time). Therefore, it is possible to arrange the various tenses on a TIME LINE in order for us to see the differences among them. We could call the center of the line "present" and number it 0:

-3	-2	-1	0	$+1$	$+2$	$+3$
PAST			PRESENT			FUTURE

Anything to the left of 0 would be considered in the "past" and be numbered negative. Anything to the right of 0 would be considered in the "future" and be numbered positive.

First of all, let's set up a model verb for reference:

TO TALK

Future
(A) will talk
(B) will be talking
(C) will have talked
(D) will have been talking

Present
(E) talk, talks
(F) is, are, am talking
(G) has, have talked
(H) has, have been talking

Past
(I) talked
(J) was, were talking
(K) had talked
(L) had been talking

Tenses, A, E, and I are our "base" tenses; they are the SIMPLE FUTURE, the SIMPLE PRESENT, and the SIMPLE PAST. When we write an essay or letter, our main action is usually based in one of these tenses—past, present, or future. For example:

> Today, Mr. Lewis *talks* to the Rotary Club.
> Last week, he *talked* to the Town Council.
> Next week, he *will talk* to the Elks.

On a time line, the SIMPLE TENSES may be arranged this way:

	I			E			A	
−3	−2	−1	0		+1	+2	+3	
PAST			PRESENT				FUTURE	

Sometimes, though, we mention secondary actions that happen before or after our main action. That's when we have to use the more complicated tenses.

Tenses B, F, and J are called the FUTURE CONTINUOUS, the PRESENT CONTINUOUS, and the PAST CONTINUOUS. This is because using the present participle (the ING-ending) implies that the action happened over a stretch of time. The continuous tenses refer to the same time as the simple tenses, but the action of a continuous tense goes on longer. For example:

> Today, Mr. Lewis *talks* to the Rotary Club.
> He *is talking* about the problem of local pollution.
>
> Next week, he *will talk* to the Elks.
> He *will be talking* about another public issue.

On the time line, the CONTINUOUS TENSES may be indicated with arrows:

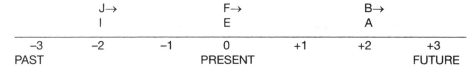

Tenses C, G, and K are called the FUTURE PERFECT, the PRESENT PERFECT, and the PAST PERFECT. They all use the helping verb *to have* plus a past participle. The PERFECT TENSES are used for actions that don't coincide in time with the main action in the SIMPLE or CONTINUOUS TENSES.

For example, Tense K is used for actions that happened even *more in the past* than Tense I:

> Last week, Mr. Lewis *talked* to the Town Council.
> The week before, he *had talked* to the mayor about his speech.

Therefore, on the time line, Tense K would be to the left of Tense I.

Similarly, Tense G is used for actions that happened sometime *between* the simple past and the simple present.

> Last week, Mr. Lewis *talked* to the Town Council.
> Since then, he *has talked* privately to several council members.
> Today, he *talks* to the Rotary Club.

Therefore, on the time line, Tense G would go between Tense I and Tense E.

Finally, Tense C is used for actions that will happen between the present and some time in the future:

Mr. Lewis *will talk* to the Elks next week.
Before then, he *will have talked* to the mayor again.

On the time line, Tense C should go between Tense E and Tense A. Our time line should now look like this:

	J→		F→		B→	
K	I	G	E	C	A	

-3	-2	-1	0	+1	+2	+3
PAST			PRESENT			FUTURE

The last tenses, Tenses D, H, and L, are called the FUTURE PERFECT CONTINUOUS, the PRESENT PERFECT CONTINUOUS, and the PAST PERFECT CONTINUOUS. And, as you may have guessed, they are used to express actions that happen at approximately the same time as the perfect tenses (Tenses C, G, and K), but they continue for a longer period.

For example, Tense L is used for actions that happen more in the past than Tense I and that continue longer than Tense K:

Last week, Mr. Lewis *talked* to the Town Council.

He *had been talking* individually to different council members the week before.

Tense H is used for actions that happen between the simple past and the simple present but that continue longer than Tense G:

Today, he *talks* to the Rotary Club.
He *has been talking* about his speech for days.

Lastly, Tense D is used for actions that will happen between the present and some point in the future but will continue longer than Tense C:

He *will talk* to the Elks next week.
By then, he *will have been talking* to local organizations over a month.

Therefore, on the time line, Tenses D, H, and L coincide with Tenses C, G, and K but are indicated with arrows:

L→	J→	H→	F→	D→	B→	
K	I	G	E	C	A	

-3	-2	-1	0	+1	+2	+3
PAST			PRESENT			FUTURE

What the time line and the preceding examples suggest is that the tenses are used in combinations with each other. That is, the perfect tenses are usually used when the simple tenses have already been assigned to an action at a different time. Some examples may make this more clear:

Past + Past Perfect
She *went* to lunch after she *had finished* the filing.
(The action that occurred first is *more in the past*.)

Present + Present Perfect
She *is* a stenographer now, but she *has held* many jobs since graduating
from high school.
(Between the present and some point in the past, a third action took place.)

Future + Future Perfect
He *will have caught* up on all his work before he *leaves* on vacation.
(Neither action has occurred yet, but one will happen first.)

> **Note:** In the last example, note the use of the simple present
> (*leaves*) to express an idea in the simple future. This phenom-
> enon in English is exemplified also by the use of *to be going
> to* (the present continuous tense):

I <u>am going</u> <u>to answer</u> the mail this afternoon.

The perfect continuous tenses are used in similar combinations to the
perfect tenses:

Past Perfect Continuous
She *had been waiting* for an hour before I *noticed* her.

Present Perfect Continuous
She *started* to wait at noon. It *is* now one o'clock.
She *has been waiting* for an hour.

Future Perfect Continuous
She *will have been waiting* for two hours by 2 P.M.

EXERCISE 6

The following pairs of sentences are almost the same; only the tenses are different. The
questions test your ability to interpret the meanings of the different tenses. Be prepared to
explain your answers.

1. Eileen will take the subway to school today.
   Sylvia took the subway to school today.
   Who is already sitting in class? _____

2. Mrs. Hartman washed her kitchen floor.
   Mrs. Ortiz has washed her kitchen floor.
   Whose floor is more likely to still be wet? _____

3. May spends her weekly paycheck on new shoes.
   June spent her weekly paycheck on new shoes.
   Who has purchased more pairs of shoes? _____

4. Sue was late for work every day.
   Max is late for work every day.
   Who is more likely to get fired? _____

5. Amy had the flu when Easter vacation started.
   Dan had had the flu when Easter vacation started.
   Who was sick during vacation? _____

6. Ann decided she didn't like her new supervisor when she met him.
   Rose had decided she didn't like her new supervisor when she
   met him.
   Who made up her mind because of what the man was really like?
   _____

7. Henry will have reached the restaurant when we get there.
   Norma will reach the restaurant when we get there.
   Who will reach the restaurant first, Henry or Norma? _____

8. Lois will be getting dressed when her date arrives.
   Judy will have gotten dressed when her date arrives.
   Who will be ready when her date arrives? _____

9. Mr. Toshiro has been president for five years.
   Mr. Svensen was president for five years.
   Who is now the company's president? _____

10. Lisa has been talking on the phone for hours.
    Steve talks on the phone for hours.
    Who makes a regular practice of talking on the phone for hours?
    _____

EXERCISE 7

These sentences are written in the present tense. First, underline the verb in each sentence. Then rewrite the sentence in the past tense. (You may have to change more than the verb.)

EXAMPLE:

I <u>have to type</u> too many letters this week.
I had to type too many letters last week.

1. Foreign investors in China have many opportunities.
   _____
   _____

2. Bureaucratic delays frequently snarl their investments.
   _____
   _____

3. The recent death of Deng Xiao Ping threatens future instability.
   _____
   _____

4. American trade sanctions also jeopardize investments.
   _____
   _____

5. American companies fear negative publicity.
   _____
   _____

6. They do not wish to be seen as profiting from Chinese repression.
   _____
   _____

7. Still, many foreign companies consider China an attractive market.
   _____
   _____

8. China has a large literate workforce willing to work for low wages.

_____

_____

9. China's domestic market offers a huge pool of consumers.

_____

_____

10. Underlying this investment boom is China's renewed rapid economic growth.

_____

_____

Passive Voice

In addition to TENSE, verbs in English also have what is known as VOICE. Voice can be either ACTIVE or PASSIVE.

In most of the sentences we have seen so far, the verbs have been ACTIVE. That is, the subjects have been *doing* the action expressed by the verbs. In our old example:

Sam sees the tree.

the subject *Sam* is doing the action of seeing. The object *tree* is what he sees.

In a sentence with a passive verb, the subject does NOT do the action. Rather, the subject *receives* the action, which is done by a different noun. The passive version of our example looks like this:

The tree is seen by Sam.

In this sentence, the verb is *is seen*; the subject is *the tree*. However, the subject is not doing anything. (Obviously, trees can't see!) Another noun (*Sam*) is doing the action, and the tree is being acted upon.

The subject of an ACTIVE VERB *acts. The subject of a* PASSIVE VERB *does not act.*

A passive verb always consists of a form of the verb *to be* followed by a past participle. Therefore, a passive verb can have as many tenses as an active verb; this is indicated by using the appropriate tense of *to be*.

ACTIVE	PASSIVE
He will see	He *will be* seen
He will be seeing	(He *will be being* seen)
He will have seen	He *will have been* seen
He will have been seeing	(He *will have been being* seen)
He sees	He *is* seen
He is seeing	He *is being* seen
He has seen	He *has been* seen
He has been seeing	(He *has been being* seen)
He saw	He *was* seen
He was seeing	He *was being* seen
He had seen	He *had been* seen
He had been seeing	(He *had been being* seen)

> **Note:** The passive verbs in parentheses are rarely used because the meaning is so confusing. For example, instead of saying:
>   He will be being seen by us.
> it is much more clear to use the active voice:
>   We will be seeing him.

To change a sentence from ACTIVE VOICE to PASSIVE VOICE involves four steps.

   Mrs. Miller hired Richard.

First, the object of the active sentence becomes the subject of the passive sentence:

   Richard _____ _____

Secondly, the subject of the active sentence becomes the AGENT (or the *doer*) of the passive sentence. Note that the agent is preceded by the word *by*:

   Richard _____ by Mrs. Miller.

Thirdly, the verb *to be* is put into the tense of the active verb. (In this case, *hired* is in the simple past tense.)

   Richard was _____ by Mrs. Miller.

Finally, the past participle of the active verb is inserted after the form of *to be*:

   Richard was hired by Mrs. Miller.

EXERCISE 8

Change each sentence from active voice to passive voice. (Be sure that you use the right tense!)

1. Allbright Enterprises ordered a new copier on Tuesday.

   _____

   _____

2. The Allied Truck Company delivered it on Thursday.

   _____

   _____

3. The manufacturer immediately sent the bill.

   _____

   _____

4. Allbright received the bill on Friday.

   _____

   _____

5. They paid it promptly.

   _____

   _____

6. However, a secretary discovered a malfunction in the machine on Monday.

_____

_____

7. Paper was jamming the mechanism.

_____

_____

8. Allbright considered stopping payment on their check.

_____

_____

9. But the manufacturer guarantees its merchandise.

_____

_____

10. They repaired the copier Tuesday afternoon.

_____

_____

To convert a sentence from PASSIVE VOICE to ACTIVE VOICE, simply reverse the process.

   Mrs. Miller was thanked by Richard.

First, the agent of the passive sentence becomes the subject of the active sentence. (Remember to eliminate the *by*.)

   Richard _____ _____

Next, the subject of the passive sentence becomes the object of the active sentence:

   Richard _____ Mrs. Miller.

Finally, the past participle of the passive sentence is put into the tense of the *to be* verb, which is not used in the active sentence. (Here, *was* is simple past.)

   Richard thanked Mrs. Miller.

EXERCISE 9

Change each sentence from passive voice to active voice, being careful to use the right tense.

1. That porch was constructed by Harold Dawson.

_____

_____

2. He was contracted by Emma Hobbs to build it.

_____

_____

3. Mr. Dawson had been taught carpentry by his father.

_____

_____

4. So the porch was expertly crafted by him.

_____

_____

5. The floorboards were evenly laid by him.

_____

_____

6. The railings were hand-notched by him.

_____

_____

7. Even the molding was hand-carved by him.

_____

_____

8. Mrs. Hobbs was pleased by his final product.

_____

_____

9. He was paid handsomely by her.

_____

_____

10. The work of a fine craftsperson cannot be matched by a machine.

_____

_____

It is important to be able to convert from PASSIVE VOICE to ACTIVE VOICE (and vice versa) because, in business writing especially, the active voice is often more effective. It is more direct and emphatic than the passive voice.

For example, when writing a collection letter, one might say:

Your bill *has not been paid* in over 90 days.

But an active version of this sentence would be stronger.

You *have not paid* your bill in over 90 days.

Putting the verb in the active voice means that the subject is acting. In this case, the emphasis is therefore placed on the person who owes the money. The recipient of the letter (*you*) is made responsible for paying the bill.

On the other hand, sometimes receivers of the action may be more important than the doer. In these cases, the passive voice would be effective. Consider these two examples from a claims letter:

ACTIVE: You made an error on invoice 7625
PASSIVE: An error was made on invoice 7625.

The first sentence is *accusatory*; it places blame for the error directly upon the recipient of the letter. However, in a situation like this, rectifying the error is more important than knowing who committed it. Therefore, the second sentence may be more effective because the recipient would not be placed in a defensive position.

The choice to use passive voice rather than active voice, clearly, depends upon the circumstances. Business judgment and a bit of insight into human psychology can help.

EXERCISE 10

Find the verbs in this letter and decide whether they are active or passive. Then, on another sheet of paper rewrite the letter, changing the voice wherever you feel a change would make the letter more effective.

Dear Mrs. Franklin:

Your credit reputation is in danger!

The balance of $319.19 on your account has not been paid. It is now ninety days past due.

Two statements and three letters regarding your balance have been sent to you by us. Yet they have been ignored.

We know that you have been a reliable customer for many years although your bills have been paid slowly on occasion. This time, however, your payment is much later than usual.

Please do not force your account to be closed by us or this matter to be turned over to our attorneys. Send us your check for $319.19 today.

Sincerely yours,

REVIEW EXERCISES

A. In each of these sentences, there is an infinitive in parentheses. Change the infinitive to the appropriate verb form and write your answer in the space provided.

1. Employment opportunities for health-care professionals are (to expect) to increase dramatically over the next decade. __________
2. For this reason, many people have (to pursue) careers as paraprofessionals in the health-care field. __________
3. These people participate in life-and-death situations, for which they are (to pay) well. __________
4. Some have (to become) emergency medical technicians. __________
5. These people are the ambulance staff who, if (to train) as paramedics, can administer first-line treatment. __________
6. Other paraprofessionals (to work) as cardiopulmonary technicians. __________
7. In high demand, these people conduct and monitor the various tests (to perform) on patients' hearts and lungs. __________
8. A third paraprofessional, the respiratory therapist, works with patients whose breathing has been (to obstruct). __________

9. Special training is (to require) of all three types of health-care para-professionals. _____

10. Such organizations as the National Association of Emergency Medical Technicians, the National Society for Cardiopulmonary Technology, and the American Association for Respiratory Therapy can (to provide) additional information on training and career opportunities._____

B. In the space provided, supply the correct verb form of the infinitives in parentheses.

1. Nydia has always (to want) to be a gym teacher. _____

2. As a child, she had (to be) very athletic. _____

3. She (to learn) how to swim before she was four years old. _____

4. In high school, she (to serve) as captain of the girls' basketball team. _____

5. She has always (to take) sports, as well as her own physical fitness, very seriously. _____

6. When she was on a team, she (to train) hard every day. _____

7. While growing up, she was (to advise) to become a teacher. _____

8. Physical Education (to seem) to be the only choice for an athletic young woman's career in those days. _____

9. So, in college, she (to combine) sports with education courses. _____

10. While playing basketball, she was also (to prepare) to take the teachers' licensing examination in her state. _____

11. In her senior year, she (to begin) to send her resume to high schools in her home town. _____

12. One day, however, a scout from the New York Stars (to arrive) at Nydia's campus. _____

13. The New York Stars (to be) a women's professional basketball team. _____

14. After watching Nydia play, the scout (to offer) her a contract with the team. _____

15. Nydia realized that, since her childhood, the world of professional athletics had (to begin) to open up to women. _____

C. 1. This paragraph is in the present tense. In the space provided, rewrite it in the past tense, changing the verbs and any other necessary words.

Example:

I want to go home early today.
I wanted to go home early yesterday.

Justin wants to become an airlines reservation agent. He enjoys working with the public, and he has the necessary qualifications. He is a high school graduate, speaks two foreign languages, types fifty-five words per minute, and has worked with computers. He has been a salesperson for the past two years, which is also helpful. Most importantly, he relates well to people.

_____

_____

_____

_____

_____

_____

_____

_____

_____

_____

_____

2. This paragraph is in the past tense. In the space provided, rewrite it in the present tense, changing the verbs and any other necessary words.

Example:

I felt confident about the interview yesterday afternoon.
I feel confident about the interview this afternoon.

Alicia was a flight attendant, a job that involved serving others. Her position required patience and tact since she dealt with potentially irritable passengers. She had to keep passengers calm as well as serve them food and beverages. She not only catered to their needs, but also maintained their safety. Because she performed her duties well and was often complimented by passengers, she has been promoted to Supervisor of Flight Training.

_____

_____

_____

_____

_____

_____

_____

_____

_____

_____

_____

3. This paragraph is in the past tense although many of the verbs are in the past perfect tense. To change the meaning of the paragraph to the present tense, shift all the verbs and write your new version in the space provided.

Example:

Keisha had dropped out of college but then decided to return to school.
Keisha dropped out of college but now has decided to return to school.

Donna had entered corporate management immediately after finishing college. She had started as a product manager and moved up to assistant vice president for finance. Then she wanted to open her own business. She was considering cosmetics, a traditionally "women's field," but she preferred to invest in a "mainstream" industry. So she investigated computer software. She found the field attractive and so was planning to quit her job in the near future.

_____

_____

_____

_____

_____

_____

_____

_____

_____

D. Proofread this letter for errors in verb forms. Then correct all the errors.

Dear Mr. Temple:

It is my great honor to informed you that you have been name Employee of the Month by the administrators of the Union Bank of Freeport.

Words cannot expressed our deep appreciation of your valiant behavior during the holdup on April 22. We feel strongly that your fast thinking and good judgment save the lives of your fellow employees as well as our customers, not to mention the thousands of dollars that would have been losted had the robbers escape.

In recognition of your heroism and the stress it must have create for you, we would like you to spent, as our guest, a weekend of your choice at Todman's Mountain Resort. In addition, we will be please to present you with a plaque commemorating the occasion at the staff luncheon to be helded on Friday, May 10, at 1 P.M.

Thank you, Mr. Temple. You're a very special man.

Sincerely yours,

E. This news release contains a number of errors in verb forms. Find and correct the errors.

<u>For Immediate Release</u>   July 16, [*year*]

FIRST NATIONAL BANK SPONSORS SENIORS
EMPLOYMENT PROGRAM

Anso, California. July 16, [*year*]. The First National Bank of Anso has announce plans to sponsor an employment program for local senior citizens. The program is schedule to begin August 1, according to Mr. Robert Delaney, bank manager.

Many senior citizens, including retire persons with many years of work experience, have trouble matching their skills to the current job market. Mr. Delaney explain: "Job descriptions change along with the times. We intend to help senior citizens rethink what they can do and convinced local employers they can do it."

Interviews with local companies are been schedule for the first two weeks of August. Any Anso senior seeking full- or part-time employment is urge to register at one of the bank's five branches. Applicants need not be experience but must be 60 years or older.

Local employers interest in hiring an Anso senior should call Mr. Delaney at 292-3334.

18.
Mechanics

Punctuation

Although we haven't focused on punctuation directly, you have already learned a great deal about it, for many of the rules of punctuation are closely related to the principles of sentence structure. You should therefore be familiar with the use of periods and semicolons, for example, and with some of the uses of commas.

This chapter will look more closely at the various marks of punctuation. As you study their uses, you should keep in mind the principles of grammar and sentence structure that you have already mastered.

The Period

The two major uses of the period are to mark the end of a sentence and to indicate an abbreviation.

When you proofread your work for sentence completeness, be sure to mark the end of each sentence with a period:

> Lorna has gone on vacation.
> I will miss her help while she is gone.

Indirect questions (see Chapter 15) should also be ended with a period:

> Before she left, she asked me if I would water her plants.
> I asked her if she would send me a postcard.

Other types of sentences that should be ended with a period are *commands:*

> Please type this letter for me.
> Answer the phone.

and requests phrased as questions:

> Would you please type this letter as soon as possible.
> May we have your response by the end of the week.

Most abbreviations (see page 268) require the use of periods:

Mr.	Co.
Ms.	Inc.
Mrs.	Corp.

Nowadays, however, periods are often omitted in the abbreviation of organizational names:

ITT   FBI
IBM   CIA
UAW   NATO
AFL-CIO   OPEC

Also, you should be careful not to confuse *abbreviations,* such as the above, with *contractions* (see Apostrophes, page 248). A contraction, which is a combined form of more than one word, requires an apostrophe to indicate the omitted letters (for example, *don't* for *do not*).

One other use for the period is called an ELLIPSIS, which consists of three spaced periods (. . .). An ellipsis is used within a quotation to indicate an omitted word or words.

President Ohashi began his address to the Board of Directors by saying, "The age of the personal computer has just begun. This company got started two years ago with just a quarter of a million dollars and 10,000 sales. Now, despite the birth of several competitors, our market is expanding phenomenally. Next year, we expect to sell 500,000 computers."

President Ohashi began his address to the Board of Directors by saying, "The age of the personal computer has just begun. . . . Next year, we expect to sell 500,000 computers."

If you restrict your use of periods to the situations just explained, you will not run into trouble. However, there are specific occasions when a period should NOT be used although you may be tempted:

- DO NOT use a period after a heading or a title.

    Chapter One: Recognizing Verbs and Subjects

- DO NOT use a period after a sentence ending in a punctuated abbreviation.

    Our guest speaker this evening is Marcus More, Ph.D.

- DO NOT use a period when the numbers or letters of a list have been enclosed in parentheses.

    The following factors will be considered: (a) attendance, (b) punctuality, and (c) performance.

    But

    The following factors will be considered:
    1. Attendance
    2. Punctuality
    3. Performance

- DO NOT use periods (or zeros) after even amounts of dollars.

    Your check for $40 has been received.
    Your check for $40.58 has been received.

- DO NOT use a period after a Roman numeral that is part of a name.

    Elizabeth II has been Queen of England since 1952.

The Exclamation Point

An exclamation point, instead of a period, is used at the end of a sentence in order to indicate emphasis or strong emotion:

Stop interrupting me!
Unauthorized personnel are not to be admitted!

In addition, an exclamation point should be used after an *interjection,* a word or phrase inserted into a sentence to indicate emphasis or surprise:

Boy! Was I angry.
Stop! Do not read any further.

The Question Mark

The question mark is used after direct questions:

Will my order be ready by Tuesday?
Have you checked your records?

Similarly, when a question is being directly quoted, the sentence may contain a question mark:

"Do you mind if I smoke?" asked the interviewer.
He then asked, "How old are you?"

Note: Question marks and exclamation points should never be followed by a period or comma.

EXERCISE 1

Terminal punctuation has been omitted from these sentences. For each, decide whether a period, exclamation point, or question mark is needed and indicate your choice in the space provided.

1. Have you any idea what it takes to become a physician ___
2. The ordeal is almost beyond belief ___
3. The work actually begins in high school, where one must work hard to qualify for a top-notch college ___
4. Once in college, the pressure really mounts ___
5. Do you think a student with less than straight As will be accepted by a medical school ___
6. Coursework in medical school demands rigorous study and the suppression of any social life ___
7. Have you heard enough ___
8. Just wait until you're an intern ___
9. You'll learn, at this stage, how to function without sleep ___
10. But after these fifteen years, from high school through your residency, you'll have the satisfaction of being called "doctor" for the rest of your life ___

Proofread this letter for errors in punctuation. Then on another sheet of paper, rewrite the letter, making all necessary corrections.

Dear Advertiser:

In response to your request, you will find enclosed our latest <u>Secretary's World</u> media kit. This kit contains all the materials you'll need to determine the appropriateness of <u>Secretary's World</u> to your product!

In addition to a rate card and a sample copy of our magazine. We have enclosed an editorial calendar that outlines upcoming articles and a readership profile which is based on a nationwide readership survey.

I hope the information contained in our media kit proves useful to you, should you decide to include <u>Secretary's World</u> in your advertising campaign, we would like to know if you'd be interested in our special money-saving rates? Our advertising sales representatives are available to help you set up the most cost-productive package for your needs.

Don't delay, call to reserve space now.

Sincerely,

The Semicolon

A semicolon may be used to join two closely related sentences:

> Sam sees the tree. Willy hears the birds.
> Sam sees the tree; Willy hears the birds.
>
> I will arrange a guest speaker. Arlene will take care of refreshments.
> I will arrange a guest speaker; Arlene will take care of refreshments.

This is the reason that a semicolon often appears before such words of transition as *however* and *therefore:*

> We have sent you three bills and two statements; however, we have not received your payment.
>
> I received your bill for consultant services performed in April; therefore, I am enclosing a check for $940.

Remember: The test for correct semicolon use is to see whether a period would be grammatically correct in its place. If not, the semicolon has been misused.

The Colon

Colons are used after formal introductory statements. They alert the reader to what follows. Some of the main uses of colons follow.

- Use a colon before *a formal list:*

    When evaluating a credit application, consider the following: credit history, employment history, and current assets.

- Use a colon before *an explanation:*

    A letter refusing credit should be positive: you hope to continue business on a cash basis.

- Use a colon before *a formal quotation:*

    Secretary's World reports: "Secretaries are members of the fastest-growing occupational group (annual average job openings are now 300,000 and expected to expand to 325,000)."

Colons are also used in these situations:

1. After the salutation in a business letter

    Dear Sir:
    Gentlemen:

2. Between a title and a subtitle

    Word Processing: An Introduction

3. Between the hour and minute of a time reference

    9:10 A.M.
    11:15 P.M.

EXERCISE 3

Punctuate each sentence by inserting a semicolon or a colon.

1. My day begins at 6 45 A.M.
2. It takes me approximately forty-five minutes to shower, dress, and have breakfast then I rush to catch the 7:45 bus.
3. I occupy myself during the bus ride in a number of ways reading a newspaper, writing a letter, or just getting a bit of extra sleep.
4. When I arrive at the office, I perform a daily routine I buy coffee and a donut and have a second breakfast at my desk.
5. I'm always ready to get started by nine o'clock that's when my boss arrives.
6. Every day, he greets me with the same remark "Ready to get this show on the road?"
7. My first task is to open all the mail this is usually interrupted by the arrival of our first appointment.
8. Some mail requires an immediate response I take care of this before I do anything else.
9. Next I do the previous day's billing I try to get this done in time for the morning mail.
10. Before long, the best time of the morning arrives my coffee break!

The Comma

Commas are used to indicate a pause. Their use is determined by sentence structure and meaning.

Two of our basic sentence patterns (see Chapter 14) required commas:

S V, ⬚coordinator⬚ S V.
Sam speaks, and Willy listens.

The second basic sentence pattern looked like this:

⬚Subordinator⬚ S V, S V.
When Sam speaks, Willy listens.

> **Note:** Be careful *not* to use a comma when a coordinator is connecting two verbs—
> S V and V.
> Sam speaks and listens.
> Basically, the rule is this: A SUBJECT SHOULD NEVER BE SEPARATED FROM ITS VERB WITH A SINGLE COMMA.

> **Remember:** When the subordinator is in the *middle,* there is usually *no* comma—

S V ⬚subordinator⬚ S V.
Sam speaks as Willy listens.

A comma may also be used after an introductory expression, such as a word of transition (see page 174).

Indeed, Sam likes to dominate a conversation.
Nevertheless, Willy doesn't understand much of what he says.

Introductory *phrases* fall into this category, too.

In general, Sam makes little sense.
Trying to sound important, he tends to make a fool of himself.

A third use of commas is to separate items in a series or list.

Latasha has studied marketing, salesmanship, and advertising.
Your report must be either in the files, on my desk, or among my other mail.
To look your best, feel your best, and be your best require a personal program of sound diet and strenuous exercise.

Note that a comma precedes the coordinator at the end of the list. However, commas should NOT be used if a coordinator appears before each item:

I am tired and hungry and annoyed.

A special case arises when adjectives are listed before a noun:

All-City Video employs courteous, knowledgeable, helpful salespeople.
They offer the lowest retail prices in town.

A comma is needed if it would be correct to insert *and* between the adjectives (as in the first example). But if *and* cannot be inserted, then do NOT use a comma (as in the second example).

EXERCISE 4

In each of these sentences, insert commas where appropriate. (More than one may be needed per sentence.)

1. When Lydia got a job as assistant to a civil engineer she knew very little about the field.
2. Like most people she knew that civil engineers design and build such structures as bridges dams and highways.
3. After getting the job Lydia researched the field further.
4. She found that some civil engineers specialize in earthquake construction and she learned that nuclear waste disposal is another area of specialization.
5. However Lydia's new firm is involved in municipal improvement.
6. The company is at work on street improvement water quality and bridge construction projects.
7. Lydia's new boss is currently overseeing the construction of a subway system so she frequently must deal with public officials.
8. Lydia finds her work very exciting and her boss is pleased with her performance.
9. In fact she has offered to send Lydia to school to take courses in business management accounting and economics.
10. Confident about her future Lydia hopes to move up quickly with the firm.

Finally, commas should be used to set off an "interrupting" expression in a sentence. These expressions are not essential to the structure or meaning of the sentence and are therefore separated from the rest. Interrupters fall into several categories:

1. Contrasted Elements

The chairman of the board, not the stockholders, made the decision.
I returned to school to improve my typing, not my English.

> **Note:** When the interrupter appears in the middle of the sentence, it is both preceded *and* followed by a comma. An interrupter at the end (or beginning) of a sentence requires only one comma to separate it from the rest.

2. Parenthetical Expressions

The affidavit, I think, is ready to be typed.

I think can be removed from the sentence without altering the meaning, so it is set off with commas.

It is, in fact, a convincing legal document.

Similarly, *in fact* can be eliminated without changing the meaning of the sentence.

3. Appositives

The president of this company, Rafa al-Habobi, started out as a sales trainee.

The president of this company and *Rafa al-Habobi* are one and the same person, so the name is set off with commas.

A woman of humble origins, Mrs. Figueroa is now the owner of a large retail chain.

A woman of humble origins is just a way of describing Mrs. Figueroa, so the description is separated from the name with a comma.

4. Explanatory Expressions

Linda Porter, M.D., performed the surgery.

Degrees and titles that follow a person's name are set off with commas.

Batale Lusangu now works for Jericho Steel, Inc.

The abbreviations *Inc.* and *Ltd.* are set off from the corporate name with commas.

Brooklyn, New York, was the original home of the Dodgers.

The state is separated from the city by commas.

Nanette graduated from high school in June, 1990, and began her first job on July 2, 1990.

The year is set off from the month or the day by commas. Although it is acceptable to omit the commas when only the month and year are referred to, be careful *not* to use a single comma. In such situations, either two commas or no commas are correct, but one comma is ALWAYS wrong.

The punctuation of numbers poses a special problem. As we have seen, the year is set off from the month or day. You probably are also aware that commas are used to separate thousands, hundred thousands, billions, etc., in figures of four or more digits: $2,642,921.

However, some numbers DO NOT take commas:

1. Street numbers and ZIP codes

   1129 Maple Street, Smithtown, Ohio 93011

2. Telephone numbers

   (914) 830-9612

3. Decimals

   49.113207

4. Serial or account numbers

   621 Z78 97

5. Weights and measures

   7 pounds 7 ounces

EXERCISE 5

Supply commas wherever needed in these sentences.

1. World Transport Ltd. is located at 241 West Decatur Street Rockville Maine 31229.
2. The company founded in 1949 is owned and operated by Diana Forman.
3. Ms. Forman a graduate of the Harvard Business School was one of the first women in the field of interstate trucking.
4. In August 1962 she hired her first female driver.
5. This woman one would imagine had to overcome strong resentment from her male peers.
6. Today Ms. Forman employs over 1200 women many of whom are truck drivers.
7. According to Ms. Forman it is the success of the female drivers not her own achievement that has contributed the most to women's progress.
8. Acceptance of women on the road she believes has contributed to the growth of women's opportunities in the rest of society.
9. World Transport of course employs many men too.
10. But it is the women not the men who are currently making the headlines.

The distinction between RESTRICTIVE and NONRESTRICTIVE expressions is confusing to many writers. A *restrictive* expression is essential to the meaning of the sentence; think of restrictive as meaning "making specific":

> Students *who are bilingual* should have no trouble finding a job.

Here the italicized words are crucial; not all students, but only those "who are bilingual" should have no trouble finding a job.

On the other hand, a *nonrestrictive* expression is NOT essential to the meaning of the sentence; think of nonrestrictive as simply "adding information" rather than "making specific."

> My mother, *who is bilingual,* should have no trouble finding a job.

Here the italicized words are *not* crucial. Since "I" can have only one mother, knowing that she is bilingual doesn't help us identify her; it simply tells us more about her.

Consider these additional examples:

> Mr. Brown's brother John works for the government; his brother Arthur is in private industry.

Since Mr. Brown has more than one brother, their names are *restrictive;* they tell us which brother is which, and so we use *no* commas.

> Mr. Brown's wife, Susan, is an attorney.

Mr. Brown, of course, can have only one wife, so her name is *nonrestrictive.* Therefore, we set *Susan* off with commas.

Some of these sentences require commas to set off nonrestrictive expressions. Insert any missing comma and mark those sentences that need no comma with a check in the space provided.

1. People who strive for professional success occasionally entertain business contacts. ____
2. Mr. Chu who strives for professional success must occasionally entertain business contacts. ____
3. Business discussions that begin over lunch may frequently result in a signed contract. ____
4. In his discussion with Mr. Alvarez which began over lunch Mr. Chu settled a major deal. ____
5. Mr. Chu's client Ms. Murphy was delighted with his success. ____
6. Mr. Chu confident of his social manner enjoys taking clients to dinner. ____
7. Businesspersons confident of their social manner enjoy taking clients to dinner. ____
8. Even breakfast which is usually overlooked can be a fruitful occasion for a business chat. ____
9. Mr. Chu has an appointment for breakfast tomorrow. ____
10. Another contract which he anticipates signing will be an enormous boost to his career. ____

The Apostrophe

The apostrophe is used in three ways.

First, it is used to indicate the possessive form of nouns and indefinite pronouns.

> The briefcase owned by Martin—Martin's briefcase
> The fault of nobody—nobody's fault
> The property owned by the company—the company's property

In each of the preceding examples, the noun being made possessive is singular and does not end in S. So the possessive form takes 's at the end.

If a singular noun already ends in S, however, there are two possibilities. If the noun has only one syllable, add 's:

> The telephone number of Bess—Bess's telephone number
> The job of my boss—my boss's job

If the singular noun has more than one syllable, add only an apostrophe:

> The disciples of Jesus—Jesus' disciples

But, if the pronunciation of the possessive gives the word an extra syllable, add 's:

> The fatigue of the waitress—the waitress's fatigue
> The car owned by Louis—Louis's car

Plural nouns may also be made possessive. If a plural noun already ends in S, form the possessive by adding only an apostrophe:

The benefits of the workers—the workers' benefits
But
The rights of women—women's rights

A confusing point of possession arises with hyphenated nouns:

The editor-in-chief's office
my father-in-law's business

Note that possession is indicated by the last word only. This is also the case for nouns in joint possession:

Ray and Sally's friend
Tom and Rita's store

If separate possession is intended, both nouns must get an *'s* ending:

Al's and Lucy's answers

EXERCISE 7

Using a possessive noun, rewrite each of these.

EXAMPLE:
the orders from my boss
my boss's orders

1. the guess of anybody

2. the responsibility of Rosemary

3. the weapons of the policemen

4. the roles of the actresses

5. the dog owned by Gus

6. the cat owned by Iris

7. the transmission of the cars

8. the tires of the bus

9. the partnership between Alex and Sid

10. the reaction of the passerby

The second use of apostrophes is with CONTRACTIONS. Contractions are shortened forms of words. The apostrophe goes where the omitted letters or numbers would be.

I would	I'd
can not	can't
they are	they're
1929	'29
because	'cause

The apostrophe is also used to form special plurals.

1. Lowercase letters

   The w's on this typewriter come out looking like u's.

2. Abbreviations ending with periods

   All the M.D.'s in the theater offered their help.

However, though acceptable, no apostrophe is needed to form these plurals:

1. Capital letters

   I recognized your briefcase by the two Rs in the monogram.

2. Abbreviations that are capitalized and unpunctuated

   Many MIAs from the Vietnam era are still unaccounted for.

Of course, an apostrophe should be used in the two above cases when it is needed to avoid misreading:

   The A's in the letterhead should all be capitalized.

Also, numbers referred to as numbers and words referred to as words similarly take an apostrophe in their plural only when needed for clarity:

   During the first round at poker, I had two 10s and two 9s but couldn't draw a third of either.

   I tend to abbreviate all my *ands.*
But
   In the new shipment of towels, the *his*'s are all blue, but the *hers*'s are turquoise.

EXERCISE 8

By inserting apostrophes where needed, correct these sentences. If a sentence is correct, put a check in the space provided.

1. This companys collection rate is rather high. ___
2. Many of our bills are c.o.d.s. ___
3. Some of our charge accounts havent been paid, however. ___
4. The M.D.s tend to be especially slow. ___
5. Dr. Adlers account, for instance, is now 90 days past due. ___
6. Weve sent him several statements. ___
7. Dr. Moses payments are also behind. ___
8. But she has been our customer since the early 1970s. ___
9. Sometimes I get tired of typing all those *please remits.* ___
10. But its worth it when the checks come in. ___

Quotation Marks

Quotation marks enclose the exact words from either someone's writing or someone's speech. They are always used in pairs.

> In an article on credit, financial advisor Jane Freund wrote: "Establishing credit before you need it is an intelligent precaution."

A quote within a quote is enclosed in single *quotation* marks:

> Freund noted: "We all have at least one friend who brags, 'I never buy anything on credit.' But that person is establishing no credit history, a hedge against the day he may need credit."

Notice that the speaker and the verb of saying (<u>Jane Freund</u> <u>wrote</u>, for example) are always *outside* the quotation marks.

> DO NOT FORGET TO CLOSE A QUOTATION WITH THE SECOND QUOTATION MARK.

Quotation marks are also used to enclose certain titles: short stories, essays, articles, poems, and chapters. Titles of full-length works (such as books, magazines, newspapers, plays, movies, and television shows) are usually underlined (to indicate italics).

> I found the article "How to Ask for a Raise," in the August issue of <u>Secretary's World</u>, very interesting.

Note that italics (or underlining) are also used for names of ships, aircraft, spacecraft, and trains; titles of works of art; and foreign words.

> The launching of *Apollo VII* was spectacular.
> The *Mona Lisa* has captured men's imaginations for centuries.
> As we parted, he waved and bid me *adieu*.

A third, but often misused, use of quotation marks is to enclose words used in a special sense:

> "Insolvent" means "unable to pay debts."
> The accountant suggested that we "amortize" our expenditures, that is, write them off by prorating them over a fixed period.

EXERCISE 9

In these sentences, insert quotation marks wherever needed. Be sure also to capitalize where required.

1. Julia Lantigua, who has written many articles on personal computers, is the author of The Affordable PC: Power to the People in the August issue of <u>PC Monthly</u>.
2. In the article, Lantigua maintains, computers enable ordinary people to do big projects that they otherwise wouldn't have the resources to do.
3. Lantigua points out, computers provide access to vast amounts of information and simple ways to store it.
4. Laptop computers, she explains further, enable people to take information wherever they go.
5. In The Affordable PC, Lantigua interviews several professionals who have become dependent on their computers.

6. One, Alan Novak, a short story writer, said, because my computer simplifies revising, I am much more prolific now than I was in my pre-computer days.
7. Similarly, Lois Bagdikian, an advertising executive, said, by storing bits of ideas for new ads on my laptop, I can work on new campaigns while travelling, with my inspiration right there on my knees.
8. Finally, Robert Ragin, a high school teacher, observed, many of my students are hooked on electronic mail and belong to bulletin-board type clubs.
9. Lantigua elaborates, without the performance pressure of school, the fear of making mistakes, electronic mail encourages people to communicate with words.
10. Reassuringly, she adds, with spelling and grammar software, they may even learn to write with accuracy and precision.

The Hyphen

The hyphen is used to join two or more words into a compound:

do-it-yourself instruction booklets
a wait-and-see attitude

The hyphen is also used with compound numbers from 21 to 99 and with fractions:

thirty-eight
eighty-two
one-quarter
four-fifths

And the hyphen is used with such prefixes as *ex-, all-, self-,* and *pro-:*

ex-convict
all-star
self-help
pro-tennis

A hyphen may also be used to divide a word at the end of a line. This should only be done between syllables. (Therefore, one-syllable words may NOT be hyphenated.)

At the end of every semester, you must take an examination.

Note: DO NOT leave a single-letter syllable at the beginning or end of a line (*e-liminate, dictionar-y*). Similarly, DO NOT begin a line with a two-letter word ending (*want-ed*).

EXERCISE 10

Revise these phrases, using hyphenated compounds.

EXAMPLE:
a vacation for three weeks
a three-week vacation

1. a movie that has been rated X

   _____

2. a restaurant that is ranked at four stars

   _____

3. a garment sewn by hand

   _____

4. a question that boggles the mind

   _____

5. vegetables that were grown at home

   _____

6. negotiations that took all night

   _____

7. a tablecloth stained with tea

   _____

8. a graduate who is seventeen years old

   _____

9. a student who is oriented toward a career

   _____

10. a dress covered with polka dots

    _____

EXERCISE 11

In the space provided, write out each word with spaces between syllables, inserting a hyphen at a suitable end-of-line break. If a word should NOT be divided, place an X in the space. Refer to the dictionary if necessary.

1. bankruptcy _____
2. corporation _____
3. price _____
4. depreciation _____
5. liability _____
6. fiscal _____
7. selling _____
8. franchise _____
9. mortgage _____
10. monopoly _____

The Dash

The dash is used to indicate a sudden change of thought or tone. To type a dash, use two unspaced hyphens; to write a dash by hand, use an unbroken line about the length of two hyphens.

> I plan to study for the exam all night--if my eyes hold out.
>
> Mr. Rodriguez—do you remember him from last year's convention?—will be joining our staff in May.

A dash should be used to break off an unfinished statement:

> Mrs. Olsen mumbled, "I can't seem to remember where—"

A dash should also be used between an introductory list and the explanatory sentence that follows:

> Calmness, confidence, and a copy of your resume—bring all of these with you to a job interview.

> **Remember:** The dash should be used discreetly. It is NOT a substitute for commas or terminal punctuation.

Parentheses

Parentheses are used to enclose statements that are completely separate from the main thought of the sentence. Such statements may serve as supplement or as reference:

> In some professions (physical therapy, for example), a dress code may be strictly enforced.
>
> Margaret Grange (1883–1966) was the author of several books on corporate finance.
>
> According to the union contract, all employees are required to have a college transcript on file (see section 6, paragraph 1).

Parentheses should also be used for enumeration within a sentence:

> You will need the following: (1) your resume, (2) letters of reference, (3) a college transcript, and (4) a pad and pencil.

Note that sentence punctuation comes AFTER the closing parenthesis:

> I have investigated various models of calculators for the office (see the attached list), but none has been purchased as yet.

However, if the parentheses enclose a whole sentence, the terminal punctuation is placed inside the closing parenthesis:

> Please submit your time cards by Wednesday evening. (Blank time cards are available in the personnel office.)

Brackets

Brackets have three uses:

1. Parentheses within parentheses

    The role of business in American life has often been the subject of our fiction (see, for example, the novels of William Dean Howells [1837–1920]).

2. Interpolations within a quotation

    In *Death of a Salesman* by Arthur Miller, Charlie pays tribute to Willy Loman: "[A salesman's] a man way out there in the blue, riding on a smile and a shoe shine. . . . A salesman is got to dream, boy. It comes with the territory."

3. Editorial corrections and comments

    The professor ended his lecture with this remark: "All of you will hopefully [*sic*] read at least some of these books."

Sic signifies here that the word *hopefully,* although used incorrectly, is being reproduced from the original quotation.

EXERCISE 12

Punctuate each of these sentences by inserting the necessary dashes, parentheses, and brackets.

1. Bernard M. Baruch 1870–1965 was born in Camden, South Carolina.
2. Because he was a renowned financier he made a fortune in the stock market before he was thirty he was often engaged by the government as a special adviser.
3. He contributed to the Allied effort during both World War I national defense adviser and World War II special adviser to James F. Byrne.
4. Later he was a member of FDR's "Brain Trust" a group of unofficial advisers that also included college professors and labor leaders.
5. He even participated in efforts toward international control of atomic energy U.S. representative to the U.N. Atomic Energy Commission.
6. In 1953, a branch of the City University of New York formerly the School of Business Administration of the City College was renamed in his honor the Bernard M. Baruch School of Business and Public Administration.
7. The details of Baruch's life and times may be found in his autobiography see *Baruch* 2 volumes, 1957–60.

Capitalization

The rules for capitalization fall into three categories:

I. The first word of a sentence should be capitalized.

> The man sees the tree.
> My mother talks while I listen.

This rule includes complete sentences *within* sentences such as:

> QUOTATIONS—My adviser says, "It is never too early to plan your career."
> CERTAIN QUESTIONS—The real issue was, What were we to do about the problem?
> STATEMENTS AFTER COLONS (when emphasis is desired)—We found a solution: We would do the job ourselves.

EXERCISE 13

Proofread this paragraph for words that should be capitalized but aren't. Then underline the letters that should be changed to capitals.

"flexible work hours" (or flextime for short) is one of the biggest innovations in employment policy in the past few decades. under flextime, employees choose the times at which they arrive at and depart from work within the limits set by management. usually core hours are established: during this midday period all employees must be present. they may choose, however to come in early or stay late. under flextime, absenteeism has dropped significantly, and productivity has risen. as a result, the Public and World Affairs Committee predicts, "flextime is going to be with us in the coming years."

II. The first and last words of *titles* and *headings* should be capitalized. So should all the other words EXCEPT:

> ARTICLES (*a, an, the*)
> COORDINATORS (*and, or, but, for, nor; so* and *yet* are flexible)
> SHORT PREPOSITIONS (such as *in, on, of*)

Consider these examples:

> *Advertising Strategy for the Small Business*
> "Tax Shelters: Are They for You?"
> *Middle Management Stress*
> "Latest News in Money Market Funds"
> *Introduction to Computer Programming*
> "The Ups and Downs of the Adjustable Mortgage"

EXERCISE 14

In the space provided, rewrite these titles, using appropriate capitalization.

1. *secretarial and office procedures for college*

_____

2. *principles of data processing*

_____

3. *how to marry a millionaire*

_____

4. "so you want to be a legal secretary?"

_____

5. "how to ask for a raise"

_____

6. "one hundred ways to supplement your income"

_____

7. *how to find the job you've always wanted*

_____

8. "avoiding three o'clock fatigue"

_____

9. "how to work around a candy machine without gaining weight"

_____

10. *take the money and run*

_____

III. The *names* of specific persons, places, and things should be capitalized.

> Michael Jordan, like many other successful athletes, also successfully maneuvered a career in advertising.
>
> A motor trip to Rome from Sicily would be an unforgettable vacation.
>
> The World Trade Center is the tallest structure in New York City.

The names of organizations and institutions are covered by this rule:

> The convention of the American Psychological Association will be held during the week of May 24.
>
> Warren earned his bachelor's degree at Yale University.

Similarly, historical periods, events, and documents are capitalized:

> Literature of the Renaissance is marked by an awareness of classical culture.
> The Revolutionary War began in 1775 and ended in 1783.
> The Declaration of Independence was adopted on July 4, 1776.

Members of national, political, religious, racial, social, and athletic groups are capitalized:

> The Republican candidate for mayor spent the morning shaking hands at the train station.
>
> Babe Ruth was one of the most famous outfielders to ever play with the Yankees.

Days of the week, months of the year, and names of holidays are capitalized, but seasons of the year are NOT.

> I will have your order ready by Tuesday.
> Winston entered law school in September.
> I always overeat on Thanksgiving.
> Every summer, the Feins rent a cottage on Cape Cod.

Note that compass directions work two ways: When used to refer to a region or place, they are capitalized.

> Voters in the Northeast are often stereotyped as liberals.

But compass points used as *directions* are NOT capitalized.

> Los Angeles is west of Las Vegas.

Finally, words referring to a deity or to religious documents are capitalized.

> In Greek mythology, Zeus was the father of Castor and Pollux.
> The Lord gives and the Lord takes away.
> The Koran is the collection of Moslem scriptural writings.

EXERCISE 15

Proofread these paragraphs for words that should be capitalized but aren't. Then underline the letters that should be changed to capitals.

1. On june 28, 1778, the battle of monmouth was fought. The last major battle in the north during the revolutionary war, it took place north of monmouth court house in new jersey. There, george washington led an army of 13,500 troops to victory against the British troops, who were led by henry clinton.

2. Born on february 11, 1847, in milan, ohio, thomas alva edison became one of america's greatest inventors. Although he produced over 1,300 inventions, the most famous remain the light bulb and the phonograph. Edison also built the first central electric power station, erected on pearl street in new york city. Known as the "wizard of menlo park," he considered his genius to be "one percent inspiration and ninety-nine percent perspiration."

A number of special considerations arise with regard to capitalization:

1. Regular nouns are capitalized when they are *part of a name,* for example:

> During lunch hour, the street was teeming with people.

But

> I work at the corner of Twelfth Street and Arthur Avenue.

> Cheryl graduated from high school in 1976.

But

> Her *alma mater* is Madison High School.

> Our office building is thirty stories high.

But

> The Empire State Building is a major New York tourist attraction.

This rule holds true for commercial brand names:

> Kellogg's Corn Flakes

But

> Ivory soap

2. Adjectives that are formed from names are capitalized.

> The American flag is a symbol of democracy.
> *Hamlet* is a frequently produced Shakespearean play.

3. Abbreviations of capitalized words should also be capitalized.

> U.P.S. (United Parcel Service)
> *But*
> c.o.d. (cash on delivery)

4. A person's title should be capitalized when used *before* the name. Titles used *after* names are not capitalized.

> Last year, Dean Douglas addressed the student body at the first assembly of the year.
> *But*
> Mr. Paul Douglas, dean of students, attended the first assembly of the year.

Titles of particularly high rank MAY be capitalized when used without a name:

> The President of the United States held a press conference.
> *But*
> The president of U.S. Steel held a press conference.

Similarly, terms of kinship MAY be capitalized when used as the person's name:

> Before I went out, I told Dad that I'd be home by ten.

5. As we have seen frequently, the pronoun *I* is always capitalized.

> I am quite proud of myself.

6. The *first* word of a complimentary closing is capitalized.

> Sincerely yours
> Yours truly

EXERCISE 16

Proofread this letter for uncapitalized words that should be capitalized. Then underline the letters that should be changed to capitals.

Dear mr. jackson:

i would like to offer my hearty congratulations on your promotion to president of the empire stove company. All of us at seymour's service centers, inc., are pleased that your years of hard work have been rewarded.

Seymour's appreciates the fine quality and serviceability of american-made stoves and appliances. That is why we have always confidently offered empire stoves to our customers.

In closing, president jackson, let me say that we look forward to a long and mutually rewarding business relationship with e.s.c.

sincerely yours,

Abbreviations

As a general rule, you should avoid abbreviations in your writing, unless the writing is technical or you are preparing lists or tables. The following abbreviations *are* acceptable in formal writing.

Titles

1. *Mr., Mrs., Ms., Dr.,* and *St.* (meaning *Saint*) are always abbreviated when used before a name.

Mr. James Cooper	Mrs. Jane Bowles
Mr. J. F. Cooper	Mrs. J. Bowles
Mr. Cooper	Mrs. Bowles
Ms. Lillian Lewis	St. Peter
Ms. L. Lewis	St. Cecilia
Ms. Lewis	

2. Such abbreviations as *Prof., Gov., Sen.,* and *Rep.* may be used before a *full* name (a first name or initial PLUS a last name).

Prof. Fred Farkas	Sen. Helen Coyne
Gov. T. P. Barnes	Rep. L. D. Woo

   When only a last name is used, however, the title must be spelled out.

Professor Farkas	Senator Coyne
Governor Barnes	Representative Woo

3. The designations *Honorable* and *Reverend,* because they indicate dignity and respect, should *not* be abbreviated except in addresses and lists. Moreover, they must be used with a first name, initial, or title in addition to the last name.

Reverend Tom Payne	Honorable Bruce Ng
Rev. Tom Payne	Hon. Bruce Ng
Rev. T. Payne	Hon. B. Ng
Rev. Dr. Payne	

   Using *the* before such designations indicates additional formality.

The Reverend Tom Payne	The Honorable Bruce Ng
The Rev. Tom Payne	The Hon. Bruce Ng

4. Titles appearing *after* names must be spelled out, except Esq., Jr., and Sr., and academic, professional, and religious designations.

   T. P. Barnes, governor

   But

   T. P. Barnes, Esq.
   Frieda Farkas, Ph.D.
   Tom Payne, D.D.
   Wayne Reed, C.P.A.

Company Names

Abbreviate firm names only when the company prefers it. The company's letterhead will provide you with this information; for example, *Con Edison* is acceptable for the *Consolidated Edison Company.* Similarly, using *&* instead of *and* should be limited to the company's official use:

A & P
Lord & Taylor

Organizations and governmental agencies that are known by their initials may be abbreviated in writing:

The OPEC nations have agreed to raise the price of oil by another $2 per barrel.

The CIA has recalled its agents from the Middle East.

Terms Used with Figures and Dates

1. The designation *A.D.* (*anno Domini* meaning "year of our Lord") or *C.E.* (common era) and *B.C.* ("before Christ") or *B.C.E.* (before common era) should always be abbreviated.

    Claudius I was born in the year 10 B.C. and died in the year A.D. 54.

    Note that *A.D.* and *C.E.* precede the year while *B.C.* follows it.

2. The abbreviations *A.M.* ("before noon") and *P.M.* ("after noon") may always be used.

    My work day begins at 9:00 A.M. and ends at 4:30 P.M.

    Note that *A.M.* and *P.M.* must always be used with figures; do not use them with words or the term *o'clock.*

    My work day begins at nine o'clock in the morning and ends at four-thirty in the afternoon.

3. *Number* and *numbers* may be abbreviated as *no.* (or *No.*) and *nos.* (or *Nos.*) respectively when used before figures.

    The model I am most interested in is no. 131.
    The following checks have not yet cleared: nos. 451, 454, and 458.

    However, spell out *number* or *numbers* at the beginning of a sentence:

    Number 62159 is the missing invoice.

4. The dollar sign ($) is permissible in writing. Instead of the cumbersome

    Sue owes Roger nineteen dollars and fifty-five cents.

    it is proper to write:

    Sue owes Roger $19.55.

Latin Expressions

The abbreviation of certain Latin expressions are acceptable though in formal writing the English version should be spelled out.

c.f.	compare
e.g.	for example
et al	and others
etc.	and so forth
i.e.	that is
viz.	namely
vs.	versus

For example:

The major oil companies (Gulf, Exxon, *et al*) are passing on the price increase to consumers.

Certain words should NOT be abbreviated in writing. (In addresses, lists, tables, invoices, and the like, abbreviations are acceptable.)

1. Names of cities, states, and countries

   Although Arnold was born in Philadelphia, Pennsylvania, he has lived in West Germany most of his life.

2. Months of the year, days of the week

   The shipment of electric yo-yos arrived Wednesday, October 1.

3. Parts of place names, such as *Street, Avenue, Road, Park, Port, Fort, Mount, River,* as well as compass directions

   The Adirondack Mountains are northeast of the Mississippi River.
   The hardware store is on the west side of Bruckner Boulevard.

4. Units of measure, courses of study, and the words *page, chapter,* and *volume*

   On page 14 of the physics textbook, the speed of light is listed as 186,000 miles per second.

EXERCISE 17

In the space provided, rewrite each of these sentences, using any abbreviations that are acceptable in formal writing. (Avoid those abbreviations that should be used only in addresses, tables, invoices, or technical writing.) Watch out for sentences in which *no* abbreviation is permissible.

1. The meeting to explore ways of increasing tourism in Greenwood, North Dakota, was called to order at seven-fifteen in the evening.

   _____

   _____

2. Mister Ashley introduced the guest speaker, the Honorable J. R. Buckley, mayor of Greenwood.

   _____

   _____

3. The members of the Greenwood Chamber of Commerce, who were present at the meeting, greeted Mayor Buckley with warm applause.

_____

_____

4. Buckley began his speech with an anecdote about ancient Rome in the year 129 before Christ.

_____

_____

5. But he quickly moved to the number one concern of everyone present, namely, how to attract more tourists to Greenwood.

_____

_____

6. The mayor surprised the audience by announcing plans to spend two million five hundred fifty thousand dollars on restoring the town's landmarks and historical sites.

_____

_____

7. He also announced the intentions of International Telephone and Telegraph to erect a Sheraton Hotel on Broad Street in the center of town.

_____

_____

8. After Buckley's address, Lana Stephens, Certified Social Worker, asked a question.

_____

_____

9. Miss Stephens wanted to know if local residents would be employed on the planned construction projects.

_____

_____

10. The mayor assured her that they would, and the meeting adjourned at ten o'clock.

_____

_____

EXERCISE 18

Proofread this letter for incorrect abbreviations and then rewrite the letter on another sheet of paper, making all necessary corrections.

Dear Mr. Poe:

On Tues., Mar. 17, which happened to be Saint Patrick's Day, I purchased four lbs. of Muenster cheese from your supermarket on Grand St. in Grahamsville, N.J.

I intended to serve the cheese to guests that night. However, when I unwrapped the cheese after getting it home, I discovered that it was green with mold!

The manager of the Grand St. store refused to refund my money. I paid $12.44 for the cheese. I would like you to know that if my claim is not satisfied, I intend to take the matter to the Dept. of Cons. Affairs.

Yours truly,

Numbers

There are some guidelines to help you know if you should spell out a number or use figures. A safe general rule is to *spell out numbers that can be expressed in one or two words;* use figures for other numbers.

six million soldiers	6,490,000 soldiers
one-fourth	82¼
fifty dollars	$49.95

Certain numbers should always be spelled out:

1. Numbers that begin a sentence

   One hundred fifty yards of wire are needed to complete the project.
   We will need 150 yards of wire to complete the project.

2. Large round numbers

   Six billion dollars (or) $6 billion
   (Using figures would imply emphasis: $6,000,000,000.)

3. Time expressed as a number alone or with the word *o'clock*

   four in the afternoon
   four o'clock

   Use figures with A.M. and P.M.

   4 A.M. (or) 4:00 P.M.
   2:30 A.M.

Other numbers should be indicated with figures:

1. Addresses: house, street, and ZIP code numbers

   252 Ash Street, Greenville, Wyoming 71226
   11 East 49 Street (or) 11 East 49th Street
   P.O. Box 72
   RFD 2

2. Decimals

> 6.293
> 0.00329

Note that commas are NOT used with decimals.

3. Dates

> January 31, 1951 (or) 31 January 1951

> May twenty-fourth (or) the twenty-fourth of May (or) May 24 (or) May 24th

Note that figures are used when the year is mentioned along with the day. Note, too, that an ordinal ending (1st, 2nd, 4th) is NOT used when the year is mentioned.

4. Expressions requiring two numbers

> 10 fifteen-cent stamps
> 2 five-dollar bills

Note that the first number is indicated in figures and the second is spelled out.

Keep in mind that *consistency* in using numbers is important. In a series, use either all words or all figures:

> On the desk were two pens, one pad, and six manila envelopes.

> I would like to order 10 reams of paper, 4 dozen pencils, and 2 boxes of erasers.

Finally, certain words and symbols often used with numbers must be considered:

1. The word *percent* should be spelled out, except on invoices and lists (in which case you may use %).

> nine percent
> 11½ percent

2. The symbol ¢ should only be used in quoting prices. Otherwise, use words or units of a dollar.

> 6¢
> six cents
> $.06

3. The symbol # should only be used in tables, invoices, etc. Instead, use *number* or the abbreviation *no.* or *No.* The symbol should NEVER be used with house numbers or RFD numbers.

EXERCISE 19

These numbers are all written as words. Some should be written as figures; others should remain words if intended for use in formal writing. In the space provided, convert those numbers that would be acceptable as figures; label CORRECT those numbers that should be left alone.

1. eight dollars and twelve cents

   _____

2. three-fifths

   _____

3. forty-nine west eleventh street

   _____

4. August tenth, 1980

   _____

5. seven billion

   _____

6. ten men, 8 women, and sixteen children

   _____

7. two sixty-cent fares

   _____

8. nine-thirty A.M.

   _____

9. ten cents

   _____

10. Post Office Box Twenty-one

    _____

■■■■■■ REVIEW EXERCISES

Proofread these letters for errors in punctuation, capitalization, abbreviation, and use of numbers. Then rewrite each letter on another sheet of paper, making all necessary corrections.

A.

TO: All Sales Representatives

FROM: Fay Sorrell

DATE: November 4, [*year*]

SUBJECT: Departmental Meeting

There will be a meeting of the sales department on friday November 8, in rm. 110. Mister Arthur Parker will address the meeting on the topic, "Improving Your Sales Through Self-Hypnosis.

Mr. Parker a certified psychoanalyst who has studied at the Alfred Adler institute, is the author of several books including the best-seller It's a Snap (New York, 1991).

Following the lecture, there will be a question and answer period.

Your attendance is required.

B.

Dear Tenant—

Please be advised, that pursuant to the 1998–99 Rent Guidelines Board, the percentages covering Lease Renewals effective July 1st, 1998, have been changed. The renewal percentages are:

 Five percent for one-year renewal
 9% for two-year renewal
 13% for 3-year renewal

Enclosed is your lease renewal. Please sign, and return both copies; along with the additional security of $20.41.

Thank you for your cooperation.

Yours truly,

C.

TO: Michael Moody

FROM: Fred Dobbs, Personnel Insurance Coordinator

DATE: May 15, 1998

SUBJECT: Medical Leave of Absence

On the basis of information provided by your Physician and at your request, you have been placed on medical leave of absence as of May 30, '98.

To maintain your leave, Company policy requires additional written statements from your physician at thirty-day-intervals. These statements, should be sent directly to the Personnel insurance Coordinator at the downtown office.

Failure to return to work on the date indicated by your physician, will be considered a Resignation.

Feel free to contact me, for further information regarding this policy.

D.

Policy Number: 43 681 345
Date: 9/5/98

Dear Mr. & Mrs. Chou:

We are sorry that we cannot provide the additional protection that you requested.

Because you made 5 claims in the past four years, we cannot provide $500.00 Deductible Comprehensive Coverage on the '98 Ford Taurus that replaced your old car. Nevertheless—Bodily Injury and Property Damage on the old car have been transferred to your new car.

Although we were temporarily providing the protection while considering your request, we will be unable to continue providing it. You will be covered by the protection only until 12:01 o'clock (A.M.) on September 26, 1998. You will, therefore have a 3-week period in which to apply for the protection elsewhere.

Please understand, Mister and Mrs. Chou, that our decision was made after thorough consideration of your case and based upon the underwriting rules and regulations of our company.

All of your other coverage, remains in full force as it was before your request.

Sincerely,

E.

Dear Doctor Christopher,

Not long ago I spoke with you on the telephone, about a possible teaching position with you next semester. You suggested, I mention this in my letter.

The man who referred me to your school was Prof. Helmsley of the accounting dept.

My most recent job was in the secretarial skills department at Bronxville Comm. College. I was a part-time instructor there, for 4 consecutive semesters.

I have enclosed my resume for your consideration.

Thank you

Sincerely Yours,

Part Three

IMPORTANT DETAILS

The final section of this book is intended to help you put the finishing touches on your correspondence.

- "Culture and Customs" is an overview of American business values, customs, and taboos that will help you to encounter a new culture with few surprises and to meet new business associates with confidence and understanding.

- "Addressing Dignitaries" is a selected list of acceptable terms of address for individuals of rank. (The reader is advised, however, that such terms are a matter of custom and vary widely with locale.)

19.
Culture and Customs

The United States is an extraordinarily diverse society. From the East Coast along the Atlantic Ocean to the West Coast along the Pacific, from our northern border with Canada to our southern border with Mexico, our topography encompasses mountains, prairies, deserts, and wetlands. We live in the wide-open, underpopulated spaces of Wyoming and the narrow, densely populated streets of Chicago. Our climate ranges from the subtropical sunshine of Florida to the long, snowy winters of Minnesota. And our people are descended from virtually every country on the planet.

Consequently, our customs and culture are similarly diverse. We can lead a driven, fast-paced lifestyle in Manhattan or a slower, more casual lifestyle in Los Angeles. We may all drink Coca-Cola and eat Big Macs, but our true regional cuisines are as different as a New England clambake and a Texas barbecue. A visitor to New York may think the only acceptable clothing color is black, whereas a visitor to Miami will find men as well as women wearing bright or pastel colors.

Thus, a discussion of American culture and customs, even specifically *business* culture and customs, must include a warning: Very little can be assumed to be true *everywhere* in the United States. Nevertheless, when it comes to business, we can safely make some generalizations.

General Values

On the whole, Americans are an optimistic people. We have a strong belief in the future. We take change for granted and assume that things will improve. We believe that hard work leads to success. We believe any child can grow up to be President. Our most deeply held values grow out of this fundamental confidence.

Work

When we Americans meet someone for the first time, one of the first questions we ask is, "What do you do?" This is because Americans place a very high value on *work*. It is virtuous in the United States to be industrious; it is healthy, we think, to be busy. Therefore, whether the idle rich or the welfare poor, the ill or the retired, those who do not work are considered of no use to society. Indeed, NOT working is considered virtually immoral. We take this so seriously that we are even pushing our retirement age later and later so that more of us will keep working longer and longer.

Time

The value we place on work shapes our attitude toward *time.* "Time is money!" is a cliché that most Americans believe. The efficient use of time is important to us. We prefer to be busy, work at a fast pace, and remain productive. Wasting time is frowned on. We have little use for ceremony or ritual; conversation not directly related to business at hand is called idle chat. We are always seeking a faster, better way to accomplish tasks.

Individualism

The optimistic belief in the future and the fruits of our own labor contributes to the high value Americans place on the *individual.* We are committed to private ownership of business and property, and we esteem the skills of entrepreneurship. We strive for independence and dream of self-employment. As employees, this translates into self-directed ambition; we expect commitment to the organization to result in personal advantage such as promotions or salary increases. On the whole, Americans do NOT place the needs of the group before the needs of the individual. We are team players as long as the team doesn't stifle our individual performance.

Family

When we Americans speak of "family values," we mean the *nuclear family,* not an extended one. Because ours is such a mobile society, few of us live in multigenerational households. It is not unusual for grandparents or aunts and uncles to reside in another city or state. Our ideal is two parents and their children living together under one roof. But we are also becoming increasingly receptive to the idea that single-parent structures *are* families.

Americans keep family and work separate. Family is protected from routine contact with the work environment. Indeed, we might work for years with the same colleagues and never meet each other's spouses. On the other hand, work is protected from family. We expect personal concerns to be left at home. Still, work generally takes precedence—requiring a family to relocate, for example, or to hire professional childcare. This priority on work over family has compelled us to legislate family protections—the right to family/childcare/maternity leave, for instance, or the provision of child daycare facilities.

Status

We Americans like to think that ours is a classless society. Surely, we do NOT define our status by birth: family does *not* confer social standing or respectability in most of our communities. We do, however, acknowledge professional standing and financial well-being. We believe that our status is self-determined. If we work hard, we can achieve professional and monetary success and thereby earn social respect. Conversely, we do not automatically acknowledge the status of others; we respect performance before position.

Interpersonal Relationships

With our fundamental values of individualism and work, we maintain a strong sense of personal responsibility. Particularly in the workplace, bonds between people are not very strong, and we limit our involvement with each other. We do not take responsibility for each other. A supervisor, for example, will not usually assume responsibility for a subordinate's errors. Similarly, we may treat each other with respect and behave with open friendliness, but there are limits to our *trust*. We like to "get things in writing." We rely on lawyers to keep our relationships (even our marriages!) on track.

Customs

On the job, American values, particularly our attitudes toward WORK and TIME, translate into specific practices.

Business Hours

"Official" business hours in the United States are 9 A.M. to 5 P.M. Monday through Friday. The typical work week is defined as forty hours, but in many professions, longer work days are customary. By working overtime, you are considered conscientious. An ambitious employee may arrive early, remain late, or work through lunch hour. (Our lunch breaks are one hour, usually noon to 1 P.M.)

Punctuality

American frown on lateness and delays. We expect employees to arrive on time. We expect meetings and other events to begin when scheduled. If kept waiting, we expect an explanation and apology. An American businessperson typically maintains a personal agenda—a daily schedule of appointments and activities. A single delay pushes an entire business day off schedule.

Holidays

There are certain national holidays on which *most* businesses close:

January 1	New Year's Day
3rd Monday of January	Martin Luther King Day
3rd Monday of February	Presidents' Day
Last Monday of May	Memorial Day
July 4	Independence Day
1st Monday of September	Labor Day
3rd Thursday of November	Thanksgiving
December 25	Christmas

In addition, there are local holidays in certain states and cities on which businesses *may* also close. But no business is *required* to close by law.

Vacations

Americans take short vacations; the typical American worker gets two weeks off a year. Even so, it is not unusual for us to split our vacation time to avoid being away from our jobs for too many consecutive days.

Our sense of individualism and the nature of our interpersonal relationships can be detected in a number of our other customs.

Greetings

The heart of an American greeting is the handshake. We stand, extend right arms, and firmly clasp each other's hand for a few seconds. Simultaneously, we make eye contact and speak a few words of greeting, preferably including the other person's name.

"It's good to see you again, Rob."
"Good morning, Ms. Lopez. Thank you for seeing me."
"Thank you for coming, Dr. Hasad. Please have a seat."

At the end of an encounter, we shake hands again before parting. Note that no distinction is made in greeting a man or a woman. Use the same firm handshake and eye contact.

Introductions

The handshake is central here, too. First, however, the introduction is spoken. Generally, we introduce the person of lesser rank to the person of higher rank.

"Dean Albright, allow me to introduce Professor Watson."
"Professor Watson, I'd like you to meet my student Sonia Tenebra."

The people introduced shake hands and speak words of greeting.

"I'm pleased to meet you, Professor Watson."

Again, do not treat men and women differently during an introduction.

Nonverbal Communication and Gestures

Americans are uncomfortable with silence. During a lull in conversation, we are likely to rush in with a remark or even begin a new topic to keep the conversation going. On the other hand, we *do* communicate nonverbally.

1. To being with, we SMILE. A smile is a courtesy during an introduction. It is a gesture of appreciation after receiving a compliment or praise. It is a means of emphasis when offering praise. It is also a defense to conceal feelings of nervousness or discomfort.

2. We NOD our heads. Nodding up and down is affirmative. Shaking side to side is negative. The vigor of the head movement determines the message. A strong shake says clearly "Yes, I agree" or "No, I disagree." But a slight nod up and down may simply mean "I'm paying careful attention to what you say," while a subtle shake from side to side may indicate moderate disapproval.

3. Use of SPACE also sends a message. Americans do NOT like to get too close and will back up if someone does come too near. This retreat is not an offense but a reflex: we like our distance. On the other hand, leaning close in conversation signals intimacy to Americans, which is considered inappropriate in a business setting and usually rude in other settings.

4. A related issue is TOUCHING. On the whole, except for the handshake, Americans do not like to be touched. A pat on the back or a hand rested on the shoulder may mean approval or comfort, but such gestures are interpreted as condescending between business associates. Between men and women, *any* touching beyond a handshake is completely unacceptable.

Gift Giving

Not only do gift-giving customs vary from country to country, but, in the United States, they vary from company to company. Some corporations forbid their employees to accept gifts from customers or suppliers. Other companies permit the acceptance of gifts *if* the gifts are modest and suggest no impropriety. Thus, if you offer a gift to an American business associate, it may be refused. Understand that the refusal of a gift is *not* an insult.

If you do give a business gift, keep these suggestions in mind:

1. Do NOT give money. Money can be interpreted as bribery, so it is always inappropriate.

2. Do NOT give an overly expensive gift. Its value should reflect the recipient's status and the size of your business dealings. For example, a $300 fountain pen might be appropriate for a corporate executive but not for a receptionist in his or her office.

3. Do NOT give personal gifts. A gift should consider the person's taste and needs, but should still remain business-related. For in-

stance, except perhaps for a man's necktie or a woman's scarf, articles of clothing are not acceptable.

In the United States, certain categories of gifts are generally acceptable:

1. Business items—pens, portfolios, small electronic gadgets
2. Flowers—bouquets or arrangements, delivered by a florist
3. Food—again, delivered by the supplier, usually in a presentation such as a gift basket
4. Liquor—a bottle (or a case, if appropriate) of wine or a bottle of hard spirits such as Scotch or brandy *if* you know the recipient drinks alcoholic beverages (not all Americans do)

Finally, do not censor your generosity. But remember your recipient's feelings. You want the person to be pleased with your gift, not embarrassed by it.

Gratuities

As in most places, it is customary in the United States to offer a gratuity when someone does you a service. Tips are generally higher in big cities than in small cities or suburbs.

U.S. restaurants usually do NOT include the tip on the bill. Instead, 15 to 20 percent of the total bill is left for the waiter and busboy. This can be included on the credit card charge or left on the table in cash. Additional tips at a restaurant may include:

Maitre d'—$10–$20 for special service
Wine steward—$3–$5 if he or she opens and serves the wine
Coatroom attendant—$1 per coat
Washroom attendant—50¢–$1
Parking attendant—$1–$2 upon retrieving your car

Of course, these amounts are suggestions and should be increased in particularly expensive or up-scale establishments.

Hotels are also places where tips are customary. The employees to tip include:

Concierge—an option of $10–$20, either on arrival to encourage special service or on departure to show appreciation. Or, tip smaller amounts for specific services performed
Bellhop—$1–$2 per bag upon checking in *and* checking out
Chambermaid—$2 per day, left on the dresser at checkout
Doorman—$1 for service beyond simply opening the door, such as hailing a taxi

In addition, always tip:

Taxi drivers—15 percent of the fare
Delivery people—$1–$2
Airport skycaps—$1 per bag

Bartenders—15 percent of the bill or at least 50 cents per drink

Barbers and hairdressers—$3–$5 depending on how many different services are performed

There are occasions when tipping would be inappropriate. In the United States, we usually do NOT tip:

Theater ushers
Bus drivers
Train conductors
Gas station attendants
Shop clerks/salespeople

When you are served by the owner of a business (such as a restaurant or shop), do NOT offer a tip. If an employee of a business associate shows you particular courtesy or help, a gift would be more appropriate than a tip. When you are someone's guest in a restaurant, the host leaves the tip. (In this situation, though, offering to leave the tip yourself is polite.) Finally, do NOT force a tip on someone who firmly refuses it; tips may be forbidden by the employer.

Eating and Dining Habits

Eating is *not* an honored ritual in the United States; rather, mealtimes are considered useful opportunities for business meetings. This can be as simple as two colleagues regularly beginning their day together with coffee and conversation, or it can mean sending out for sandwiches so that a meeting may continue uninterrupted. It can also mean a meal in a restaurant where the discussion will range from polite social topics to serious business issues.

Except perhaps on weekends, Americans eat a light *breakfast*—orange juice, coffee or tea, and something baked (bread or pastry). It is common to arrive at the job with coffee and a pastry and consume this breakfast while beginning the day's work. American *lunch* is also light, usually a sandwich and a beverage. We eat our lunches quickly, typically using most of our one-hour lunch break to do other activities. Our main meal is *dinner,* eaten either at home after the day's work or as a social occasion. We might dine in a restaurant with friends or invite friends to dine in our home. Because it is the longest meal of the day, dinner is also a favored business occasion.

American table manners are varied. We have taboos, but they are not always obeyed. For example, we frown upon touching food with one's hands, but we do eat sandwiches and pizza without a knife and fork. In general, manners are more formal during meals in a restaurant or dinner in someone's home. Manners are more relaxed at fast-food places or when eating at the office.

When dining with business associates at a restaurant, we do follow some rules:

1. The person who extends the invitation to dine is considered the host.

2. The host pays the bill. However, a guest may offer to *share* the expense without offending the host. A senior colleague may also pay even when the junior colleague initiated the occasion.

3. The host sets the guidelines—where everyone sits, how many courses to order, when to end the meal. A guest who must leave early does so politely by offering an explanation and apology.

Dining with business acquaintances also involves a few sensitive issues:

1. *Smoking*—While many American do smoke, it has become illegal to smoke almost anywhere in public. If local laws *do* allow smoking in a workplace or a restaurant, it is nevertheless customary to ask the other people present if the smoke would disturb them. Do NOT smoke if anyone objects.

2. *Drinking*—America was once thought of as the land of the two-martini lunch because businesspeople on expense accounts would drink heavily at a business lunch or dinner. This is no longer the case. The *discreet* consumption of alcohol is now preferred: *one* (or no) drink at lunch, *one* drink or a moderate amount of wine with dinner. The guideline is TO NOT DRINK ENOUGH ALCOHOL TO AFFECT ONE'S BEHAVIOR.

3. *Cellular Phones and Pagers*—Some people consider their cellular phone a status symbol; they think it is impressive to speak on their phone in public. THEY ARE WRONG! Telephone conversations at the dinner table disturb everyone else. During a business meal, turn off your cellular phone. If you are paged for an emergency, politely excuse yourself from the table to return the call.

Taboos

The fervor with which we Americans approach work can be seen in our approach to other issues, too. Deep convictions and passionate beliefs make certain topics very sensitive. A discreet businessperson will avoid discussing these topics.

Religion

Not all Americans attend a house of worship, but most of us believe in God. Our religious beliefs inform every part of daily life from our drinking habits to our sexual mores. We turn to religion to guide us through personal relationships, business decisions, and health problems. Some of us even rely on prayer to lose weight.

All the world's religions are represented in the United States. We were founded by the Pilgrims, and our value system is often called the Protestant Ethic, but we are a nation not just of a wide variety of Protestants. We are also Roman Catholics, Jews, Muslims, and Buddhists, among many other creeds. Recent years have seen the rise of evangelical "megachurches," huge buildings that accommodate congregations of thousands of people. With such a variety of religions, American generally have a live-and-let-live attitude; that is, "I will live according to my beliefs, you according to yours." Sometimes this tolerance for each others' beliefs is threatened, and if our beliefs are contradictory, there can be distrust. If one person (or group) attempts to force his or her beliefs upon others, there will be conflict.

For these reasons, religion is a taboo subject among business associates. It is an easy topic on which to give offense.

Politics

Just as most Americans identify with a particular religious denomination, so we also identify with a particular political party. We consider ourselves Republican, Democrat, or Independent, for example, and usually remain so our entire lives. Sometimes this political identity goes back many generations in a family.

Most Americans hold strong political opinions that are sometimes consistent with party positions. We take politics personally, seeing social issues in terms of our own lives. Because we feel directly affected by actions that our political leaders take, we can become quite aggressive when we discuss politics. Such topics as gun control and abortion are recent examples of how ferociously divided Americans can be over political issues.

We Americans greatly value our freedom of religion; we value just as highly our political freedom and freedom of speech. In business situations, it is prudent not to discuss politics—public issues not directly related to business can cause arguments that disrupt business relations.

Humor

Americans have a sense of humor. We tell each other jokes; we laugh at comic performances on television and in the movies. But humor is rarely cross-cultural. What is considered funny in Tokyo may not be amusing in Paris. Indeed, what is humorous in Boston may appear inane in Seattle. What a twenty-five-year-old salesperson laughs at a fifty-five-year-old executive may find offensive.

Telling a joke is risky; if your listener doesn't see the humor, you will feel foolish. Worse, if your listener misinterprets the joke, you may seem offensive. Unless you know your companions well, it is best to avoid humor. Even when you *do* know your companions, however, absolutely avoid jokes about sex, religion, or specific ethnic groups.

Relations Between Men and Women

There is no ambiguity here. American businesswomen expect to be treated the same as businessmen. Like men, women occupy every level of business organizations. A woman and a man in equal positions should interact as equals. A woman in a supervisory position to a man should be treated as a superior. It is not acceptable to consider gender when assigning responsibilities. It is not acceptable to consider women secondary to men in any capacity.

Furthermore, it is not advisable for men and women to mix social and business relations. Men should not consider women business associates potential social companions. The emotional nature of personal relationships will likely interfere with business dealings. Moreover, any suggestion of sexual contact is *completely taboo.* Not only can a sexual relationship damage a business relationship, but in the United States, unwelcome sexual advances can be grounds for legal action. It cannot be emphasized too strongly: AMERICAN BUSINESSWOMEN EXPECT BUSINESS RELATIONSHIPS TO BE ABOUT BUSINESS.

20.
Addressing Dignitaries

CLERGY	
Term of Address	*Mode of Salutation*

(Alternatives are listed in order of decreasing formality.)

Abbot

The Right Reverend Abbott Scott (*plus initials of his order*)	Right Reverend and Dear Father: Dear Father Abbott:

Archbishop

The Most Reverend John P. Doohan Archbishop of (*place name*)	Your Excellency: Your Grace:

Archdeacon

The Venerable the Archdeacon of (*place name*)	Venerable Sir:
The Venerable Walter Frank Archdeacon of (*place name*)	

Bishop (Anglican)

The Right Reverend the Lord Bishop of (*place name*)	My Lord Bishop: My Lord:
The Lord Bishop of (*place name*)	

Bishop (Methodist)

The Reverend Aaron Jones Bishop of (*place name*)	Reverend Sir: Dear Sir: Dear Bishop Jones:

Bishop (Protestant Episcopal)

The Right Reverend Thomas Watt Bishop of (*place name*)	Right Reverend Sir: Dear Bishop Watt:

Bishop (Roman Catholic)
The Most Reverend Samuel
    Keen
Bishop of (*place name*)

Your Excellency:

Bishop (Scottish)
The Right Reverend Bishop
    Alan Crane

Right Reverend Sir:

Canon
The Very Reverend Canon John
    Steed

Very Reverend Canon:
Dear Canon Steed:

The Very Reverend John Steed
Canon of (*place name*)

Cardinal
His Eminence Ralph Cardinal
    Peel

Your Eminence:

His Eminence Cardinal Peel

Cardinal/Archbishop
His Eminence the Cardinal,
Archbishop of (*place name*)

Your Eminence:

His Eminence Cardinal Pierce,
Archbishop of (*place name*)

Clergyman or Clergywoman
The Reverend Richard North

Dear Sir:

The Reverend Dr. Priscilla North
    (*If Doctor of Divinity*)

Dear Dr. North:

Dean (Ecclesiastical)
The Very Reverend the Dean of
    St. John's

Sir:
Very Reverend Sir:
Very Reverend Father: (*Roman
    Catholic*)

The Very Reverend William Hart

Monsignor
The Right Reverend Monsignor
    Horace Wall

The Right Reverend and Dear
    Monsignor:
The Right Reverend Monsignor
    Horace Wall:
Dear Monsignor Wall:

Mother Superior

The Reverend Mother, Superior
    Convent of (*name*)

Mother Mary Frances, Superior
    Convent of (*name*)

The Reverend Mother Mary
    Frances (*plus initials of her
    order*)

Reverend Mother:
Dear Madam:
Dear Reverend Mother:
Dear Reverend Mother Mary
    Frances:

Nun

Sister Mary Theresa (*plus
    initials of her order*)

Dear Sister:
Dear Sister Mary Theresa:

Pope

His Holiness Pope John Paul II

His Holiness the Pope

Most Holy Father:
Your Holiness:

Priest (Episcopal)

The Reverend William Long

Dear Father Long:

Priest (Roman Catholic)

The Reverend Father Anthony
    Roma (*plus initials of his
    order*)

Reverend Father:
Dear Father Roma:

1) Benedictine, Cistercian, or
    Canon Regular
    The Very Reverend Dom
    Anthony Roma (*plus
    initials of his order*)

Reverend Father:
Dear Father Roma:

2) Carthusian
    The Venerable Father
    Anthony Roma, O. Cart.

Venerable Father:
Dear Father Roma:

3) Secular
    The Reverend Anthony
    Roma (*plus initials of his
    order*)

Reverend Sir:
Dear Sir:
Dear Father Roma:

Rabbi

Rabbi Hyman Marcus

Reverend Sir:
Dear Sir:

The Reverend Hyman Marcus

Dear Rabbi Marcus:
Dear Dr. Marcus:

Dr. Hyman Marcus

MILITARY	
Term of Address	*Mode of Salutation*
Admiral The Admiral of the Navy of the United States Admiral Frank Scrod Chief of Naval Operations	Dear Sir: Dear Admiral Scrod:
Brigadier General Brigadier General David P. Small	Dear Sir: Dear General Small:
Captain Captain Jesse Jones (*plus branch of military*)	Dear Sir: Dear Captain Jones:
Colonel Colonel Nathan Borman (*plus branch of military*)	Dear Sir: Dear Colonel Borman:
Commander Commander Morris Rosen United States Navy	Dear Sir: Dear Commander Rosen:
General General Jose Jerez United States Army	Sir: Dear Sir: Dear General Jerez:
Lieutenant Colonel Lieutenant Colonel Albert Robb United States Army	Dear Sir: Dear Colonel Robb:
Lieutenant General Lieutenant General Robert Howe	Dear Sir: Dear General Howe:
Major Major Susan Savan United States Army	Dear Madam: Dear Major Savan:
Major General Major General Clarence King United States Army	Dear Sir: Dear General King:
Rear Admiral Rear Admiral Evan Wyeth United States Navy	Dear Sir: Dear Admiral Wyeth:

GOVERNMENT/POLITICS

Term of Address	*Mode of Salutation*
Alderman or Alderwoman	
Alderman Clark Cook	Dear Sir:
	Dear Alderman Cook:
The Honorable Clark Cook Alderman	
Ambassador (American)	
The American Ambassador to (*place name*)	Sir:
	Your Excellency:
	Dear Madam Ambassador:
The American Embassy (*place name*)	
The Honorable Carol Eames The American Ambassador to (*place name*)	
Ambassador (Foreign)	
His Excellency The Ambassador of (*place name*) (*Place name*) Embassy Washington, D.C.	Sir: Excellency: Your Excellency:
His Excellency Christopher Latour Ambassador of (*place name*)	
Assemblyman or Assembly- woman	
The Honorable Marianne Glace Member of Assembly	Dear Madam: Dear Ms. Glace:
Assemblywoman Marianne Glace	
Associate Justice of the Supreme Court	
The Honorable Ruth Bader Ginsburg Associate Justice of the Supreme Court	Madam Justice: Your Honor: Dear Justice Ginsburg: Mr. Justice:
The Honorable Thurgood Marshall Justice, Supreme Court of the United States	

Cabinet Officer
The Honorable Kevin Black   Sir:
Secretary of (*department name*)   Dear Sir:
                                   Dear Mr. Secretary:

The Secretary of (*title*)

Chief Justice of the United
    States
The Honorable William H.   Sir:
    Rehnquist   Mr. Chief Justice:
Chief Justice of the Supreme   Dear Justice Rehnquist:
    Court of the United States

Chief Justice Rehnquist
United States Supreme Court

The Chief Justice of the United
    States

Commissioner
The Honorable Thelma Dole   Madam:
Commissioner of (*bureau name*)   Dear Madam:
                                   Dear Ms. Dole:

Congressman or Congress-
    woman
The Honorable Stuart Larson   Sir:
House of Representatives   Dear Sir:
                                   Dear Congressman Larson:
The Honorable Stuart Larson   Dear Representative Larson:
Representative in Congress   Dear Mr. Larson:
(*when out of Washington*)

Representative Stuart Larson
House of Representatives

Consul
Miss Rhonda Marley   Dear Madam:
United States Consul at (*place*
    name)

Governor
His Excellency   Sir:
The Governor of (*state name*)   Dear Sir:
                                   Dear Governor Brown:
The Honorable the Governor of
    (*state name*)

The Honorable Howard Brown
Governor of (*state name*)

Judge
The Honorable Laura Gordon
Judge of the Circuit Court
(*or other title*)

Dear Madam:
Dear Judge Gordon:

Lieutenant Governor
The Honorable Sydney Blunt
Lieutenant Governor of (*state name*)

Sir:
Dear Sir:
Dear Mr. Blunt:

Mayor
The Mayor of (*place name*)

Sir:
Dear Sir:

The Honorable Lawrence
  O'Rourke
Mayor of (*place name*)

Dear Mr. Mayor:
Dear Mayor O'Rourke:

Minister (Diplomatic)
The Honorable Bertram Blyth
Minister of (*place name*)

Sir:
Dear Mr. Minister:

President of the United States
The President
The White House

Mr. President:
Dear Mr. President:

Senator
The Honorable Chester L. Fried
United States Senator

Dear Sir:
Dear Senator Fried:

The Honorable Regina Lukas
The Senate of (*state name*)

Dear Senator Lukas:

Speaker of the House
The Honorable Thomas Southey
Speaker of the House of Representatives

Mr. Speaker:
Dear Mr. Southey:

Vice President of the United States
The Vice President of the United States
United States Senate

Mr. Vice President:
Sir:

The Honorable Gary Cross
Vice President of the United States

NOBILITY	
Term of Address	*Mode of Salutation*
Baron	
The Right Honorable Lord Chichester	My Lord:
	Dear Lord Chichester:
The Lord Chichester	
Baroness	
The Right Honorable Lady Chichester	Madam:
	Dear Lady Chichester:
The Lady Chichester	
Baronet	
Sir Richard Bartlett, Bart.	Sir:
Countess	
The Right Honorable the Countess of (*place name*)	Madam:
	Dear Lady (*place name*):
Duchess	
Her Grace the Duchess of (*place name*)	Madam:
	Your Grace:
Duke	
His Grace the Duke of (*place name*)	My Lord Duke:
	Your Grace:
Earl	
The Right Honorable the Earl of (*place name*)	My Lord:
King	
The King's Most Excellent Majesty	Sir:
	May it please your Majesty:
His Most Gracious Majesty King John	
Knight	
Sir Edward Leigh (*plus initials of his order*)	Sir:
	Dear Sir Edward:
Queen	
The Queen's Most Excellent Majesty	Madam:
	May it please your Majesty:
Her Gracious Majesty, The Queen	

APPENDICES

Some additional information is presented here for your reference, along with the answers to the Review Exercises in Part Two.

- "State Abbreviations" in Appendix I offers an easy reference for the traditional and the officially approved ZIP Code abbreviations of the states.

- Appendix II, "A Glossary of Business Terms," will help you make certain that you are using words correctly.

- Answers, with explanations where appropriate, are given in Appendix III, beginning on page 305.

Appendix I

State Abbreviations

State	Traditional Abbreviation	Postal Service Abbreviation
Alabama	Ala.	AL
Alaska	—	AK
Arizona	Ariz.	AZ
Arkansas	Ark.	AR
California	Calif.	CA
Colorado	Colo.	CO
Connecticut	Conn.	CT
Delaware	Del.	DE
District of Columbia	D.C.	DC
Florida	Fla.	FL
Georgia	Ga.	GA
Hawaii	Haw.	HI
Idaho	Ida.	ID
Illinois	Ill.	IL
Indiana	Ind.	IN
Iowa	—	IA
Kansas	Kans.	KS
Kentucky	Ky.	KY
Louisiana	La.	LA
Maine	—	ME
Maryland	Md.	MD
Massachusetts	Mass.	MA
Michigan	Mich.	MI
Minnesota	Minn.	MN
Mississippi	Miss.	MS
Missouri	Mo.	MO
Montana	Mont.	MT
Nebraska	Nebr.	NE
Nevada	Nev.	NV
New Hampshire	N.H.	NH
New Jersey	N.J.	NJ
New Mexico	N.Mex.	NM
New York	N.Y.	NY
North Carolina	N.C.	NC
North Dakota	N.Dak.	ND
Ohio	—	OH
Oklahoma	Okla.	OK
Oregon	Oreg.	OR
Pennsylvania	Pa.	PA
Rhode Island	R.I.	RI
South Carolina	S.C.	SC
South Dakota	S.Dak.	SD
Tennessee	Tenn.	TN
Texas	Tex.	TX
Utah	—	UT
Vermont	Vt.	VT
Virginia	Va.	VA
Washington	Wash.	WA
West Virginia	W.Va.	WV
Wisconsin	Wis.	WI
Wyoming	Wyo.	WY

Appendix II

A Glossary of Business Terms

account *n.* (1) a bookkeeping record of business transactions; (2) a customer or client.

accrue *v.* to accumulate, as interest.

affidavit *n.* a written oath.

amortization *n.* the gradual paying off of a debt at regular intervals.

annuity *n.* an investment that provides fixed yearly payments.

appraise *v.* to evaluate

appreciate *v.* to increase in value.

arbitration *n.* settlement of a dispute through a third party.

arrears *n.* overdue debts.

assessment *n.* evaluation for the purpose of taxation.

asset *n.* something that is owned and has value.

audit (1) *n.* the checking of a business's financial records. (2) *v.* to check a business's financial records.

backup (1) *v.* to copy a file from a computer hard drive to floppy disks or tapes. (2) *n.* a duplicate copy of a computer file.

balance (1) *n.* the difference between debits and credits. (2) *v.* to reconcile the difference between debits and credits.

bankruptcy *n.* the legally declared state of being unable to pay debts.

beneficiary *n.* a person stipulated to receive benefits from a will, insurance policy, and so on.

bond *n.* a long-term debt security issued by a public or private borrower.

boot *v.* to turn on a computer.

brokerage *n.* a business licensed to sell stocks and securities.

browser *n.* a computer program used to search the Internet for information.

Bulletin Board Service *n.* a place on the Internet to list requests, answer questions, and so on.

byte *n.* a measure of computer capacity to store information, one byte being equivalent to one character.

capacity *n.* the total number of bytes that can be stored in a computer's memory.

capital *n.* money or property owned or used by a business.

cash flow *n.* a measure of a company's liquidity

CD-ROM *n.* acronym for compact disk-read only memory, an optical computer storage device containing millions of byes of information.

click stream *n.* the path followed to find information on the Internet.

collateral *n.* property used as security for a loan.

compensation *n.* payment, reimbursement.

consignment *n.* shipment of goods to be paid for after they are sold.

corporation *n.* a business operating under a charter.

credit (1) *n.* the entry of a payment in an account. (2) *v.* to enter a payment in an account.

data processing *n.* the handling of information, especially statistical information, by computer.

debit (1) *n.* the entry of money owed in an account. (2) *v.* to enter money owed in an account.

debt *n.* money owed.

debug *v.* to remove errors from a computer program.

deficit *n.* a money shortage.

depreciate *v.* to decrease in value.

direct mail *n.* the sale of goods and services through the mail.

dividend *n.* a share of profits divided among the stockholders of a corporation.

DOS *n.* acronym for data operating system, a main program for controlling a computer.

download *v.* to move information from the memory of one computer to that of another or to a tape, disk, or printer.

endorse *v.* to sign the back of a check.

endowment *n.* money given, as a bequest.

equity *n.* the amount of maney no longer owed on a purchase.

escrow *n.* written evidence of ownership held by a third party until specified conditions are met.

executor *n.* a person named to carry out someone else's will.

exemption *n.* money not subject to taxation.

expenditure *n.* an amount of money spent.

fiscal *adj.* financial.

flextime *n.* a system of flexible work hours.

forfeiture *n.* loss of property as a penalty for default or neglect.

franchise *n.* a special right to operate a business granted by the government or a corporation.

goodwill *n.* the value of a business's public image and reputation.

gross (1) *adj.* total, before deductions. (2) *v.* to earn a certain amount before deductions. (3) *n.* the total before deductions. (4) *n.* twelve dozen.

hardware *n.* the physical machinery of a computer.

home page *n.* the screen that serves as the entrance to an organization's Web site.

hypertext *n.* highlighted or underlined text on a Web page that, when clicked on, leads to a new screen with additional information.

information processing *n.* the "marriage" of data processing and word processing.

input *n.* data fed into a computer.

insurance *n.* the guarantee of compensation for a specified loss.

interest *n.* the fee charged for borrowing money.

inventory *n.* an itemized list of property or merchandise.

investment *n.* money put into a business or transaction to reap a profit.

invoice *n.* a list of goods shipped.

journal *n.* a written record of financial transactions.

kilobyte *n.* approximately 1,000 bytes.

laptop *n.* a compact, portable computer.

lease (1) *n.* a contract for renting property. (2) *v.* to rent or let.

ledger *n.* a record book of debits and credits.

legacy *n.* money or property left in a will.

liability *n.* a debt or obligation.

lien *n.* a claim on property as security against a debt.

liquidity *n.* ability to turn assets into cash.

list price *n.* retail price as listed in a catalog.

load *v.* to move information into a computer's memory.

margin *n.* difference between cost and selling price.

markup *n.* the percentage by which the selling price is more than the cost.

megabyte *n.* approximately one million bytes.

memory *n.* information stored in a computer.

merger *n.* the combining of two or more companies into one.

middleman *n.* a businessperson who buys from a producer and resells at wholesale or retail in smaller quantities.

modem *n.* a device for linking computers by telephone line.

monetary *adj.* relating to money.

monopoly *n.* exclusive control of a commodity or service.

mortgage (1) *n.* the pledging of property as security for a loan. (2) *v.* to pledge property as security for a loan.

negotiable *adj.* transferable.

net (1) *n.* an amount left after deductions. (2) *v.* to clear as profit.

networking *n.* the establishing of business and professional contacts.

option *n.* the right to act on an offer at an established price within a limited time.

output *n.* data provided by a computer.

overhead *n.* the costs of running a business.

par value *n.* the face value of a share of stock or a bond.

payable *adj.* owed.

personnel *n.* employees, staff.

petty cash *n.* money kept on hand for incidental purchases.

portfolio *n.* the various securities held by an investor.

power of attorney *n.* the written right to legally represent another person.

premium *n.* a payment, usually for an insurance policy.

productivity *n.* rate of yield or output.

proprietor *n.* owner.

prospectus *n.* a statement describing a business.

proxy *n.* authorization to vote for a stockholder at a meeting.

quorum *n.* the minimum number of persons required to be present for the transaction of business at a meeting.

receivable *adj.* due.

remittance *n.* the sending of money in payment.

requisition *n.* a written request for supplies.

resume *n.* an outline of a job applicant's qualifications and experience.

rider *n.* an amendment to a document.

royalty *n.* a share of the profits from a book or invention paid to the author or patent holder.

security *n.* (1) funds or property held as a pledge of repayment. (2) a stock or bond.

shareholder *n.* one who owns shares of a corporation's stock.

software *n.* set of programs for a computer.

solvent *adj.* able to pay debts.

spreadsheet *n.* a table of numbers arranged in rows and columns for computer calculations.

stockholder *n.* one who owns stock in a company.

subsidy *n.* a monetary grant.

tariff *n.* a tax on imports or exports.

telecommunications *n.* high-speed communications via wire or microwave.

turnaround time *n.* time taken to complete a task.

trust *n.* a monopoly formed by a combination of corporations.

vita *n.* an outline of a job applicant's qualifications and experience, a resume.

word processing *n.* the handling of narrative information by computer.

World Wide Web *n.* a uniform information system made up of hypertext documents and links between those documents.

Appendix III

Answers to Exercises in Part Two: Usage

Chapter 13: The Basic Sentence

Exercise 1

1. (John) <u>is</u>
2. (He) <u>likes</u>
3. (He) <u>had planned</u>
4. (computer science) <u>is</u>
5. (His plans) <u>had to be changed</u>
6. (Marie) <u>is</u>
7. (She) <u>enjoys</u>
8. (Mathematics) <u>had been</u>
9. (she) <u>went</u>, <u>developed</u>
10. (The atmosphere and salary) <u>are satisfying</u>

Exercise 2

1. (Mr. and Mrs. Price) <u>are buying</u>
2. (Their real estate agent and their banker) <u>are helping</u>
3. (The agent and the Prices' lawyer) <u>disagree</u>
4. (The Prices and the banker) <u>are</u>
5. (The agent, the banker, the lawyer, and the Prices) <u>will be</u>
6. (Regina and her boss) <u>were discussing</u>
7. (Accuracy, thoroughness, and conscientiousness) <u>were</u>
8. (Poor sales and high expenses) <u>were</u>
9. (Regina and her employer) <u>met</u>
10. (Her raise) <u>will begin</u>

Exercise 3

(We) would like

(Dark Lady) is named

(Its bouquet) is steeped

(One drop) mingles

(Rosemary, violets, and pansies) evoke

(loves and lyrics) blend

(perfume and cologne) are

(we) are offering

(purse-atomizer and pouch) are

(this and all your purchases) can be charged ordered

Exercise 4

1. Bicycling keeps
2. Writing makes
3. Balancing makes
4. To answer is
5. To admit indicates
6. To lose is
7. Waiting infuriates
8. Smoking is
9. To find demands
10. To operate requires

Exercise 5

(*Answers may vary.*)

1. a. Walter is selling insurance.
   b. Selling insurance has been his job for the last ten years.
   c. The selling point of his insurance is its low premium.
2. a. I will be speaking to the Chamber of Commerce next Friday.
   b. Speaking to groups is not my strongest skill.
   c. Speaking engagements make me nervous.
3. a. The customer is paying cash for her purchase.
   b. Paying bills is always unpleasant.
   c. Paying customers deserve courteous service.
4. a. Mary is writing a novel.
   b. Writing can be a highly marketable skill.
   c. My writing skills need improvement.
5. a. I was looking at myself in a mirror.
   b. Looking at one's reflection is enlightening.
   c. My looking glass is broken now.

Exercise 6

(Answers may vary.)

1. a. My dog was lost.
   b. The lost dog found his way home.
2. a. Having danced all night, Wendy was tired.
   b. The tired dancer went home to sleep.
3. a. The wedding invitations were printed on parchment.
   b. The printed word is a powerful tool.
4. a. The old jar was opened after much prying.
   b. The opened jar required refrigeration.
5. a. The job was advertised in the newspaper.
   b. The advertised vacancy was filled quickly.

Exercise 7

1. roving (reporter)
2. growing (controversy)
3. demanding (editor)
4. (politician) accused
5. provoking (questions)
6. alleged (criminal)
7. tempting (bribe)
8. Refusing (he)
9. suspected (politician)
10. honest (man)

Exercise 8

1. difficult (job)
2. good (boss)
3. quiet (boss)
4. low (profile)
5. dynamic (boss)
6. long (hours)
7. high (salaries)
8. fair (situation)
9. smart (individuals)
10. rare (positions)

Exercise 9

(Answers may vary.)

1. careful: The careful bookkeeper double-checked her figures.
2. expressive: The expressive child described her experience thoroughly.
3. lovely: The lovely room was tastefully furnished.
4. lucky: The lucky gambler won a lot of money.
5. boastful: The boastful salesman was disliked by his peers.
6. photographic: The photographic equipment was quite valuable.
7. senseless: The senseless lyrics of the song bored the audience.
8. magical: The magical atmosphere in the theater kept the audience enthralled.
9. moody: My moody boss is difficult to get along with.
10. planetary: Planetary events are studied by astronomers.

Exercise 10

(*Answers may vary.*)

1. in
2. of
3. on
4. inside
5. around
6. at
7. of
8. at
9. of
10. of

Exercise 11

(*Answers may vary.*)

1. silently: The lovers looked at each other silently.
2. excitedly: I opened the package excitedly.
3. merrily: The children sang merrily.
4. horribly: He died horribly in a plane crash.
5. wearily: We worked on wearily till dawn.
6. patiently: I explained the answer patiently.
7. studiously: She prepared studiously for the exam.
8. correctly: She answered every question correctly.
9. joyfully: We celebrated the holidays joyfully.
10. boastingly: He told us boastingly of his accomplishments.

Exercise 12

1. memo
2. it
3. topic
4. information
5. copy
6. memo
7. questions
8. copy
9. details
10. memo

Review Exercises

A. ordered
   was
   cost
   received
   arrived
   listed
   is
   enclose
   credit
   appreciate

B. Americans
   I
   readers
   article
   It
   restaurants
   places

prices
consideration
You

C. High
overdue
personal
outstanding
current
great
prompt
delayed
troublesome
sound

D. carefully
belatedly
improperly
initially
later
efficiently
slowly
promptly
immediately
daily

Chapter 14: Building Sentences

Exercise 1

(*Answers may vary.*)

1. accountant, *or* he
2. job, *and* he
3. carefully, *so* he
4. discouraged, *but* he
5. job, *so* she
6. relieved, *but* she
7. unemployed, *and* she
8. job, *for* she
9. back, *or* she
10. secretary, *yet* she
11. advance, *and* she
12. boss, *for* he
13. plans, *and* she
14. her, *so* she
15. careers, *or* nothing
16. jobs, *and* they
17. patient, *but* they
18. large, *so* you
19. workers, *but* first
20. best, *and* you

Exercise 2

1. gold *because* they
2. gold *although* its
3. funds *while* others
4. gold *before* a social
5. crisis *since* it has
6. value *when* inflation
7. gold *because* they
8. caution *because* gold
9. return *when* the stock
10. safety *if* you

Exercise 3

(*Answers may vary.*)

1. wardrobe *before* you
2. thought *because* first
3. best *since* you
4. comfortable *because* you
5. choice *although* a
6. idea *unless* they
7. tie *whether* the
8. chances *before* you
9. mirror *before* you
10. best *so that* you

Exercise 4

(*Answers may vary.*)

1. *Although* James . . . immediately, he
2. *Because* he . . . forgotten, he
3. *So that* he . . . practice, he
4. *When* he . . . job, he
5. *Because* Judy . . . school, she
6. *While* that . . . weeks, she
7. *As* she . . . interviews, she
8. *When* the . . . along, she
9. *Because* she . . . practice, nervousness
10. *Because* James . . . ahead, their

Exercise 5

(*Answers may vary.*)

1. *While* some . . . time, others
2. *If* you . . . done, effective
3. *Unless* you . . . planning, you
4. *After* you . . . planning, you
5. *If* you . . . deadlines, you
6. *When* you . . . activity, you
7. *Unless* you . . . relaxation, you
8. *Because* overcommitment . . . ineffectiveness, you
9. *If* you . . . morning, schedule
10. *If* you . . . time, you

Review Exercises

A. You must prepare carefully before you go on a job interview. You should anticipate questions that you may be asked about items on your resume. You should dress conservatively but feel comfortable about your appearance. You should take with you a pen, a pad, and your resume. Also, you should be sure to arrive on time to make a good impression.

B. Some businesses grow substantially even when the economy as a whole suffers from recession. They proper because they benefit from the recessionary situation. Employment agencies are busy when more unemployed people are looking for jobs. Repair services do well whether the stock market goes up or down. People try to repair their old possessions before they spend money on new ones. Discount stores show increased sales although department store sales drop. When people are worried about the future, they want to get more for their money now. Clever entrepreneurs discover that recession can work to their advantage if they provide goods and services that people in a recessionary economy demand. These businesspersons use a difficult situation while other people complain and wait.

C. Even before the American Revolution, the American labor movement had begun. The first unions were associations of skilled artisans whose aim was to provide each other with mutual help in the event of misfortune. As unions grew in the early nineteenth century, small locals were isolated within their communities but gradually began to unite, forming national associations. More than thirty-two national unions were formed by the end of the Civil War. Some of them are still in existence. Their original purpose, which was to improve working conditions and wages, continues to exist as well.

D. Public relations letters, a highly specialized mode of business communications, are written to influence public opinion. A public relations writer prepares news releases as well as advertisements, speeches, and other written forms that promote an organization's positive image. To become a public relations writer, one must be clever with words, but a knowledge of sales technique and a sense of timing are further requirements. A persistent competitive spirit will also help, for public relations is a difficult field to break into.

E. Experiencing rapid growth in the past decade, the paralegal profession offers many opportunities. To become a paralegal can take as little as three months in one of the hundreds of paralegal training programs across the country. Paralegals are legal assistants who work with lawyers and other legal professionals. The paralegal's duties include legal research as well as drafting and indexing legal documents and assisting in trial preparation. Employed by local, state, and federal governments, by private law firms, and by corporations, there are over 80,000 paralegals in the United States. Nearly 80 percent of them are women.

Chapter 15: Advanced Sentence Structure

Exercise 1

1. flexibility
2. registering with employment agencies
3. vast competition
4. supervision
5. help-wanted ads
6. personality
7. overhead costs

8. good benefits
9. advancement
10. achieve his own career goals in time

Exercise 2

(*Answers may vary.*)

1. Having started a family and been able to finish school at the same time, Beth was prepared for the pressures of her new job.
2. Still, holding a job and trying to raise her family were difficult.
3. Her ambitions were to nurture her children, her career, and her husband.
4. Beth succeeded because of her children's understanding, her husband's support, and her family's respect.
5. Sometimes Beth's husband was the housekeeper, dishwasher, baby-sitter, and also cook.
6. Beth reciprocated by doing the shopping and the laundry and making time to be alone with her husband.
7. The children learned to clean their own room, make their own lunch, and be independent.
8. On weekends, they all made a point of spending time together and discussing their feelings.
9. Beth had explained her hopes for the family, her goals for her career, and her reasons for wanting to work in the first place.
10. As a result of Beth's working, the family has benefited socially, financially, and emotionally.

Exercise 3

(*Answers may vary.*)

1. Many small investors would rather save their money than risk it in the stock market.
2. They are more interested in financial security than large profits.
3. They think they must either jeopardize all they own in the stock market or settle for 3½ percent interest.
4. Actually, small investors can afford neither low interest rates nor the risk of the stock market.
5. So, both recession and low-interest savings accounts have led many people to other areas of investment.
6. These people are looking not only for security but for a high return.
7. Many, therefore, have put their money into mutual funds rather than savings accounts.
8. Mutual funds not only provide high yield but offer reasonable security.
9. They provide the investor with not only professional management but also diversification.
10. Thus, the investor is neither taking an enormous risk nor giving up to recession.

Exercise 4

(*Answers may vary.*)

1. Employees all through the company were curious about the executive board meeting.
2. Secretaries around the water cooler could not figure out why the president had been so nervous.
3. On Monday, he had explained to his assistant why the company was in trouble.
4. He began the meeting by saying, "Customers who buy our products are frequently discovering defects."
5. The meeting, which stretched on for hours, was attended by all executive personnel.
6. An assistant delivered cold dinners in cardboard boxes to hungry board members.
7. After much discussion behind locked doors, they pinpointed the source of the problem.
8. They agreed to institute new procedures on the following day.
9. The board decided that each product, after going through the assembly line, would be inspected by an expert.
10. They are trying to devise a set of foolproof standards for employees.

Exercise 5

(*Answers may vary.*)

1, 2. C
3. They fixed the terminal, only six months old but already unreliable, in our reception area.
4. C
5. The precision of this man, who seemed to know exactly what he was doing, greatly impressed our office manager.
6. We watched as he returned the machine to perfect working order in less than ten minutes.
7. So little company time was lost due to a damaged computer.
8, 9. C
10. Their bill, which was very reasonable, was on our office manager's desk Tuesday.

Exercise 6

(*Answers may vary.*)

1. As I was settling down at my desk, the day started.
2. The morning passed quietly while I prepared reports and filed them away.
3. When I was nearly finished with the last report, the telephone rang.
4. I answered it promptly as a salesman walked in.
5. To run an office smoothly often requires tact.
6. Asking the salesman to have a seat, I took the caller's message.

7. As the salesman was about to give his sales pitch, two customers arrived.
8. As I was listening to one customer's complaint, the salesman continued pushing his products.
9. I tried to keep an eye on the second customer, who was wandering around the showroom.
10. I finally handled each in turn, and the day resumed its leisurely pace.

Exercise 7

(*Answers may vary.*)
1. C
2. Al single-handedly served dozens of customers who were walking in and out all day long.
3. C
4. However, when first starting up the business, he required help.
5. C
6. Also, pricing and displaying the merchandise himself, he set up the boutique for opening day.
7. But, to incorporate the operation, he needed legal assistance.
8. To set up his system of record keeping, he relied on an accountant's advice, too.
9. C
10. To get a business going, one should not avoid the expense of a team of professionals.

Exercise 8

1. Pat told the personnel officer that she was applying for a position as an administrative assistant.
2. The personnel officer replied that they had no such opening at that time.
3. Pat said that she would like to make out an application for their waiting list anyway.
4. While she was waiting, the man said that they were looking for an executive secretary.
5. He explained that the position was with the assistant vice president of marketing.
6. Pat said that she was willing to begin as a secretary if there were opportunities for advancement.
7. The personnel officer assured her that they filled most higher positions from within the company.
8. Then he added that, if her skills were appropriate, he would arrange an interview for her.
9. Pat informed him that she could type 80 words a minute and take dictation at 120.
10. Now, she tells people that within an hour she had the job.

Exercise 9

1. The program director began by asking me if I had had any previous experience in an old age home.
2. Then she asked if I could tell them about my relevant education.
3. The director's assistant wanted to know how I found working with people much older than myself.
4. A third person queried about what special approaches were necessary when working with an elderly population.
5. Next, the director asked what I would do if I thought someone were having a heart attack.
6. Another member of the panel inquired into what musical instruments I play.
7. Then the assistant asked if I felt I could work on my own.
8. She further questioned if I was willing to work long hours.
9. The director then asked what salary range I would consider acceptable.
10. Finally, she inquired when I could start.

Review Exercises

(Answers may vary.)

A. I would like to order a desk advertised in your fall catalog. The model is number 15C-2J, comes in solid oak, and is priced at $495.

Please charge the desk to my account, number 7651-38-801, and send it immediately to the following address:

    96 Lakeview Drive
    Riverdale, New York 11232

B. It is with great pleasure that we have contracted with your executive council to provide refrigeration and stove repair services. . . .

We have agreed to assume responsibility for all malfunctions of refrigerators, freezers, and gas ranges for an annual fee of $150 per apartment. There will be no additional charge to you for repairs, even if the cost of these services should exceed $150.

Therefore, please let us know if you are interested in securing our Kitchen Insurance for your home. . . .

C. . . . In checking our records, we find you have indeed owned the set for only six weeks.

We can clearly understand your anger at having a television break down so soon after purchase. . . .

On your behalf, we have contacted the factory repair service, who informed us that they will get in touch with you immediately to arrange for free repair of your set. . . .

D. . . . A standard review of credit applications includes checking accounts, savings accounts, and outstanding debts. Having investigated your ability to assume such credit, we find that your current obligations are substantial. . . .

E. On Tuesday, October 12, you instructed me to find out which telephone-answering equipment will best suit our office needs. You asked me to find the three top models. . . .

1. Dictaphone, model #108B—equipped with 30-second announcement cartridge, 90-minute message cassette, and remote control message receiver; available at Berkeley's Office Equipment, Inc., for $165.

2. Ansaphone, model #26-60—equipped with 30-second announcement cartridge, 60-minute message cassette, fast-forward device, and remote control message receiver; available at Audrey's Audio for $100.

3. Quadraphone, model #XJ9—equipped with 20-second announcement cartridge, 90-minute message cassette, message length switch, and remote control message receiver; available at all Taylor Discount Stores for $125. . . .

Chapter 16: Subject-Verb Agreement

Exercise 1

Singular	Plural	Singular	Plural
cost	costs	factory	factories
journey	journeys	safe	safes
buzz	buzzes	life	lives
inquiry	inquiries	fox	foxes
holiday	holidays	banana	bananas
anniversary	anniversaries	loss	losses
request	requests	cargo	cargoes
finance	finances	trustee	trustees
success	successes	phony	phonies
ax	axes	banjo	banjos

Exercise 2

1. This company's policy
2. All employees' salaries
3. An employee's performance
4. An immediate superior's opinion
5. The administration's objectivity
6. An employee's loyal service
7. A raise's merit
8. someone's outstanding performance
9. This company's employees
10. their workers' satisfaction

Exercise 3

1. Airports employ
2. The pilots fly jets
3. The navigators keep
4. The flight attendant takes
5. The ground crews check
6. The baggage handler tosses
7. The ticket agent arranges
8. The customs officials open
9. Tower control directs
10. The security agent watches

Exercise 4

1. offers
2. hire
3. need
4. clean
5. employs
6. have
7. comes
8. pay
9. employ
10. is

Exercise 5

1. is
2. are
3. are
4. are
5. are
6. are
7. were
8. are
9. were
10. are

Exercise 6

1. is
2. travel
3. take
4. drive
5. has
6. walk
7. rains
8. take
9. is
10. have

Exercise 7

1. satisfy
2. are
3. covers
4. are
5. have
6. augment
7. help
8. meets
9. break
10. are

Exercise 8

1. is
2. are
3. does
4. makes
5. provides
6. is
7. prepares
8. say
9. help
10. are

Exercise 9

1. wants
2. pays
3. is
4. remains
5. has
6. seems
7. volunteers
8. is
9. moves
10. is

Exercise 10

1. have
2. are
3. qualify
4. seem
5. have
6. is
7. are
8. contribute
9. are
10. are

Exercise 11

1. has
2. were
3. are
4. is
5. has
6. are
7. was
8. need
9. is
10. are

Exercise 12

1. seems
2. are
3. is
4. appears
5. are
6. is
7. has
8. seems
9. are
10. is

Exercise 13

1. have
2. were
3. were
4. was
5. appears
6. has
7. are
8. is
9. are
10. has

Exercise 14

1. offers
2. feel
3. disagrees
4. has
5. feel
6. are
7. provides
8. obstructs
9. wants
10. is

Exercise 15

1. have
2. is
3. has
4. induce
5. are
6. needs
7. put
8. leads
9. encourage
10. depends

Exercise 16

1. is
2. were
3. has
4. is
5. provide

6. increases
7. grow
8. require
9. are
10. makes

Exercise 17

1. offer
2. include
3. was
4. supplies
5. show

6. provides
7. are
8. is
9. meet
10. is

Review Exercises

A.
1. consist
2. is
3. frighten
4. discourage
5. prefer
6. are
7. make
8. worries

9. wait
10. depends
11. is
12. is
13. have
14. realizes
15. is

B.
1. is
2. are
3. are
4. put
5. are
6. ceases
7. provides
8. is

9. reduces
10. compounds
11. plans
12. alleviate
13. enriches
14. does
15. becomes

C. As you know, job hunting in this day and age is a difficult proposition. . . .

Now, Integrity Careers, Inc., has the help you need. Our career guidance kit, "Know Thyself," provides the answers to your biggest questions: What job do I really want? What are my most marketable skills? What factors have kept me from reaching my goals up to now? What do I do to finally land the job of my dreams?

This kit, including job lists and model resumes, is not available in any store. . . . Only those who receive this letter even know the kit exists.

So why not send us $50 postage paid to receive your Integrity Career Guidance Kit? . . .

D. Corro Communications <u>is</u> pleased to announce the promotion of Augusta Samuels to assistant vice president of marketing. The former advertising director of our South and Midwest divisions bring<u>s</u> to her new job a wealth of dedication and experience.

Ms. Samuel<u>s</u>' new office will be located in the New York headquarters building at 1 Sixth Avenue.

To mark the occasion, Corro request<u>s</u> the pleasure of your company at a reception honoring Ms. Samuel<u>s</u>. . . .

E. . . . We appreciate your interes<u>t</u> in a position with our company.

Although we received over 200 respons<u>es</u> to our advertisement for an administrative assistant, we have given each applicant<u>'s</u> resume careful consideration. Because your background and experience mee<u>t</u> our company<u>'s</u> criteria, we would like to invite you to come in for an interview. . . .

Chapter 17: Verb Forms

Exercise 1

1. spoken   done   forgotten
   written   said   gone
   been   taken

2. types   laughs   argues
   works   knows   speaks
   says

3. answering   typing   speaking
   laughing   filing   working
        trying

4. typed   worked   transcribed
   filed   decided   corrected
   forgot

5. fought   argued   cooperated
        bickered   disagreed
        conferred

Exercise 2

Present Tense	Past Tense	Past Participle
arise	arose	arisen
bear	bore	born
begin	began	begun
bend	bent	bent
bet	bet	bet

bid	bid	bid
bind	bound	bound
bleed	bled	bled
blow	blew	blown
break	broke	broken
bring	brought	brought
burst	burst	burst
buy	bought	bought
cast	cast	cast
catch	caught	caught
choose	chose	chosen
come	came	come
cost	cost	cost
creep	crept	crept
cut	cut	cut
dig	dug	dug
do	did	done
draw	drew	drawn
drink	drank	drunk
drive	drove	driven
eat	ate	eaten
feed	fed	fed
feel	felt	felt
fight	fought	fought
find	found	found
flee	fled	fled
fly	flew	flown
forget	forgot	forgotten
get	got	gotten
give	gave	given
go	went	gone
grow	grew	grown
hang	hung	hung

have	had	had
hear	heard	heard
hit	hit	hit
hold	held	held
hurt	hurt	hurt
keep	kept	kept
know	knew	known
lay	laid	laid
lead	led	led
lend	lent	lent
lie	lay	lain
lie	lied	lied
light	lit	lit
lose	lost	lost
make	made	made
mean	meant	meant
meet	met	met
pay	paid	paid
put	put	put
quit	quit	quit
read	read	read
rid	rid	rid
ride	rode	ridden
ring	rang	rung
rise	rose	risen
run	ran	run
say	said	said
see	saw	seen
seek	sought	sought
sell	sold	sold
send	sent	sent
set	set	set
shake	shook	shaken

shed	shed	shed
shine	shone	shone
shoot	shot	shot
sing	sang	sung
sit	sat	sat
sleep	slept	slept
slide	slid	slid
speak	spoke	spoken
speed	sped	sped
spend	spent	spent
split	split	split
spread	spread	spread
stand	stood	stood
steal	stole	stolen
stick	stuck	stuck
swear	swore	sworn
sweep	swept	swept
swim	swam	swum
swing	swung	swung
take	took	taken
teach	taught	taught
tear	tore	torn
tell	told	told
throw	threw	thrown
win	won	won
wind	wound	wound
write	wrote	written

Exercise 3

1. wanted
2. loved
3. read
4. asked
5. majored
6. changed
7. been
8. continued
9. attends
10. studying

Exercise 4

1. work	meet	prepare
rest	study	apologize
try		

2. sleeping	typing	writing
planning	cooking	studying
		working

3. gone	finished	graduated
tried	learned	rested
recovered		

4. talking	walking	writing
typing	working	studying
sleeping		trying

Exercise 5

(Answers may vary.)

1. can	6. should
2. would	7. will
3. must	8. may
4. should	9. should
5. had better	10. could

Exercise 6

1. Sylvia	6. Ann
2. Mrs. Ortiz	7. Henry
3. May	8. Judy
4. Max	9. Mr. Toshiro
5. Amy	10. Steve

Exercise 7

1. <u>have</u>: Foreign investors in China <u>had</u> . . .
2. <u>snarl</u>: Bureaucratic delays frequently <u>snarled</u> . . .
3. <u>threatens</u>: The recent death of Deng Xiao Ping <u>threatened</u> . . .
4. <u>jeopardize</u>: American trade sanctions also <u>jeopardized</u> . . .
5. <u>fear</u>: American companies <u>feared</u> . . .
6. <u>do</u>: They <u>did</u> . . .
7. <u>consider</u>: Still, many foreign companies <u>considered</u> . . .
8. <u>has</u>: China <u>has</u> . . .
9. <u>offers</u>: China's domestic market <u>offered</u> . . .
10. <u>is</u>: Underlying this investment boom <u>was</u> . . .

Exercise 8

1. A new copier was ordered by Allbright Enterprises on Tuesday.
2. It was delivered by the Allied Trucking Company on Thursday.
3. The bill was sent by the manufacturer immediately.

4. The bill was received by Allbright on Friday.
5. It was paid by them promptly.
6. However, a malfunction in the machine was discovered by a secretary on Monday.
7. The mechanism was being jammed by paper.
8. Stopping payment on their check was considered by Allbright.
9. But its merchandise is guaranteed by the manufacturer.
10. The copier was repaired by them Tuesday afternoon.

Exercise 9

1. Harold Dawson constructed their porch.
2. Emma Hobbs contracted him to build it.
3. Mr. Dawson's father had taught him carpentry.
4. So he crafted the porch expertly.
5. He laid the floorboards evenly.
6. He hand-notched the railings.
7. He even hand-carved the molding.
8. His final product pleased Mrs. Hobbs.
9. She paid him handsomely.
10. A machine cannot match the work of a fine craftsperson.

Exercise 10

is   (active)
has not been paid   (passive)
is   (active)
have been sent   (passive)
have been ignored   (passive)
know   (active)
have been   (active)
have been paid   (passive)
is   (active)
do force   (active)
send   (active)

. . . We have sent you two statements and three letters regarding your balance. Yet you have ignored them.

We know that you have been a reliable customer for many years although you have paid your bills slowly on occasion. . . .

Please do not force us to close your account or to turn this matter over to our attorneys. . . .

Review Exercises

A.
1. expected
2. pursued
3. paid
4. become
5. trained
6. work
7. performed
8. obstructed
9. required
10. provide

B.

1. wanted
2. been
3. learned
4. served
5. taken
6. trained
7. advised
8. seemed
9. combined
10. preparing
11. began
12. arrived
13. were
14. offered
15. begun

C.

1. Justin <u>wanted</u> to become an airline reservations agent. He <u>enjoyed</u> working with the public, and he <u>had</u> the necessary qualifications. He <u>was</u> a high school graduate, <u>spoke</u> two foreign languages, <u>typed</u> fifty-five words per minute, and <u>had worked</u> with computers. He <u>had been</u> a salesperson for the <u>previous</u> two years, which <u>was</u> also helpful. Most importantly, he <u>related</u> well to people.

2. Alicia <u>is</u> a flight attendant, a job that <u>involves</u> serving others. Her position <u>requires</u> patience and tact since she <u>deals</u> with potentially irritable passengers. She <u>has</u> to keep passengers calm as well as serve them food and beverages. She not only <u>caters</u> to their needs, but also <u>maintains</u> their safety. Because she <u>performs</u> her duties well and <u>has</u> often <u>been</u> complimented by passengers, she <u>is being</u> promoted to Supervisor of Flight Training.

3. Donna <u>entered</u> corporate management immediately after finishing college. She <u>started</u> as a product manager and moved up to assistant vice president for finance. <u>Now</u> she <u>wants</u> to open her own business. She <u>has considered</u> cosmetics, a traditionally "women's field," but she <u>prefers</u> to invest in a "mainstream" industry. So she <u>has investigated</u> computer software. She <u>has found</u> the field attractive and so <u>is planning</u> to quit her job in the near future.

D. It is my great honor to infor<u>m</u> you that you have been nam<u>ed</u> . . .

Words cannot expres<u>s</u> our deep appreciation . . . and good judgment sav<u>ed</u> . . . that would have been los<u>t</u> had the robbers escap<u>ed</u>.

. . . it must have creat<u>ed</u> . . . you to spen<u>d</u> . . . we will be pleas<u>ed</u> . . . to be hel<u>d</u> on Friday . . .

E. . . . has announce<u>d</u> plans . . . is schedule<u>d</u> to . . .

including retire<u>d</u> persons . . . Delaney explain<u>ed</u>: "Job . . . and convinc<u>e</u> local. . . ."

are bei<u>ng</u> schedule<u>d</u> for . . . is urge<u>d</u> to . . . be experience<u>d</u> but . . . employers intereste<u>d</u> in. . . .

Chapter 18: Mechanics

Exercise 1

1. ?
2. !
3. .
4. .
5. ?

6. .
7. ?
8. !
9. .
10. .

Exercise 2

product.
magazine, we
you. Should
rates. Our
delay! Call

Exercise 3

1. 6:45
2. breakfast;
3. ways:
4. routine:
5. o'clock;

6. remark:
7. mail;
8. response;
9. billing;
10. arrives:

Exercise 4

1. engineer, she
2. people, she . . . bridges, dams, and
3. job, Lydia
4. construction, and
5. However, Lydia's
6. improvement, water quality, and
7. system, so
8. exciting, and
9. fact, she . . . management, accounting, and
10. future, Lydia

Exercise 5

1. Transport, Ltd., is . . . Street, Rockville, Maine
2. company, founded in 1949, is
3. Forman, a . . . School, was
4. August, 1962, she [or August 1962 she]
5. woman, one would imagine, had
6. Today, Ms. . . . 1,200 women, many
7. Forman, it . . . drivers, not her own achievement, that
8. road, she believes, has
9. Transport, of course, employs . . . men, too.
10. women, not the men, who

Exercise 6

1. √
2. Mr. Chu, who . . . success, must
3. √
4. Mr. Alvarez, which . . . lunch, Mr. Chu
5. client, Ms. Murphy, was
6. Mr. Chu, confident . . . manner, enjoys
7. √
8. breakfast, which . . . overlooked, can
9. √
10. contract, which . . . signing, will

Exercise 7

1. anybody's guess
2. Rosemary's responsibility
3. the policemen's weapons
4. the actresses' roles
5. Gus's dog
6. Iris's cat
7. the cars' transmission
8. the bus's tires
9. Alex and Sid's partnership
10. the passerby's reaction

Exercise 8

1. company's
2. c.o.d.'s
3. haven't
4. M.D.'s
5. Adler's
6. We've
7. Moses'
8. √
9. √
10. it's

Exercise 9

1. "The Affordable . . . the People"
2. "Computers enable . . . to do."
3. "Computers provide . . . store it."
4. "Laptop computers," she explains further, "enable . . . go."
5. "The Affordable PC,"
6. "Because my . . . days."
7. "By storing . . . my knees."
8. "Many . . . clubs."
9. "Without . . . with words."
10. "With spelling . . . and precision."

Exercise 10

1. an X-rated movie
2. a four-star restaurant
3. a hand-sewn garment
4. a mind-boggling question
5. home-grown vegetables
6. all-night negotiations

7. a tea-stained tablecloth
8. a seventeen-year-old graduate
9. a career-oriented student
10. a polka-dotted dress

Exercise 11

1. bank-rupt-cy
2. cor-por-a-tion
3. X
4. de-pre-ci-a-tion
5. li-a-bi-li-ty

6. fis-cal
7. sell-ing
8. fran-chise
9. mort-gage
10. mo-nop-o-ly

Exercise 12

1. (1870–1965)
2. financier—he . . . thirty—he
3. (national defense adviser)
   (special . . . Byrne).
4. Trust"—a
5. (U.S. . . . Commission).
6. (formerly . . . College)
7. (see *Baruch* [2 volumes, 1957–60]).

Exercise 13

"<u>F</u>lexible <u>W</u>ork <u>H</u>ours" (or <u>F</u>lextime for short) is one of the biggest inno-vations in employment policy in the past few decades. <u>U</u>nder <u>F</u>lextime, employees choose the times at which they arrive at and depart from work within limits set by management. <u>U</u>sually core hours are estab-lished: during this midday period all employees must be present. <u>T</u>hey may choose, however, to come in early or to stay late. <u>U</u>nder <u>F</u>lextime, absenteeism has dropped significantly, and productivity has risen. <u>A</u>s a result, the Public and World Affairs Committee predicts, "<u>F</u>lextime is going to be with us in the coming years."

Exercise 14

1. <u>Secretarial and Office Procedures for College</u>
2. <u>Principles of Data Processing</u>
3. <u>How to Marry a Millionaire</u>
4. "So You Want to Be a Legal Secretary?"
5. "How to Ask for a Raise"
6. "One Hundred Ways to Supplement Your Income"
7. <u>How to Find the Job You've Always Wanted</u>
8. "Avoiding Three O'Clock Fatigue"
9. "How to Work Around a Candy Machine Without Gaining Weight"
10. <u>Take the Money and Run</u>

Exercise 15

1. On June 28, 1778, the Battle of Monmouth was fought. The last major battle in the North during the Revolutionary War, it took place north of Monmouth Court House in New Jersey. There, George Washington led an army of 13,500 troops to victory against the British troops, who were led by Henry Clinton.
2. Born on February 11, 1847, in Milan, Ohio, Thomas Alva Edison became one of America's greatest inventors. . . . Edison also built the first central electric power station, erected on Pearl Street in New York City. Known as the "Wizard of Menlo Park," he considered his genius to be "one percent inspiration and ninety-nine percent perspiration."

Exercise 16

Dear Mr. Jackson:

I would like to offer my hearty congratulations on your promotion to president of the Empire Stove Company. All of us at Seymour's Service Centers, Inc., are pleased that your years of hard work have been rewarded.

Seymour's appreciates the fine quality and serviceability of American-made stoves and appliances. That is why we have always confidently offered Empire Stoves to our customers.

In closing, President Jackson, let me say that we look forward to a long and mutually rewarding business relationship with E.S.C.

Sincerely yours,

Exercise 17

1. The meeting to explore ways of increasing tourism in Greenwood, North Dakota, was called to order at 7:15 P.M.
2. Mr. Ashley introduced the guest speaker, the Honorable J. R. Buckley, mayor of Greenwood.
3. CORRECT
4. Buckley began his speech with an anecdote about ancient Rome in the year 129 B.C.
5. CORRECT
6. The mayor surprised the audience by announcing plans to spend $2,550,000 on restoring the town's landmarks and historical sites.
7. He also announced the intentions of ITT to erect a Sheraton Hotel on Broad Street in the center of town.
8. After Buckley's address, Lana Stephens, C.S.W., asked a question.
9, 10. CORRECT

Exercise 18

On <u>Tuesday,</u> <u>March</u> 17, which happened to be <u>St.</u> Patrick's Day, I purchased four <u>pounds</u> of Muenster cheese from your supermarket on Grand <u>Street</u> in Grahamsville, <u>New Jersey.</u> . . .

The manager of the Grand <u>Street</u> store refused to refund my money. . . . I would like you to know that if my claim is not satisfied, I intend to take the matter to the <u>Department</u> of <u>Consumer</u> Affairs.

Exercise 19

1. $8.12
2. CORRECT
3. 49 West 11 Street
4. August 10, 1980
5. CORRECT
6. ten men, eight women, and sixteen children *or* 10 men, 8 women, and 16 children
7. 2 sixty-cent fares
8. 9:30 A.M.
9. CORRECT
10. P.O. Box 21

Review Exercises

A. There will be a meeting of the <u>Sales</u> <u>Department</u> on <u>Friday,</u> November 8, in <u>room</u> 110. <u>Mr.</u> Arthur Parker will address the meeting on the topic, "Improving Your Sales Through Self-Hypnosis."

Mr. Parker, a certified psychoanalyst who has studied at the Alfred Adler <u>I</u>nstitute, is the author of several books, including the bestseller *It's a Snap* (New York, 1991). . . .

B. Dear Tenant:

Please be advise<u>d</u> that, pursuant to the 1998–99 Rent Guidelines Board, the percentages covering <u>l</u>ease <u>r</u>enewals effective July <u>1</u>, 1998, have been changed. . . .

<u>5%</u> for one-year renewal

<u>9%</u> for two-year renewal

<u>13%</u> for <u>three</u>-year renewal

. . . Please sig<u>n</u> and return both copies, along with the additional security of $20.41. . . .

C. On the basis of information provided by your physician and at your request, you have been placed on medical leave of absence as of May 30, 1998.

To maintain your leave, company policy requires additional written statements from your physician at thirty-day intervals. These statements should be sent directly to the Personnel Insurance Coordinator, at the downtown office.

Failure to return to work on the date indicated by your physician will be considered a resignation.

Feel free to contact me for further information regarding this policy.

D. Policy No. 43 681 345

Date: September 5, 1998

Dear Mr. and Mrs. Chou:

. . . Because you made five claims in the past four years, we cannot provide $500 deductible comprehensive coverage on the 1998 Ford Taurus that replaced your old car. Nevertheless, bodily injury and property damage on the old car have been transferred to your new car. . . .

You will be covered by the protection only until 12:01 A.M. on September 26, 1998. You will therefore have a three-week period in which to apply for the protection elsewhere.

Please understand, Mr. and Mrs. Chou, that our decision was made after thorough consideration of your case and based upon the underwriting rules and regulations of our company.

All of your other coverage remains in full force as it was before your request.

E. Dear Dr. Christopher:

Not long ago, I spoke with you on the telephone about a possible teaching position with you next semester. You suggested I mention this in my letter.

The man who referred me to your school was Professor Helmsley of the Accounting Department.

My most recent job was in the Secretarial Skills Department at Bronxville Community College. I was a part-time instructor there for four consecutive semesters. . . .

Thank you,

Sincerely yours,

INDEX

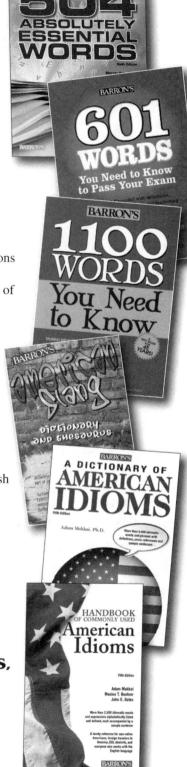

NOTES